AROUND THE WORLD THROUGH A CHILD'S EYES

A Memoir of Travel, Cultures, and Our Shared Humanity

BRIAN J. FABBRI
WITH SASHA FABBRI

River Grove
BOOKS

This book is a memoir reflecting the author's present recollections of experiences over time. Its story and its words are the author's alone. Some details and characteristics may be changed, some events may be compressed, and some dialogue may be re-created.

Published by River Grove Books
Austin, TX
www.rivergrovebooks.com

Copyright © 2025 Brian J. Fabbri

All rights reserved.

Thank you for purchasing an authorized edition of this book and for complying with copyright law. No part of this book may be reproduced, stored in a retrieval system, or transmitted by any means, electronic, mechanical, photocopying, recording, or otherwise, without written permission from the copyright holder.

Distributed by River Grove Books

Design and composition by Greenleaf Book Group and Kim Lance
Cover design by Greenleaf Book Group and Kim Lance

Publisher's Cataloging-in-Publication data is available.

Print ISBN: 978-1-63299-929-0

eBook ISBN: 978-1-63299-930-6

First Edition

To my loving wife and mother of Sasha, Natalia, whose eternal wanderlust and consummate dedication to career advancement made these family journeys possible, necessary, and desirable. It was her inspiration that encouraged me to collect my extensive notes from all of our trips and fashion them together into a memoir for our daughter, to recapture memorable moments from her youth that she might have otherwise forgotten and to instill in her psyche the pleasures and advantages of having a global perspective like both of her parents.

Contents

    Introduction... 1

1   Singapore: The Modern Door to the Orient............... 5

2   The Start of Sasha's Travels in Asia...................... 15

3   Hokkaido, Japan.. 25

4   Sabah Borneo, Indonesia.................................. 41

5   Shanghai, China.. 49

6   New Year's in Australia................................... 63

7   Bintan Island, Indonesia.................................. 79

8   A Visit with Friends to Angkor Wat..................... 83

9   St. Petersburg, Russia..................................... 91

10 Summer in Switzerland................................... 97

11 Boracay Island, the Philippines......................... 129

12 Da Nang, Vietnam.. 137

13 Algarve, Portugal... 145

14 Jimbaran Bay, Bali, Indonesia........................... 149

15 India: The Golden Triangle.............................. 155

16 Langkawi: The Beach in the Rainforest................ 167

17 Tuscany and Rome....................................... 171

18 A Final Trip to Hokkaido................................ 183

19	Deer Valley, Park City, Utah	189
20	Eleuthera: The Bahamas' Beautiful Beaches	195
21	Thanksgiving in Havana	201
22	Skiing in Aspen	211
23	Summer in the United States	215
24	Europe's Urban Capitals: Paris and London	235
25	New Year's in Punta Cana	247
26	Ski Weeks in Vail	255
27	Life in the Heart of Europe: Brussels, Belgium	265
28	Skiing at the Top: St. Moritz	273
29	Easter Week in Spain	279
30	Mother's Day on Santorini	283
31	Mom's Birthday on the Côte d'Azur	287
32	Back to Pine Crest	293
33	Sasha's Words	297
	About the Authors	*301*

Introduction

THESE MANY EPISODES IN a young girl's life, written initially from her own childlike perspective by her father and gaining substance and detail as she ages into a teenager, trace a journey through Asia, Australia, North America, and Europe. The journey exposed this young girl to a vast quantity of varied cultures, peoples, and languages, which incrementally helped her form a distinct vision of oneness with the peoples of the world. She understood and spoke a few words in many languages, studied several non-native languages in more depth, and generally learned different ways of communicating. She observed different styles of dressing, watched many ethnic and cultural performances, and gained an appetite for an extensive selection of diverse cuisines.

Seeing diverse peoples in their natural environment allowed her to notice small physical differences and perceive the ultimate sameness in people, especially children around her own age. She also absorbed many vast differences in terrain, temperature, humidity, and vegetation throughout the world and began to grasp its immense size and diversity.

Now, as an older teenager, she has had the opportunity to look back and read about these episodes of her life, some of which she may have forgotten, and to reflect on her adventures and experiences. Most importantly she was able to express in her own words how they shaped her life, her relationships with friends and classmates, and her understanding of people, cultures, and places. Her youthful exposure to the world and its people has helped her form a vision of how she might make a positive contribution to the international community now, and more crucially, later, when her studies are complete and she embarks on her career.

Traveling through distant lands is never easy with a small child, and it often becomes more challenging as children age. However, the advantages that such exposure to a wider world than the one they initially grew up in outweigh any of the minor inconveniences that such travel necessitates. The exposure of children to different peoples, places, and cultures is particularly rewarding at a young age because it opens their minds to a limitless scope of possibilities to pursue.

The world becomes this child's stage, and its many evident problems become inspirations for this child to seek solutions for as she shapes her career path. Journey through these episodes, and they will eventually reveal how such youthful travel could enlarge a child's concepts of what's possible and extend their thoughts beyond the boundaries of their everyday life.

Along this fascinating journey through time and space, Sasha was accompanied by her mother, Natalia Shuman Fabbri, and her father, Brian Fabbri. Natalia was, and still is, a working mom managing huge international companies across the world, while her father recently retired from his role of international chief economist and professor. Both parents were highly academically motivated, having spent many years in advanced study, and both were highly appreciative of the profound role formal education would have on their child's future. Their careers reflected this, and it predicated their commitment to expand Sasha's education and global experience. Because he had the luxury of more time, Sasha's father was designated to be the author recounting this odyssey, sometimes in Sasha's words and often in his own.

Sasha begins this journey as a five-year-old girl who ventured from her home in New Jersey the day after her fifth birthday and moved to Singapore because her mother's career brought them there. This meant that Sasha had to advance from preschool, learning to read and write in English, to listening to and speaking Mandarin in Singapore's preschool. Mandarin was also taught as a basic subject throughout Sasha's years spent in kindergarten through the fourth grade. She supplemented her language learning by attending Mandarin classes during summers with her dad in Shanghai, China.

Life changed for Sasha again when her mom changed jobs, industries, and location. This time her mom's career progression brought everyone back to Fort Lauderdale in the United States. Dad's role was to find a suitable school for this precocious child that would continue to challenge her. His choice was Pine Crest, a nationally regarded private institution with a reputation for a challenging academic curriculum. Sasha started fifth grade in her new school and quickly adjusted to the new environment and school. She made many new American friends and soaked up the advanced curriculum easily. The most onerous adjustment was finding a Mandarin tutor in South Florida until her school began offering Mandarin instruction in the sixth grade. Middle school should have passed routinely for Sasha, but it did not because of COVID-19. The pandemic caused schools in South Florida to offer online instruction and therefore, for more than a year, classes were conducted at home on a laptop. Sasha overcame this impediment gracefully.

At the conclusion of middle school, another obstacle confronted Sasha: Her mom changed jobs again, bringing the family this time to Brussels, Belgium. This change was far more difficult for Sasha, who had grown to love Pine Crest and all the friends she had made there. As a teenager, leaving her friends behind was a very difficult challenge to overcome, one that she intensely resisted. The problems in her new environment were manifest. First, her new school in Brussels was not as rigorous as Pine Crest was and did not have an equally robust reputation among US universities. Second, it did not offer Mandarin, and thus Sasha was forced to enter first-year French as she started high school. And third, her classmates were no longer all American, but came from disparate nationalities speaking different native languages, which made making new friends more arduous, even for a girl who had a gift for creating large numbers of friends in separate groups.

Sasha's unhappiness motivated a final change. Sasha's mom recognized Sasha's dejection and realized she would not live up to her potential living in Brussels. Natalia had to confront Sasha's despair, and she made the painful decision to send Sasha back to their home in Fort Lauderdale and to Pine Crest with her dad while she maintained her role in her new firm and continued to live in Brussels. It was a loving sacrifice for a mother to make, and the brave decision proved to be very beneficial for Sasha, who proceeded to earn high academic grades and form a happy circle of friends in her sophomore year back at Pine Crest.

As you travel through this book visiting countries in Europe, Asia, Australia, and North America, you will see how famous and magnificent historical sites, natural and man-made, come alive through a child's eyes. Each site is seen with its authentic cultural backdrop of clothing, sounds, languages, food, and ceremonies, which add texture and significance to the descriptions of these places. Such specific insights cannot be gleaned from learning about them even in the most well-written textbooks. Being there is indisputably more valuable than reading. Not only for children but for everyone—being present aids immensely in opening our eyes to the curious distinctions that make up our world. Sasha and her parents hope their family's journey will inspire you to follow them throughout this widely varied world and bring your children with you.

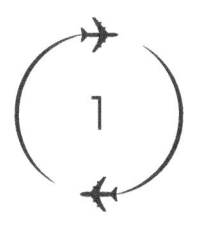

Singapore: The Modern Door to the Orient

THIS WAS THE FARTHEST SASHA would ever be from home. "Home" for Sasha, up to that point, meant New Jersey. But as her parents closed the door on emptied rooms and lugged their suitcases filled with more than a vacation's worth of clothes, Sasha knew that home would soon be somewhere completely different. On the other side of the world, in fact. Sasha's family was moving to Singapore for Sasha's mother to take on her new responsibility of creating and expanding a pan-Asian business for her domestically focused employment services firm, Kelly Services.

For several centuries, Hong Kong was the door to the orient for Western nations to commence trade with China and the principal financial center for capital transactions and investment in Asian companies. That door began to slowly close after 1996 when the British withdrew and the Chinese government incrementally increased their control and authority over the island. As the hand of government was changing in Hong Kong, another independent city-state was rapidly gaining global attention: Singapore.

This modern island nation has achieved much in its fifty-eight years of existence: global respect for its institutions (because of its strict adherence to the rule of law); an absence of public corruption, drugs, and violence; a dedication to pursuing financial due diligence; and nurturing harmony among its diverse ethnic populations. In part because of its announced independence from global political influences, it has recently become the new financial center of Asia.

For these reasons, it was this country that Sasha's family chose over other, bigger and better-known Asian metropolises such as Hong Kong and Tokyo. A weeklong visit to each city was enough to convince them of Singapore's merits and long-term potential. It was a bilingual country—English and Mandarin were the two official languages—which made travel, communication, shopping, education, and relations with government bureaucracy manageable. Singapore was also a relatively safe country. The government established very strict rules from its earliest days forbidding drugs, guns, and violence. There was even a ban against chewing gum; using it was a punishable offense. Sasha hated being denied chewing gum and had to learn to live without it during her years in Singapore. Her craving for something sweet to chew on intensified once she realized that it was unavailable, and she tried to sneak gum into her life each time she left Singapore for a vacation or when she returned to the United States. Despite the lack of chewing gum, it was visibly evident that Singaporean citizens enjoyed their current economic prosperity, appreciated the political success the country achieved, and overwhelmingly believed in the destiny of their tiny nation. They voluntarily chose to uphold the government's rules.

Once Singapore was selected as their new Asian base, Sasha's dad immediately connected with several former colleagues who lived in Singapore, and they introduced him to the dean of the business school at the National University of Singapore, one of the most highly ranked universities in Asia. This introduction led to a lasting relationship with the business school that involved teaching classes, giving speeches on behalf of the school throughout Asia, attending conferences in Singapore, interacting with guests at the university's school of public policy, and writing a monthly economic review that was distributed to the school's constituents.

Sasha's mom, while intensely busy jetting off to all the major countries in Asia—from Korea to India and everywhere in between—and building and expanding her company's profile in Asia, was also a member of the Singapore chapter of the Young Presidents' Organization. This interaction with other business leaders living in Singapore provided a wealth of opportunities for networking and attending educational and motivational conferences in Singapore. Her frequent travel schedule also afforded Sasha the opportunity to tag along with her to visit many cities, particularly those in China where her efforts to expand her company's business were largely based.

Sasha's parents also had to quickly find a preschool for Sasha to attend. The choices were copious, as Singapore stresses a high quality of education. They eventually chose a preschool called EtonHouse, and the environment proved very beneficial for Sasha. Of course, entering a new school is always somewhat stressful for youngsters, but Sasha adjusted quickly and looked forward each day to her new classes. The school was housed in a large colonial mansion perched on top of a hill near the Ministry for International Affairs. Sasha loved trying to climb the steps to reach her classroom faster than her classmates (which she often did!) and running with them through the extensive lawns that surrounded the building. It was a warm and inviting building for all who attended school there, and it spread its glow to the teachers and parents too. EtonHouse was filled with children of expats from all over the world.

In the years Sasha's family lived there and just before, Singapore was building its reputation as a trade and financial hub for Asia. Consequently, most major international companies were trying to build their presence in Singapore to participate in that growth. It created a continuous flow of new international students for Sasha to mingle with.

Sasha at EtonHouse preschool in Singapore

It was the first of many times Sasha would make friends with children from other nationalities and ethnic backgrounds.

This was also Sasha's first introduction to Mandarin, which was taught as the school's mandatory foreign language along with intense exposure to Chinese culture. Sasha's first Chinese teacher at EtonHouse went by the Western name of Crystal. This young woman would eventually become Sasha's Chinese language tutor, visiting her home every week. Chinese instruction beginning at five years old made an impression on Sasha, and she has continued to study Mandarin through her present high school years.

Chinese holidays were important events at the preschool, and they were well planned and celebrated along with a few key international holidays such as Christmas for the Westerners, the Japanese Cherry Blossom Festival to honor the few Japanese children in Sasha's class, and many Indian Hindu holidays. All holidays were observed unusually early by American standards and were celebrated with colorful, culturally specific clothing, some with bands and parades, and many with fireworks. The biggest celebration, however, was for Chinese New Year. It was a very memorable event with children donning traditional Chinese outfits, singing songs in Mandarin, and indulging in traditional holiday dishes. For Sasha, Chinese New Year was symbolized by a large, family-sized platter of *lo hei*, a mélange of crispy fried noodles piled high over fish, dumplings, pineapple slices, mandarin orange sections, and cabbage in special sauces specific to each restaurant. While in Singapore, Chinese New Year celebrations were always enjoyed with Sasha's new friends and their families at a classic Chinese restaurant.

Many Singaporeans, however, preferred eating at the inexpensive hawker arcades. These tiny, family-run restaurants were bundled side by side and offered a vast array of foods such as fish, shrimp, prawns, rice, soups, sugar cane, stir-fry vegetables, egg rolls, and dumplings. They were always takeout only, as the restaurants were too small to fit tables and chairs. Usually the arcades had a central space filled with large common tables and chairs where people consumed their food. They were everywhere on the island, from parks by the sea to the downtown financial district. Sasha enjoyed the dumplings and egg rolls, but she most loved the lamb satay and begged to stop for a bite whenever she and her family (and sometimes friends) went bike riding on weekends past the hawker arcade in the vast park that extended almost to the airport along the sea.

Upon graduation from EtonHouse, Sasha was enrolled in the Singapore American School (SAS), which was regarded as one of the best full-time international schools in Singapore for first through twelfth grade. Mandarin lessons continued throughout Sasha's years at SAS, but the competition to excel at Mandarin was quite intense since so many of Sasha's classmates were Chinese. The tables turned for some of them in other subjects though, since all children had to learn math and to read and write in English.

SAS was also filled with students from a broad swath of countries across the world, and this continued to push Sasha into befriending many children with different ethnic backgrounds. Her two best friends were Asian. One, Misa, was Japanese, and her parents, like Sasha's, came to Singapore to pursue business opportunities. Their friendship introduced Sasha to the fine art of origami and the homey taste of miso soup. Sasha's other best friend at SAS was Indonesian. She lived in a huge colonial house outside the business district. There Sasha encountered a trampoline, and a new passion was born, one that would propel Sasha into pursuing gymnastics and later competing at the local and national levels.

Sasha made many other friends in Singapore, and it seemed like friends were always coming and going because of the highly transitory nature of their parents' jobs. But the beautiful thing about having friends from all over the world, which Sasha would learn, is the adventure of visiting one another and traveling together. One such friend was Mia, a Greek girl who would later enjoy skiing with Sasha in Hokkaido. Mia also taught Sasha the pleasures of eating Greek food. There was a lively Greek restaurant called Blu Kouzina on Dempsey Road, an upscale collection of restaurants and art stores not far from where Sasha and Mia lived. The food there was so good that Sasha penned a poem about it and gave it to the owner, who framed it and hung it on the wall of his restaurant.

Society in Singapore made it very convenient to interact with all the other international expats through visiting the many Asian art exhibits in the various museums, attending the abundant live sporting events and outdoor concerts, and going to ballet performances and symphony recitals in the many theaters and concert halls. It seemed as though every well-known global performer wanted to appear live in Singapore, and as a result, Sasha's family had numerous opportunities to enjoy many top-level international performances while living there. Singapore has become a cultural mecca with a plethora of performance and art spaces supported by the relatively high-income class of expats and native citizens.

Not everyone who lived in Singapore was wealthy, though. International business brought many wealthy executives to Singapore, and this produced a building boom that many Singaporean citizens took lucrative advantage of. It also created labor opportunities for people from less prosperous surrounding nations. For example, household assistants were abundant and relatively inexpensive. Singapore had a very open policy with regard to permitting workers from other countries in Asia access to temporary work permits. Most of the construction trades were staffed by Indian workers, and many Filipina women entered Singapore to work as domestic housekeepers. As native Singaporeans became wealthier, the demand for domestic helpers also rose. As a result, all of the newer, multistory residential buildings included a helper's room in every unit so the domestic help had a place to live and work. Sports instructors and academic tutors were plentiful, too, making it inexpensive to receive instruction in many activities that would be prohibitively expensive in the United States.

Sasha took complete advantage of the opportunities that Singapore provided, filling her days with extracurriculars. Her family employed a live-in housekeeper who cooked, cleaned, and occasionally babysat Sasha. Sasha began training in gymnastics, took swimming lessons, and received individual tennis and golf instruction once a week. To round out her after-school activities, Sasha started art classes, and took piano lessons and later switched to guitar lessons. She also trained in Tae Kwon Do and was quite advanced in it by the time her family left Singapore.

When Sasha wasn't in school or pursuing one of her many extracurricular activities, one might find her exploring the elaborate complex of underground shopping that complemented Singapore's rapid transit system. Singapore experiences two monsoon seasons every year, and anyone who has lived through one knows it is imperative to conduct daily shopping underground during these rainy seasons. Therefore, soon after Singapore's rapid transit system was constructed, an immense tri-level shopping area was completed alongside it and above and below it. All the well-known department stores on Orchid Road had levels of merchandise on display below ground, squeezed in next to mom-and-pop shops, piercing and tattoo parlors, and inexpensive restaurants, giving Sasha and her friends an enormous variety of spots to explore. Here Sasha wandered, seeking out inexpensive jewelry, candy, hats, flip-flops, sunglasses, and cheap food. Sasha would lose her parents as quickly as they took their eyes away from her. Getting lost was a given in the multiple levels of shops and department stores. More than once Sasha would get on the wrong escalator, mistaking it for the one she had started down, and would end up well away from her chosen entrance.

On the more upscale side of things, Singapore boasted the Marina Bay Sands: a hotel with an infinity pool shaped like a surfboard on the top, a casino, an arcade of expensive shops, and fine-dining restaurants. Nearby were the twin botanic domes featuring plants and orchids of all Asian species in glass-sealed, climate-controlled enclosures. The adjacent colorful garden park contained more tropical trees and flowering plants, and a large hilly green park occasionally hosted live performances. There were also many museums specializing in Asian themes, and theaters that attracted artists from around the world. And too many high-quality restaurants to mention! A towering Ferris wheel and a beach that extended from midtown almost to the airport were among the city's most striking features. Sasha spent much of her time exploring these places and enjoyed taking relatives and friends to visit some of them. She even went there on school trips intended to teach students some of the unique history of this vibrant, modern, first-world city.

Of course, the highly efficient transit system in Singapore, built to complement its world-class airport and airline, was a huge benefit to Sasha and her family as well. It made international travel convenient, affordable, and attractive. This was another key ingredient in their decision to choose Singapore over other potential homes in Asia, and it led them to entertain the opportunity to investigate as much of Asia as they could. It was always Sasha's parents' intent to travel as widely as they could and observe and embrace as many cultures as possible, with their distinct festivals, cuisines, and architecture, and to expose their daughter to all of it.

This jet-setting book filled with exotic places, diverse people, and magnificent landscapes began when Sasha's family moved to Singapore from New Jersey immediately following Sasha's fifth birthday party. However, this wasn't the beginning of Sasha's vagabond life. It just marked the beginning of recording her experiences and probably her first memories of her travels. Sasha's parents applied for her US passport before she was six months old, and she made her first international trip from the United States to Costa Rica that same month. She had also made several trips to Michigan when she first started to walk; had a fun-filled week on Hawaii's big island; visited Sarasota, Florida, where she had her first dinner alone with her father in a fancy adult restaurant; took a trip or two to Puerto Rico; and made two trips to Paris before the family left for Singapore. But Sasha's adventures were only just beginning.

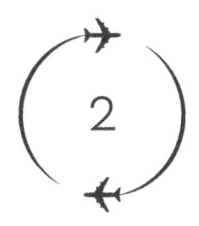

The Start of Sasha's Travels in Asia

THE TRIPS STARTED IMMEDIATELY and simply at first. Sasha's first destination was Sentosa, the adjacent island within the country of Singapore. It is where the wealthy relax in modern five-star hotels and enjoy the privileges of a famous golf course that hosts professional tournaments every year. Sasha would visit this famous golf course when the Ladies Professional Golf Association conducted their annual tournament there. Sasha and her parents celebrated their first New Year, 2012, in a beach resort on Sentosa. It had a huge enticing pool and, to Sasha's great amusement, peacocks that roamed everywhere on the island. Since it was less than an hour's drive from their Singapore home, the family visited this resort many times.

The food at the Sentosa resort and at all of the many Asian places they visited was also very different from the food Sasha ate in New Jersey. It took Sasha a while to break from prior eating habits to begin enjoying the vast array of Asian cuisine. Breakfasts always started with platters of exotic fruits that Sasha had never seen or even heard of before. Lunches and dinners were amalgams of Chinese dumplings, Indonesian satays, Thai bowls, Japanese sushi and sashimi, and much more.

The first big adventure Sasha had in Asia was to travel to Bali, one of the thousands of islands in the Indonesian chain, perhaps the most famous one. Nearly everyone knows that Indonesia has the largest population of Muslims in the world—more than 200 million. However, it is little known that Bali specifically is populated mainly by Hindus practicing Agama Hindu Dharma. Sasha's family wasn't aware of this, or that the final week of March, when they decided to visit, happened to be the Hindu New Year, which the Balinese celebrate intensely. Sasha's parents decided to split the trip to Bali into two parts: first they would visit the famous beaches in Denpasar, and then they would ride up into the mountains to the well-known art village of Ubud.

The weather when they arrived in Bali was cloudy, misty, and chilly—not at all conducive to enjoying the beach. While Sasha took some time to wander around the village looking at the colorful clothes and the multitude of art in the many modern retail stores, she preferred walking along the beach despite the cold, inclement weather. Sasha's parents were warned one day by the hotel staff to leave Denpasar before the beginning of the island celebration for Hindu New Year because everything would close down, including electricity, food preparation, and any service the Balinese performed. Thus, Sasha and her parents set out for Ubud earlier than they'd originally planned so they could arrive at their next hotel before it closed for the holiday.

The drive up the mountains proved to be much more cumbersome and complicated than expected, and much more entertaining than Sasha could ever have imagined. As their local driver took the family through all of the tiny villages along the path to Ubud, hundreds of young and old were moving giant constructs of Hindu gods and images of villains on wheeled flats from their barns and garages, where they had no doubt spent a good deal of time and imagination constructing them. Naturally, on the narrow roads that led to Ubud, the driver had to stop many

Hindu New Year's Eve parade in Bali

times to let these homemade sculptures pass or at least slow down for Sasha to see them. Many were quite scary, and some did frighten young Sasha, but as the van passed more of them along the way, she grew more amused than afraid.

After a very laborious, long, and slow ride up the mountain, the family finally reached the hotel and was quickly shown to their room. Hotel staff excitedly told them of the plans the village had for the evening. They were fed immediately and early because all of the staff and the other hotel guests wanted to go out to the main street and observe the colossal constructions as the village children began to tear them apart. Then the fires were lit and the sculptures were set aflame in a ceremony to symbolize the destroying of all the bad things that occurred in the old year and to chase the demons away before the start of the new. The local boys would run through the hot coals, manifesting their bravery, and then began to throw the burning coals at one another. It was quite a sight for Sasha to absorb, and she watched with wide eyes until darkness finally overcame the exuberance of the village children and began to put Sasha to sleep.

The next day was Hindu New Year, and there were no civil services extended throughout the entire island. Food was left over from the prior day, beds were unmade, and all the guests had to fend for themselves. It was like a party for Sasha to be in a hotel without electric lights, only candles, and no air conditioning, only the warm breezes that blew through the open windows and doors. It was something she'd never experienced before, and she had great fun.

The resort was built on top of one of the mountain peaks and therefore afforded wonderful views of the surrounding mountains and valleys in between. The family's hotel room included a tiny private pool surrounded by magnificent floral vegetation, which Sasha enjoyed to no end. It also provided a partial view of the valley below. But the view was best enjoyed from the dining space built on the highest spot in the resort. The flowering trees and surrounding gardens were spectacular, as was the natural vegetation that surrounded the resort. The food served there was simple: fresh exotic fruits, tasty salads of locally grown ingredients, and meat satays. Eating here, Sasha was becoming more accustomed to the Asian diet. The resort had its own large pool, which was also a major source of pleasure for Sasha, and she spent hours paddling around in it.

The day after Hindu New Year, Sasha's parents decided to go on an art excursion through the town's numerous art stores and galleries. Sasha was initially amazed, and later bored, seeing all the various high and low arts and crafts made and displayed throughout this region of Bali.

All too soon it was time to leave to return to school and everyday life in Singapore. The ride down the mountain to the airport was much tamer and a great deal shorter than the incredible ride Sasha had driving up to Ubud on Hindu New Year's Eve. She experienced many novel sights in Bali and Ubud, and she left knowing and appreciating that there was more than one way to celebrate the New Year.

The second major trip in Sasha's first year in Singapore was to Koh Samui, one of Thailand's small islands located south of the mainland and just north of Malaysia. Thailand was one of Sasha's parent's favorite places, and they couldn't wait to bring her there, especially to celebrate her mother's birthday. Thai food is universally known for its unique flavors and colorful presentations, and Sasha needed to try it to extend her developing Asian taste buds.

The hotel's staff loved Sasha, who was very cute with her bright blue eyes and very blonde hair, and who was highly energetic. The dining room staff would constantly bring freshly created treats for her to try. In spite of their kind efforts, it was the dining room's resident cat who always stole Sasha's affection, especially if she let her baby kittens creep into view.

Sasha and her family spent their days in Koh Samui sampling delicious cuisine, splashing in their hotel room's private pool, or enjoying time at the beach, which was only a few yards away. One afternoon, Sasha and her mom paid a short visit to the local beach shop where they both bought large wide-brimmed hats and proceeded to engage in an impromptu fashion show at the pool's edge. Sasha was the star.

With all the activities of swimming in the pools and playing on the sandy beach, it was impossible for Sasha to stay awake through dinner, even on her mother's birthday. The only night Sasha stayed awake through dinner was when a troupe of Thai dancers appeared to entertain the dinner guests. They were dressed elaborately in fine Thai silks with innovatively styled headdresses. They performed traditional Thai dance accompanied by a tiny band that played authentic Thai percussion instruments. Sasha was intrigued by the sight of the dancers and the sounds made by the band and, as the family left the open-air dining room, she began to emulate the Thai dancers' moves and gestures. As the music faded and the night wound down, too soon it was time to leave the beautiful villa by the sea in Koh Samui and return to Singapore.

Philip and Julia Ohm with Sasha in Indonesia

The next short, but important, trip for Sasha was to Jakarta, the capital of Indonesia and one of the most populous places on earth, where more than 11 million people crowd into a city that is very slowly sinking. There Sasha was to meet Philip, who would become one of her best friends in Singapore, and his family, the Ohms. The two families would travel together in later years to see some of Asia's most iconic places like Angkor Wat in Cambodia and the Taj Mahal in India. On this trip, Sasha stayed in the Ohms' residence in Jakarta. It had a pool, and this is where the children bonded. The Ohms' children are half German and half Russian, somewhat similar to Sasha in ethnic origins.

In addition to traveling through the heavy traffic of this city to observe the sites, the Ohms took Sasha to visit a fabulous zoo in Cisarua, Bogor, about two hours from their home. The zoo was unique in that it allowed visitors to drive through and observe animals in a more natural habitat, similar to a safari. The zoo housed an incredible array of large and small Asian animals, such as many types of antelopes, some rare rhinoceros, orangutans, and wild cats of all kinds, including a white tiger. One tense moment for all occurred when Sasha was asked to sit next to a sleepy Siberian tiger. Sasha also had an opportunity to ride a horse and then, much more adventuresome, ride a large Asian camel. She also walked through a jungle to view a very high waterfall.

The next day was Sunday and public bazaars sprung up in all open spaces. The Ohms took Sasha to the old customs house by the wharf. The colonial-style building was still in service, and on this day it had a large open courtyard filled with stalls selling mainly local creations. Since

Natalia, Sasha, and a tiger in Indonesia

the building was near the wharf, Sasha could see the huge commercial sailboats that filled the harbor and were used to transport products throughout the islands of this immense country.

Her parents purchased some snorkeling gear in preparation for a boat trip they would take the next day. Sasha, full of excitement, refused to remove hers, even at dinner. Morning came, and the boat ride took Sasha and her companions to another deserted island near Java for some crystal-clear shallow water snorkeling. Sasha and the group ate lunch on the beach at rough picnic tables and benches created for visitors to enjoy an authentic island experience. They then sailed back to the small boat harbor in which this rented boat was docked and looked around at more local retail stands and some extremely large old banyan trees before driving home. At the end of the trip, Sasha said goodbye to Philip as she and her parents left the Ohms' residence. Sasha said she was very happy to have made a new friend.

The next birthday was Sasha's, and her parents decided to take her to Lombok, another Indonesian island, to celebrate. Lombok is the next island over from Bali, but in many ways, it couldn't be more different. It is predominantly Muslim, much less populated, and comparatively underdeveloped as a tourist destination compared with Bali. Some believe it will be the next island to be developed, but when Sasha visited, it was a sparsely populated island with no serious industry, just small-scale farming among some larger rice fields. On her way to the resort, Sasha drove through tiny villages with people sitting indolently by the side of the road, some selling a few inexpensive goods. The local markets were open air, as were most of the villagers' housing. The scene suddenly changed when Sasha and her parents reached their destination and drove through the guarded gates of this beautiful resort. She began to realize how different the resort was in its modernity, with manicured foliage and uniformed personnel working all over, from the surrounding places on the island. To ease her concern about the social inequity, her father pointed out that the resort helped the community by providing jobs and spreading income to many on the island.

The resort was magnificent, with many open-air spaces for dining and relaxing where guests could enjoy the gentle warm breeze blowing in from the sea. The hotel was situated in the middle of a large bay filled with the clear, warm waters of the Bali Sea, a land-sheltered part of the Indian Ocean. There were several large swimming pools running next to a long sandy beach. Sasha would alternate between the pools and the bay for most of the day. The hotel management took an interest in Sasha's sixth birthday celebration and baked a cake for her. Since the hotel was less than half full, the manager had time to speak with Sasha and her family. This was significant as it marked the beginning of Sasha's thoughts about pursuing hotel management as a career later in life. She was greatly inspired by the hotel manager's major goal to educate his Indonesian staff to adopt the manners and behavior of the staff of their sister hotel in Thailand, a world-renowned resort known for its courteous and ever-attentive service. With this in mind, Sasha would remark about hotel service throughout her young life at each hotel she visited.

Sasha releasing a baby endangered turtle into the South China Sea

In addition to enjoying the pools, the beach, glorious sunsets, and interesting Indonesian foods, Sasha's biggest treat came when the manager of pool and beach services showed her a large water basin containing a dozen scarce, baby hawksbill sea turtles. When he learned it was her birthday, he filled a small pail with seawater, took two baby turtles, and instructed Sasha to put them back into the sea. These turtles are endangered, and the hotel staff occasionally intervenes to enhance their chances of survival. Sasha has always remembered what this manager told her—that the two baby sea turtles would return to this beach someday to lay their eggs for the next generation.

3

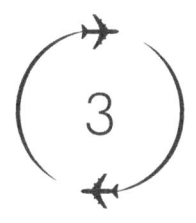

Hokkaido, Japan

WINTER WEATHER IN SINGAPORE was nearly the same as in summer except it rained harder and more often. Sasha wanted to experience the cold and snow of a northern hemisphere winter, so she and her parents traveled to Hokkaido, Japan's northernmost island. Hokkaido is famous for its near constant snowfall, and it was a perfect setting for a very successful winter Olympics back in 1972. It was an equally perfect setting for Sasha to engage in winter sports, and that is what brought Sasha to Hokkaido for multiple winters between 2013 and 2017. Before the family moved to Singapore, Sasha had had only one experience with skiing. It was on a bunny slope in New Jersey when she was four years old, and she detested it. Cold and wet conditions required too many clothes, tight-fitting boots, and awkward, sliding skies. That, coupled with no ski training, caused lots of crying and complaining. Two years later, Sasha wanted to give skiing another try.

The airplane trip from Singapore to Tokyo took nearly ten hours, followed by an overnight layover and then a flight to Asahikawa Airport on Hokkaido Island. When the airplane started flying over the northern island, Sasha was overjoyed to see the ground below covered under a thick blanket of snow. But as soon as the family deplaned, the experience of real cold hit them head on. They had just left Singapore, one of the hottest year-round climates on earth, where temperatures usually hover around thirty-three degrees Celsius, and although they had been advised that weather in Hokkaido would be frigid, they were unprepared for the reality. Outside of the airport, the temperature was minus eighteen degrees Celsius, and snow was piled high everywhere. They quickly dove into their luggage for ski hats, gloves, and scarfs. Fortunately they didn't have to wait long for the lavender-colored bus that would take them from the airport, through the tiny towns in the middle of Hokkaido, and over the frozen roads to the Prince Hotel in Furano. Along the way, snow was everywhere. The recently plowed two-lane road on which the bus was driving had walls of snow on either side piled up to the windows of the bus. As Sasha looked out of the windows at all the snow, she realized that the walls of snow on the sides of the road were taller than she was! Eventually she called out, "I see ski lifts and skiers going down the mountain!" By the time the bus arrived at the hotel about an hour later, Sasha was thoroughly cold and needed some warm soup.

The New Furano Prince Hotel was a tall, modern, glass-walled building. The highlight of the resort was the natural hot spring that sprang from a pool of super-heated water under the surface. The resort built a spa and bathroom around the hot spring, a short walk off the main floor of the hotel, and this was the most popular place after skiing on the mountain. It was very crowded at times, but always relaxing for sore muscles after a day of skiing.

Most of the restaurants were on the top floor of this twelve-story building. Breakfast was served in the basement, although it was located in a different basement from the ski-in ski-out locker room. Because the hotel layout was so vertical, navigating it required the help of four elevators, and they were always crowded. Sasha took up the challenge each morning of seeing who could navigate the passageway fastest: she or her parents.

In spite of its logistical issues the rooms on one side of the hotel offered breathtaking views of the mountains and the ski runs. On clear days, when the clouds blew away and the snow stopped falling, the wide-open blue skies and snow-covered mountaintops made for a truly magnificent sight. The west side of the hotel looked upon the picturesque antique Japanese village situated across the road from the hotel that Sasha looked forward to visiting every night.

As soon as Sasha and her parents settled into their assigned room, the first thing they had to do was to arrange for rentals of skis, boots, poles, and lessons for Sasha. The advantage of skiing in Hokkaido is that it is always done on fresh snow. On nearly all of Sasha's trips to Hokkaido it snowed a few inches every day, usually in the evening, creating extremely good ski conditions, especially for cruising. There was corduroy to ski every morning. However, there was never enough snow for proper powder skiing, and the mountain had very few mogul runs. Also, the mountain is relatively short; therefore, the runs are not long, and only a few qualify for a truly steep, black-run experience. On the bright side, the lift lines were always short and sometimes completely empty, except for holiday weeks like on Chinese Lunar New Year, which Sasha's family generally tried to avoid, or when the ski conditions were perfect from a blanketing of new fallen snow that brought out the locals. There was a high-speed cable car, locally called "the rope," that took most skiers to the top of the mountain, and this was always crowded. Thus, the mountain was perfect for beginners and intermediate skiers, with just a touch of challenge to expand their experience. Sasha learned to ski on these slopes, and her skill and confidence grew with each season.

Each year, Sasha and her parents started on the primary lift to get their legs and feet back into ski mode, to test their balance and awaken their ski technique from a year's slumber. Once assured they would stay upright, they headed to "the rope" and took it to the top of the mountain where the temperature was colder, the snow was falling harder, and the runs were steeper and more difficult. On some days when the weather was especially harsh, the sky dark gray and the wind blowing fiercely, whipping cold snow into everyone's faces, the ropeway would be closed because of the high winds and poor visibility at the top. On those days, the usually empty lift lines would be crowded, as everyone wanted to get as high as possible to ski in the freshly falling snow.

Sasha learned from a number of ski instructors in her five winters in Hokkaido. Her first ski instructor, Satosi, spoke English and quickly became her best friend at the resort. He was patient, cheerful, and quite adept at teaching young beginners to ski. She not only learned the rudiments of downhill skiing, turning, and stopping but also had fun doing it with Satosi. Each day she looked forward to a new adventure with him, and she looked forward to the challenge of skiing more advanced terrain. With Satosi's support, she skied on a red intermediate run before the end of her first season in Hokkaido.

Sasha's confidence in skiing was growing faster than her parents' confidence in her ability. The three of them went skiing together one day after her ski lesson, and Sasha was eager to demonstrate her new skill. She went hurtling down the mountain far ahead of her parents. It felt grand, the wind whipping in her face, the snowy landscape flying by, when out of nowhere her father turned right in front of her causing a giant crash. As Sasha picked herself up, her mother caught up. It turns out she had been the one who had implored Sasha's father to catch her, believing that Sasha wouldn't know how to stop before the end of the run. Sasha was so mad she wouldn't speak to either parent for the rest of the day.

On her second year there, Sasha was pleased to find Satosi was also there again. Her first morning back in Hokkaido, after wolfing down a healthy breakfast, Sasha ran downstairs to the dressing room to don her ski clothes and wait to see her favorite instructor. When Satosi arrived, they were very happy to see each other and took off for parts unknown as soon as they locked into their skis. Eventually her parents found them

Sasha's ski instructor in Hokkaido

on the highest ski lift on the mountain, happy and having a good time. Apparently Sasha's friendly relationship with Satosi overcame any skiing trepidation she had as she started her second season. She was skiing down steeper slopes from the top of the mountain and making turns, albeit with legs wide apart in semi-snowplow fashion.

Parallel ski turns are the *bête noir* of amateur skiers. An older coach named Osama helped Sasha tackle this task in her next year at Hokkaido. He proceeded along very old-fashioned standards: first some calisthenics to loosen up the muscles, and always a focus on learning technique. By the end of Sasha's first morning of ski instruction with him, she was nearly blue from the cold and wind-blown snow. However, she was proud to demonstrate that she could make preliminary parallel turns on skis. Everyone was happy because he was such a competent, technically inclined ski instructor. Sasha's skiing kept improving, her turns becoming more parallel and down-slope facing. She looked fearless and skied very well under his constant instruction.

In between skiing, Sasha had interesting conversations with Coach Osama. She learned that bears and foxes inhabit the mountain during the summer; in winter they burrow higher up in the mountain, not to be seen again until spring. She also learned that the foxes carry disease, and the locals will not touch them.

By the end of Sasha's second season in Hokkaido, the high terrain no longer bothered her. On her last day there in 2014, she and her family went up to the higher runs, and she then proceeded to ski the entire length of the trail to the bottom without stopping.

Sasha took lessons from Osama again on her third trip to Hokkaido in 2015. She skied okay on her first day that year, with her feet spread well apart and making wedge turns, but by her second day on the slopes, Sasha was skiing surprisingly well. After her lesson ended, Osama commented that Sasha had grown and was much stronger.

The next day, he took her almost to the top of the mountain with several trips on the tram and one trip on the highest lift, which took her close to the very top. The air at the top was much colder, and the trees were covered in snow. It was a winter wonderland, made especially beautiful that day as the sun shone through the snow-covered trees and made the ground glisten. It was picture-perfect, and Sasha mastered all the runs Osama took her on. It arguably was her best day as she skied new terrain, learned new techniques, and enjoyed a sunny, relatively warm, windless day.

The day after that, Osama guided her onto a black run, her first ever. Along with her parents, they took the quad and the tram twice, and again Sasha wanted to show off and took a black run twice. That run ultimately joined Sailor, a red run that courses its way down to the bottom of the lifts.

Sasha navigated the black run perfectly the first time, but fell three times on her second try, once because one of her skis was not attached properly. After the falls, the family skied to the bottom and took a short run off a lower lift to help Sasha regain her confidence. She wound up with a headache, and everyone was glad she wore a helmet. Sasha demonstrated a strong resolve to overcome her skiing mistakes and quickly regained her confidence by continuing to ski in spite of her headache.

In Sasha's fourth year going to Hokkaido, she decided to try snowboarding. She learned the rudiments from a new coach named Paka, who was just about twenty years old. It was tough to learn, and Sasha fell many times and became very tired by the end of her two-hour lesson. Nevertheless, she claimed to like snowboarding more than skiing.

Sasha's snowboarding instructor in Hokkaido

During that trip, Sasha's snowboarding skills improved rapidly. She progressed enough to take her first lift on a snowboard and then made her way all the way to the bottom of the mountain. She continued to do this, and finally after the third decline, she managed to cut her falls down to just one! It was a sterling performance for her. When the final day of that winter's trip came, she hated to have to give up her snowboard. She had made significant and impressive progress after just two two-hour lessons. Her proud parents attributed her success to the innate sense of balance she developed from her years of performing in gymnastics. She also developed some character since she had to endure many falls but rose each time to try again. By the end of the trip, Sasha declared that she wanted to do more snowboarding.

Most of the skiing Sasha did was on the private resort side of the mountain, but the mountain had another side closer to the town of Furano that she hadn't explored in the first couple of years the family traveled to Hokkaido. One afternoon, Sasha and her parents decided to ski to the town side of the mountain. They wanted to investigate the older Furano Prince Hotel at the bottom of the mountain at the entrance to the town. The journey to the other side began on the tram and required a very fast ski downhill to the traverse that led to the other side of the mountain. In spite of the speed they built up on the downhill portion, the traverse still required some exhaustive poling to get to the link to the other side. Sasha and her parents finally reached the link and the main run that would take them to the bottom of the other side of the mountain. It was rolling and banked and thoroughly enjoyable. While in the area, they skied some green and red runs, and as Sasha rode the new chair lifts, she spotted a company from the Japanese army training on one of these same slopes. They were training on telemark skis, which made the runs much more challenging for the soldiers than for Sasha on her parabolic skis. Sasha was amused to watch these grown army men have the same kind of difficulty she had learning to ski without falling. A little farther on, she also saw a team of Japanese Olympic hopefuls training on a steep giant slalom run. Their fast turns and easy motions demonstrated years of training and talent. It gave Sasha something to think about and planted the seed for a possible future ambition.

Sasha's days in Hokkaido took on a routine year after year. The morning would start with a mixed Western-Japanese breakfast taken at the hotel, followed by a full day of skiing, with a break in the middle for lunch. Sasha's favorite luncheon spot on the mountain was a tiny bakery located at the base of the mountain on the far side of the hotel. She and her parents had lunch there often, munching on various types of homemade pastries. Some were filled with sausages, some with cheese, some with pumpkin, and others with potatoes. Everything was delicious, so they often overate and had to ski extra hard to work off the calories. This cute, casual restaurant resembled a fast-food take-out joint along some US highway, but it wasn't. It was typically Japanese: tiny and extremely efficiently designed to fit into the small space it occupied. The restaurant had six tiny tables and no facilities for hanging bulky ski parkas, scarfs, gloves, goggles, and helmets. Thus, everything had to be stowed somehow on or under the tiny table and chairs. It was always crowded with customers eager to warm up after a long morning of skiing in the frigid cold. Entering this crowded space taught Sasha to be courteous and considerate of other customers. Since most of the customers were Japanese and demonstrated abundant patience and courtesy, Sasha merely had to follow their exemplary behavior to enjoy the warmth and wonderful tastes of this special place.

Another favorite lunch spot was Restaurant Downhill, located at the top of the tram to the right of the quad. Lunch at this Japanese-style restaurant was self-service and consisted mostly of hot soup dishes, such as ramen, and hot Japanese green tea. When the snow stopped falling and the sky was clear, the views from this small, Alpine-like cabin at the top of the mountain were well worth the effort to get there and the sacrifice of choosing from a more complete lunch menu elsewhere.

When it was snowing too hard and the sky was dark gray, Sasha and her parents would ski all the way to the bottom of the mountain to have lunch at the soup restaurant by the rope. Everyone would be cold and go for the usual order of ramen. This traditional Japanese soup, made from fish or chicken with miso and several Japanese spices, is served piping hot and filled with chewy round noodles. Ramen is widely served in the cold north of Japan to keep skiers, field workers, and fishermen warm through the extremely cold winter. Sasha learned to love this staple food and still likes to order it many years later.

After a day skiing, Sasha's sore muscles cried out for a visit to the steaming pools of the hot springs in and outside of the hotel, followed by dinner in one of the resort's Japanese restaurants. The hotel had been built on top of an underground hot spring, and bathing in these naturally heated waters is a favorite custom of the Japanese. The hot springs among the snowy mountains made this a convenient site on which to build the hotel, since it combined easy access to skiing and bathing.

The pools and spa facilities were segregated by sex, with each having access to their own outdoor hot spring pool and larger indoor pool. Keeping the sexes separate was also important as the traditional Japanese way of bathing required one to be fully naked. It took Sasha maybe a day to get used to this and to test out being in the outdoor pool while it was snowing. Bathing in the open was another source of challenge for a young girl to take on, but Sasha soon grew accustomed to it and then thoroughly enjoyed the experience. She liked to jump between the hot pool and the very cold plunge pool to liven up the after-ski therapy. Only Sasha could jump back and forth between hot and cold this way. Her parents preferred to watch the swirling snow float down until it dissolved on to the heated surface of the pool or enjoy a soothing massage at the adjoining spa, which was necessary to relax the muscles after the strains of a full day of skiing.

Following a relaxing soak in the hot springs, it would be time for dinner. Food in Hokkaido was fresh and highlighted the variety of Japanese cuisine. The seating at the restaurants around the hotel varied between traditional Japanese style, with floor-level cushions, and modern tables and chairs. Sushi and sashimi were a staple cuisine, and all the fish was very fresh and quite flavorful. Other Japanese specialties were also served authentically including soups, noodles, fried and fresh vegetables, and many preparations of fish. Being unaccustomed to Japanese cuisine, Sasha had to broaden her horizons and learn to try new foods (she leaned toward eating the fresh vegetables and away from fish). Even the hotel's breakfast selection highlighted miso soup with squid and seaweed in addition to eggs and toast.

Hokkaido Island is famous in Japan for its fish and vegetable harvests, and these typical—and very tasty—local garden varieties were served at every meal. Because Hokkaido is located in the far north, the water around the island is remarkably clear and unpolluted. As a result, the abundant harvests from the oceans surrounding Hokkaido are world-famous for their quality, especially the fish, crabs, and scallops.

Sasha and her family's favorite restaurant for dinner most nights was an izakaya-style restaurant called Sumiyakidokoro Kitaguni, in another section of the basement of the hotel. This restaurant was set up in the traditional Japanese style with low tables and floor-level seating. For those not accustomed to sitting on the floor, some tables had sunken pits below them which allowed non-locals the opportunity to stretch out their legs, and there were cushions for everyone to sit on. Sasha loved this restaurant because when the sushi chefs saw her coming, they immediately yelled out their greeting in Japanese for all to hear. She also learned a lesson in Japanese etiquette here. Before entering the restaurant, everyone had to take off their shoes and place them next to the sliding wood doors at the front of the restaurant, laces facing front.

Kitaguni specialized in sushi and sashimi. They served only the freshest local fish from the ice-cold local waters surrounding Hokkaido. They also made the best baked potatoes, locally grown and loaded with local sweet butter. Occasionally, Sasha's parents ordered some sake to wash down the fish, shrimp, and potatoes. Sasha and her parents liked this restaurant so much that they ate dinner there most nights while they stayed in Furano.

Other nights, they ate at the restaurant at the top of the hotel. The highlight of those dinners was the gorgeous view of the mountain and its ski trails from the massive picture windows of the twelfth-floor restaurant. Because Furano offered night skiing until eight o'clock, the trails were illuminated, and Sasha could intermittently make out a skier quickly navigating the slopes. The menu in this main dining room was a mixture of Japanese and Western; however, the food choices came in Japanese-style set menus. The portions were small, but the food was very good, especially the delicious venison. Sasha and her parents would order sukiyaki, or sashimi and miso soup, or other nights, crispy tempura. The beef sukiyaki and shabu shabu were cooked in a large pot at the table over a Bunsen burner, which was a new experience for Sasha. She enjoyed eating her dinner by fishing in the steaming hot pot looking for some savory morsels of beef and occasionally she would spear a carrot or piece of potato. Each year that Sasha visited Hokkaido, she promised to vary her choices of foods. She kept her promise and tried everything, even the foods she didn't like.

After dinner, Sasha and her parents would bundle up in extra sweaters, scarves, hats, and gloves for their nightly walk through the quaint village across the road from the hotel. This replica of an old Japanese village was one of the resort's pleasant surprises. It consisted of two dozen wooden shops, constructed in the style of centuries past, set deep in the snow-covered forest on a boardwalk that needed constant shoveling. The shops sold handmade artisan items, and in most shops the artists could be seen working their craft. Everyone wanted some of these precious keepsakes, and Sasha and her parents would buy little holiday presents for one another from these unique shops. There were also two cozy coffee shops amid the artist's buildings where Sasha and her parents would stop for dessert and tea on those cold days, especially after a vigorous round of snowball fights.

Path through the wooden shops (Ningle Terrace)
in the New Furano Prince Hotel

Snowball fights were a common pastime for Sasha and her parents on these nightly walks through the village. The snow was fresh and easy to pack into snowballs. Sasha learned how to make them quickly even as a young child. Snowballs flew everywhere amid screams, shrieks, and even some falls into very deep snow. Curiously, Sasha did not observe any of the other tourists, mainly Japanese, indulging in similar fun. She considered that perhaps they felt it would be disrespectful to the artisans who maintained the shops along the wooden paths, and she made sure to be mindful not to hit any of the storefronts or the occasional tourist passing by. Although once, to her delight, one of them returned fire by throwing a snowball at Sasha. Snowball fights in the village were Sasha's second favorite activity during her trips to Hokkaido.

Her favorite activity took place at the edge of the village where the Kan Kan Mura was located. The Kan Kan Mura was a snowy fantasy world of snow tubing and ice sculptures. Here, Sasha quickly created a new routine: She would immediately grab a huge rubber inner tube and hurl herself down the snow-covered track, paying little heed to her worried parents. Next was snow rafting. Sasha would take several long toboggan rides, staying until the track closed. At this point, most of the other excited children would go back to the hotel with their parents, but Sasha was never finished. She felt she could go on forever! So she would grab a plastic can cover and tumble down more snow piles, fearless as ever.

As they were less enthusiastic about snow rides, Sasha's frozen parents took shelter in a small igloo nearby made of blocks of ice, in the middle of which was an authentic ice bar. Here they sampled some semi-frozen sake to keep warm during the bone-chilling nights. Other evenings, they enjoyed drinks at a rustic dwelling similar in style to the wooden shops in the artists' village that today serves as a modern bar and lounge. Soh's Bar was set deeper in the same forest and well past the end of the wooden platform supporting the shops. The trail leading down was steep and snow-covered, with drifts piled three feet high on either side. The journey on a frosty, moonlit night was treacherous, and usually included at least one slippery fall, but it was more than worth the effort, as a warm drink waited at a very modern, handsome wooden bar inside the ancient dwelling. Smoking was permitted here, and that was probably why it was hidden so deeply in the forest.

Although Sasha did not experience it, summer in Furano provides another treat. It is home to immense fields of lavender and other seasonal flowers. The scent, Sasha was told, is worth the visit, and her parents purchased many lavender-scented items in the hotel gift shop to bring back home to Singapore. The resort also had a golf course that Sasha could not see because it was under several feet of snow. But she was able to traverse the fairways on snow sleds and tubes powered by fast snowmobiles. Sasha loved the thrilling rides at twilight, and this added another dimension to her enjoyment after a day of skiing.

Sasha's love for Hokkaido grew with each visit to the island, as did her skiing skills. She loved the gently falling snow and the complete snow cover everywhere she looked—so different from the warmth and humidity of Singapore. As each day ended, it would begin to snow again, promising fresh powder for those lucky skiers in the morning. But all too soon, it would be time for Sasha to pack her bags and leave.

Each year as the lavender bus drove north toward the airport, she would gaze out at the mounds of snow that lined the streets of central Hokkaido. It was a wonderful reminder of how much snow falls in this cold, faraway skier's paradise. All Sasha could say repeatedly as she and her parents waited for the plane to take them home was that she wanted to ski more and couldn't wait to return the next year to Hokkaido.

4

Sabah Borneo, Indonesia

IN MAY 2014, SASHA WENT TO one of the world's most exotic and least-traveled places: Borneo, Indonesia. It probably won't qualify as least traveled for long because it has some first-class five-star resorts; and the expectation among resort professionals is that it is on the cusp of some major development projects, as is nearly all of Asia. Sasha's destination was Sabah, which is one of two Malaysian provinces in Borneo. Sabah claims the lion's share of land area and population in Borneo, while the remaining regions belong to the tiny, oil-rich kingdom of Brunei.

Sasha and her parents flew in to the newly constructed airport in Kota Kinabalu, the third-largest city in Malaysia. The airport itself loudly hinted at Borneo's preparations for the expected wave of tourists to the area in the near future. Sasha's eyes were wide open as she traveled from the airport to the Gaya Island Resort, a five-star resort on a mostly uninhabited island in the South China Sea. The journey started by taxi, which drove to a tiny, palm-thatched building that served as the departure point for a fast boat ride across the Gaya Sound in the South China Sea. Sasha saw few other vehicles on the road as they passed through tiny villages that were probably formed centuries ago and hadn't changed since. She watched the people eating or selling modest articles of clothes by the roadside, and they seemed as interested in Sasha as she was in them.

The boat was modest in size but fairly speedy, churning up small waves and splashing Sasha with seawater. The sea voyage took Sasha and her parents past the bustling modern city of Kota Kinabalu, which stood in dramatic contrast to the large tracts of stilt houses built over the water. Sasha never saw the people in the tall modern buildings, but she did see the humble people living footsteps above the water. She saw them bathing and doing laundry in the sea, their lives inextricably tied to the water as it had been for centuries past. It was a way of life Sasha had never seen before, and she looked on with curiosity. She must have wondered whether these people ever crossed the bay to visit the modern buildings on the other side.

An attentive staff waited for Sasha's family on Gaya Island, took their luggage, and escorted them from the dock to the open-walled lobby with a gorgeous view of the main island and Mount Kinabalu, the tallest mountain on Borneo, reaching some 4,095 meters high. Sasha was immediately impressed with their attentiveness and began to form a fond view of this island. When the staff realized how young Sasha was, they offered the family a choice of rooms. The original room they had selected was situated at the end of the property, which offered much desired privacy and a superb view of Mount Kinabalu across the tranquil lagoon, but it proved too long a walk for little Sasha, so her parents chose a similar room closer to the beach and main facilities of the resort. The room was splendid, with an L-shaped wraparound balcony. The air conditioning was more than was needed, infrequently used, and supplemented by a large ceiling fan over the king-sized bed. The room service was exceptional, with fresh towels and accompaniments provided twice a day. Through the windows, Sasha could see the beach and the magnificent foliage spreading down to the water's edge. She couldn't wait to start exploring.

The path that led from their room to the beach and the main hotel facilities was an attractive, hardwood boardwalk. It led to a large, open-kitchen dining room with one wall open to views of the sea. Breakfast was served there each day and included a large array of Western and Eastern options. It started with freshly squeezed juices from several different kinds of fruits, many of which Sasha had never seen before. There were also many types of baked breads and pastries, eggs, pancakes, several types of roti, and other rice-and-noodle-based Asian foods. The dinner menu was similarly a collection of Asian-inspired, native Borneo specialties, and some typical Western selections, and the dessert bar had surprisingly bountiful and delicious options as well. All were individually prepared and delivered by a smiling staff.

The friendly, hardworking chef was exceptional. He took a liking to Sasha and prepared many special treats for her for breakfast and dinner from his repertoire of native Borneo dishes. When he did, his choices were delicious; the most memorable was local lobster in citrus sauce, roasted prawns in their own sauce, a pungent eggplant salad, lime-cured ceviche, a wonderful duck in a thick, dark sauce, and sea bass cooked in a leaf with spicy sauce. Sasha's only regret was that the number of dishes brought to the table was overwhelming and she could not sample all of them. Since she had not yet formed opinions about the various foods, she was open to trying most everything.

Dinner was served either in the main dining room with its open kitchen on the beach that boasted a large roaring fire for barbecue, or above all the rooms in an open-air dining room that looked out at the distant lights on the main island over the pitch-black lagoon. Service everywhere was attentive, friendly, and very helpful, and it continued to impress Sasha as she was forming her impression of Borneo.

All the main public rooms of the resort opened onto either the beach, the sea, or the very long, narrow swimming pool situated parallel to the beach and only a few footsteps from the sea. While narrow, it was long enough to give even the most ardent swimmer a healthy workout. The long pool included a swim-up bar, complete with common bar games like chess on a magnetized board that Sasha found fascinating. She learned to play rudimentary chess because of the magnetic pieces.

Sasha engaged in numerous other activities during her stay at this beautiful resort. Her day started on a spacious deck located at the fringe of the jungle where morning yoga classes were held. Sasha, however, went every morning to see the multitude of beautifully colored and unusual tropical birds, some of which are unique to Borneo, such as the rhinoceros hornbill. Because it was at the edge of the forest, the deck was also host to swarms of mosquitos who constantly interrupted the more serious yoga enthusiasts. The resort's design is a green one that remains kind to the natural environment, so mosquitos were prevalent.

The jungle environment was exactly why Sasha and her parents were here—so that they could fully experience it. Sasha was most excited for a guided nature walk on their first afternoon. A local trained naturalist led them high up into the mountains behind the resort on a narrow, twisting dirt path past new and old trees. One was a fig tree that was more than four hundred years old. They climbed up past thick vines, which Sasha found fascinating. Their guide informed them the natives cut pieces from these vines and placed them in ponds to kill all the resident fish for their own consumption. As they continued down paths with steps hewed out of the mountain and strewn with exposed giant tree roots, their guide pointed out trees that secrete a sap that would harden and when burned would yield a frankincense aroma that would drive away pesky mosquitos. Sasha also saw and learned about ginseng trees, whose leaves are considered an aphrodisiac, and funguses that aid in cancer relief. She even got a glimpse of a pit viper high up in a tree only because the local guide had spied him on a trek the day before. The jungle was full of lizards of all sizes, and it had a few natural streams fed from underground sources. They passed the entrance of a second trail designed for more ambitious, experienced hikers that would take them to the private beach about two long hours away. That trail required an advanced reservation and a private guide because the resort was concerned about unexpected encounters with poisonous snakes and aggressive monkeys. Sasha realized that out here, the swarms of ravenous mosquitos were the least of their worries.

Sasha and her parents also went on a guided snorkeling trip over the nearby reefs in the lagoon to the right of the resort. They were accompanied by a couple of marine biologists who described everything Sasha saw. She became fascinated with one of the biologists who was desperate to tell a willing listener of his activities on the reef and in his private aquarium. He was of unknown European extraction but spoke English well and took a liking to Sasha's inquisitiveness. He loved showing Sasha all of his aquariums, which were housed in a cement block shed and were filled with marine life that he and his team collected from the lagoon. Sasha was enthralled and often trailed after him in the following days to see if he had brought any new marine creatures in from the sea to place in his aquariums.

Fish tank and biologist on Gaya Island in Borneo

The aquariums were funded by the hotel to teach guests about the various life forms present on the reef, but for our biologist, they were part of his research for a PhD in marine biology. He also led Sasha on several snorkeling trips along the reef and showed her the many places he would find such interesting creatures. These were her first experiences of underwater exploration, and he was a great resource for her to learn from. Snorkeling was also the first time Sasha had occasion to use her newly learned swimming skills. Up until then, she thought that being in the water was only useful for splashing contests and swimming lessons.

The water in the lagoon was exceptionally clear, as there had never been any industrial activity in this region and the population was relatively small. The coral was the highlight of the reef. It was blessed with an incredible array of seemingly endless varieties of living coral. It supported a healthy population of small coral reef fish, which Sasha discovered as she and the guide snorkeled. Though she heard of larger fish out there, on all her snorkeling trips she saw nothing larger than a medium-sized grouper.

Another day, Sasha's family went on a scuba diving trip over reefs on the undeveloped side of Gaya Island accompanied by the same marine biologist. Sasha was far too young to engage in scuba lessons; however, she did enjoy snorkeling above her scuba-diving parents. This side of the island fronts the South China Sea, which was incredibly clear and warm, making diving a real pleasure. It was also uncommonly placid for a large body of open water, and it had only a modest current to factor into dive calculations. Sasha and her parents eagerly jumped into the sea to snorkel and scuba and traversed a long bay fringed by a large, highly variegated coral reef. They were delighted to happen on two schools of small barracuda and a group of large squid possibly mating. The squid were ghostlike in appearance with long, trailing tentacles and huge black eyes that at first frightened Sasha until the biologist informed her what they were. While the dive was memorable, the real indulgence was the boat that brought Sasha and her family to the dive site: a two-month-old, twin diesel, thirty-nine-foot yacht with the most advanced electronic navigation technology. The friendly and hospitable captain invited Sasha to steer the boat, which she thoroughly enjoyed.

Sasha was even more elated to get to go on a sunset cruise aboard that boat's bigger brother, a sixty-four-foot yacht that slept eight in princely comfort. From this yacht's bridge, Sasha looked out on a broad view of the surrounding islands. The magic of the water and South Sea Islands was magnified by the sun's vividly colorful setting over the South China Sea. Sasha's only regret that evening was that this yacht's captain would not let her drive the boat.

The resort also had two lesser crafts that transported guests to a private beach, located several hundred kilometers away around a promontory. When Sasha and her family arrived at this beach, it was nearly deserted. There was a small kitchen under a palm-thatched roof and a dining room that was totally open-air, sandwiched between the verdant jungle and the sea-green lagoon. The water at the private beach was clear, warm, and inviting, and it was home to many tiny fish and crabs. Sasha enjoyed the feel of the sand beneath her feet, soft and free from shells, coral, and assorted debris, which made wading into the sea very comfortable. Farther up the beach, the sand was clean, not hot, and useful for building elaborate sandcastles.

However, the real attraction for Sasha, once she overcame her initial fear of him, was the semi-domesticated wild boar circling the kitchen in the afternoons looking for a handout. Equally frightening for Sasha and her parents was a large tribe of Macaw monkeys that would swoop down onto the beach in search of anything the tide would wash in or hotel guests would leave unattended. It became Sasha's principle occupation to stand guard watching for the monkeys and to shout out that the monkeys were coming. To complete the scene were many large and small lizards that darted through the sand and the trees, alternatingly frightening and fascinating Sasha.

Chef on Gaya Island in Borneo

Sasha enjoyed the many conversations she had with the marine team, the chef, and the restaurant and bar manager. They nurtured in her a first ambition: to become the general manager of a five-star resort. Her ambition was given a big boost when she and her family had a conversation with Paul, the GM of Gaya Island Resort. He described his lengthy path to becoming a GM and told many anecdotes from his years working in hotels, including some of the pitfalls. When he told Sasha that his job was twenty-four hours a day, seven days a week, and required that he lived on the resort, that only propelled her aspirations. When he then offered Sasha the opportunity to become an apprentice in his hotel twelve years later, her eyes positively lit up.

Sasha's biggest regret was having to leave on a sun-drenched beach day. She loved the tropical climate on Gaya Island, which was less humid and milder than in Singapore. She could get used to the warm sun in the morning, the clouds forming in early afternoon, and the rain showers later in the day, she thought, and could not wait to return one day to fulfill her longtime ambition of becoming a resort general manager.

5

Shanghai, China

IT HAS OFTEN BEEN SAID that the easiest way to learn a foreign language is to be immersed in it. Sasha's first task was to learn Mandarin. She had short classes in Mandarin every day in her school in Singapore and a one-hour Chinese tutor each week, but what better way to learn Mandarin than to attend a Chinese language program in Shanghai? This is exactly what Sasha did for two summers while living in Singapore.

Sasha and her dad flew to Shanghai from Singapore and arrived at Shanghai Pudong International Airport. The Pudong side of Shanghai is ultra-modern and the huge airport was built to support at least a decade's expansion. The ride across the river into the more historic Puxi side of Shanghai later that night took them past darkened buildings on an elevated highway that extended from the airport all the way into the heart of the city. As Sasha passed over the Huangpu River, a tributary of the great Yangtze, she caught her first glimpse of the famous Shanghai skyline.

The Chinese planners had a great deal of space and bundles of ambition when they began recreating the Bund, Shanghai's famous riverfront walkway, and its signature skyline view of the Pudong side of the river. Although still unfinished, it was already truly one of the most memorable skylines in the world, and when lit up at night, the colorful spires rival those of any other city. Sasha was constantly drawn to it, whether at night or during the day. One day Sasha and her father took a tiny train that traversed under the river to the Pudong side of Shanghai so they could observe the skyline from the opposite side. The Puxi skyline is older and less dramatic than the Pudong side. It offers a view of older Shanghai before the modern renovations. The key feature of the Pudong skyline as seen from the Bund is the diversity of architectural styles that populate the waterfront and beyond, a testament to the artistic flair used in their construction.

Prior to Sasha's arrival in Shanghai, her father had travelled there to explore the city's expat-oriented schools for children. He had liked several, but the one that impressed him most was the Shanghai American School, especially their recently expanded Puxi campus. The new campus was a large, sprawling school with separate buildings for primary, elementary, and high school. It also boasted a large, ultra-modern auditorium/theater with Broadway-style lighting and moving stages. It had buildings for swimming, reading, and other activities, plus spacious fields for outdoor sport activities. Consequently, he enrolled Sasha in a four-week summer course in Chinese and Chinese culture. The choice of school in Shanghai would not only fulfill her parents' plan for Sasha to be educated in Chinese but also give Sasha the opportunity to live in one of the most modern and dynamic metropolises in the world.

The school taught its students using a mixture of English and Chinese with an emphasis on culture and language. Sasha's classmates consisted of non-Chinese Asian and expats from America, Australia, and Europe. Culture instruction stressed Chinese food, clothes, holidays, music, and musical instruments. Sasha and her classmates were asked to dress in traditional Chinese garments on several days, eat Chinese food at lunch, and at the end of the program perform songs and make presentations in Chinese with their parents in the audience. In addition to her hours in school, Sasha also enjoyed seeing rural and urban parts of Shanghai on her long bus ride home to the Ascott Residence, where she lived both summers while in Shanghai. She saw scenes of still-rural sections of Shanghai that she would never have been exposed to had she attended a local expat school in the Puxi section of Shanghai.

On the next-to-last weekend of SAS school in Shanghai, Sasha's mother invited Sasha and her father to join her in Beijing for a brief excursion in this famous city. Sasha's mother was in Beijing to expand her company's footprint in Asia, particularly in China. She planned this quick trip for Sasha meticulously, with a short list of essential highlights to explore. Sasha left SAS school and hurried from her bus to meet her father, who had a limousine waiting to take them both to the Hongqiao airport. The plane trip was relatively quick; however, it was already very dark in Beijing. Immediately upon deplaning, Sasha and her parents encountered Beijing's infamous pollution, which quickly interfered with their breathing.

Sasha was thrilled to see her mother and explain to her all the school activities she had been doing. Meanwhile, her mother began to recite the compact and energetic agenda she created for the next two days. The brief trip would begin in Tiananmen Square, where they would be able to see in the distance the Forbidden City. Sasha was impressed at the scale of the square, having never seen such a large open space in the middle of a major urban center. She was also amazed at the number of people walking within the confines of the square and the number of uniformed soldiers controlling everyone's movements.

They hiked from the gigantic square across the main thoroughfare and kept walking until they reached the gates to the Forbidden City. After some huffing and puffing and consuming a bottle of water, Sasha reached the gates, entered the Forbidden City, and looked up at the immense height of the buildings. She was quite puzzled by the enormity of the buildings and the lavishness of thrones and altars inside but most pleased at seeing the deep red colors of the buildings' wooden sides.

Fortunately, Sasha's mother hired a driver so they wouldn't have to walk back through Tiananmen Square to its other side to reach the Palace Museum. After Sasha climbed all the stairs to the top of the palace, she said that she thought it was more beautiful than the Forbidden City. Maybe it was simply the scale of the palace, which is more accessible to a child's eye than the Forbidden City is. Their day was nearly finished, and everyone was tired. They headed back to their hotel and thought about dinner. Everyone wanted to sample Peking duck from its origins. And so they did.

Sasha at the Great Wall of China

The next morning started very early because Sasha's parents were informed that it is best to view the Great Wall early, before the crowds form and swarm over all parts of it. They arrived soon after it opened and climbed many stairs to the top. As Sasha began walking along it, she imagined how it was a buttress against nomadic tribes that were trying to gain access to the forbidden city in years gone by. They left the wall in wonderment at the amount of time and the number of people involved in its massive construction. After purchasing a few souvenirs from the multitude of stands that lined the street leading to the entrance of the wall, they entered their taxi to return to the center of Beijing.

Their first stop was to walk around the new opera house, with its moat, and observe the most artistic and modern public monument in China. The opera is inside the National Center for Performing Arts, along with theaters and music halls. Sasha exclaimed, "It looks like a giant egg split in half!" She later learned that the other half is underground. By Chinese law, the building could not be taller than the Forbidden City. Sasha asked several times why there was water surrounding the building, and a guide told her that the entire building is floating on the water beneath it. Inside, the immense scope of the arts center and its unique shape was very impressive. Unfortunately, there were no performances scheduled for the day they were there, and they reluctantly left.

After consuming a quick lunch of duck and dumplings, it was time to return to the hotel, pack their things, say goodbye to Sasha's mom, drive to the international airport, and make the short flight back to Shanghai. During the flight, Sasha had much to ruminate about, and she reflected on the convergence of old Chinese and modern Chinese buildings and their unique differences. She had much to share with her fellow students.

Sasha's second summer in Shanghai was spent at the YK Pao School located in Puxi, much closer to the Ascott Residence. At her first-day orientation in her new school, the school's cofounder spoke about the institution's goal to instill a desire to learn Chinese language and culture. Sasha liked everything about her new school, especially the swimming pool and the big swimming race they had, in which she came in third out of eleven. She made a new friend in her class, Rachael, a Korean girl who also lived in Singapore and attended Singapore American School. She made another friend named Isabella, a half-Chinese girl who lived in Virginia, on the yellow bus coming home from school.

Homework was assigned, so before leaving for dinner, Sasha did her first night's homework, which was to read a Chinese book. When she finished reading the story in Chinese, she had to retell it in English to demonstrate her understanding. Already Sasha could feel her Chinese improving, as it had the previous summer.

One aspect of the school's curriculum called for the teachers to take their classes to the maritime museum, where they observed several real Chinese vessels. There Sasha saw a memorable 4D movie about Chinese ships, and she came home with a great amount of Chinese paraphernalia.

End-of-school play in Shanghai

The school produced its annual talent show on the last day of its summer school program. The show began at one-thirty in the afternoon, and eager parents frantically snapped pictures of the class, their children, and the performances. Sasha was in three of the acts, including a kung fu demonstration and another in which she had a speaking role. Sasha's part in the third presentation was to sit in a plastic bowl and swivel around the stage. Other classmates had to perform similar physical tasks, all while one of the Chinese instructors danced among them in an ancient theme.

◉

SASHA REALLY LIKED HER SHANGHAI RESIDENCE. The hotel where she stayed, the Ascott Residence, was a modern, glass-walled building with thirty-three floors. The room she shared with her father was quite spacious, especially for China. It included a small serviceable kitchen and dining table. The large, east-facing windows gave Sasha a panoramic view of an extensive, pretty park with many multicolored blooming plants; and above that, a large network of busy elevated highways.

The best feature of this hotel is its location; it is just a few short steps away from the entrance to the locally famous Xintiandi area. This is a refurbished part of the city that had been one of the nearly one-hundred-year-old French colonial quarters. The urban planners preserved the short, narrow streets and the two- to three-story brick buildings, but the buildings' interiors had been completed gutted and modernized. Today, most of these buildings are home to upscale Asian and Western restaurants and retail boutiques. Sasha considered it to be a daily or nightly ritual to wander through these streets with her father, either to satisfy her craving for good food or simply to window-shop.

During her summers exploring Shanghai, Sasha also visited three other neighborhoods (called *concessions*) that once housed European colonists nearly one hundred years ago. These concessions were also modernized, but Sasha thought that none of them was as posh as Xintiandi. They were composed mainly of small retailers selling primarily tourist-oriented fare and smaller, less expensive restaurants. While walking through these tight quarters Sasha's dad began to inform her that these narrow streets, which were often jammed with shoppers and tourists, probably presented a more authentic image of the way streets in Shanghai used to be in the twentieth-century Chinese Republic era.

Usually after Sasha finished her after-school snack at the local tea shop, she and her father took a very long walk that covered most of the streets north of Huaihai Road. The sidewalks in Shanghai are not safe for pedestrians since motorized bikes and motorcycles are permitted to drive on the sidewalks. Scooters and motorcycles ride up and down on the sidewalks and often startle and nearly collide with pedestrians who are walking absent-mindedly. One afternoon, Sasha was on a quest to find a shop that sold Chinese garments for children. But she couldn't find any since all the shops in the area sold only modern, Western-designed clothes. Chinese women with medium- to upper-level income apparently had forsaken traditional styles and adopted Western ones.

The modernization program in Shanghai was proceeding at breakneck pace following the government's declaration that Shanghai would be a free-trade zone with relatively open financial markets. The city was changing profoundly, as Sasha learned from conversations with hotel staff and English-speaking taxi drivers. She also watched the construction of many high-rise buildings from the windows of her apartment. It seemed to Sasha that new construction was springing up everywhere, especially in Shanghai's outer circles.

In the center of the city, the government was tearing down all of the older quarters. One day, Sasha learned that the current government's plans would destroy one of the ancient villages in the middle of Puxi within six months. This old village, filled with many small antique stores, was one of Sasha's favorite destinations. She would wander through the colorful shops on her own—sometimes losing sight of her father. The many, often noisy stalls and tiny shops selling oriental clothes and artifacts were a huge tourist attraction. The government's plan for this area was to make it resemble Xintiandi, filled with expensive restaurants and international designer retail stores. Soon the quaintness and uniqueness of the old city would disappear, much to Sasha's dismay.

On occasional walks toward the west side of the city, Sasha became more aware that there were hundreds of urban renewal projects taking place throughout central Shanghai. Many of the old shop houses, dilapidated residences, and sprawling stores were being destroyed and cleared for new, modern, high-rise buildings littered with expensive stores and restaurants. These were poor neighborhoods where Sasha saw people eating noodles from soup bowls on the streets. Her dad wondered out loud where a more affluent group of people would come from to partake in the refined restaurants and designer stores since the people who were being displaced did not seem to have enough money to enjoy the bounty found in the new projects.

If there's something the Shanghai city planners did well, it was to provide many open green spaces that were widely scattered across the huge city. Sasha and her dad often took long walks through these parks, sometimes traveling from one park to another. Most of the parks boasted at least one very large bed of highly colorful flowers. Sasha loved to pick the flowers and then watch the ducks and swans swim gracefully in the parks' many lakes. She also liked to seek out the resident cats that would occasionally reveal themselves after hiding somewhere in the terrain.

The most impressive relic in the city that Sasha stumbled upon, and that she would return to often, was the Yuyuan Gardens. These gardens were created during the Ming Dynasty in 1577. Today, they can be found tucked behind an old-fashioned shopping district made up of many aged multistory retail buildings. The architecture of the traditional gardens is old-fashioned, with impressive figures of animals and gods lining the curved roofs that are quintessentially Chinese: pillared walkways over water, a red pagoda, and intricate carvings everywhere. Sasha never would have guessed that within the maze of retail shops was this large temple with a fat Buddha and a small lake filled with carp.

The gardens themselves are a treasure of water, stone, and wood, and easily create a perfect backdrop for photographers. On each of her visits, Sasha was able to witness a professional photo session with Chinese models in traditional Chinese dress. Although the gardens were always crowded with visitors, one could easily imagine how beautiful and serene the setting once was, and might still be, on a quiet afternoon.

Picture-taking on the Bund in Shanghai

Walking the streets of Shanghai often led Sasha back to the Bund, with its glorious view of the city skyline, one of the most photographed sites in all of China. And every time Sasha walked along the Bund looking at the ships sailing past or up at the tall buildings on the other side, other visitors' cameras would turn toward her. Sasha, with her blonde hair and blue eyes, created a stir among the Chinese tourists who clamored to take her picture—especially next to their children. She indulged the Chinese sightseers' petitions with a gracious smile and then moved on, wondering why everyone wanted to take her picture.

Sasha with her dad, Uncle Steve, and Aunt Tatiana on the Bund

After walking along the upper wall of the Bund and experiencing the influx of tourists mostly from western China, Sasha and her father would eventually come to Nanjing Street, a famous street lined with stores and filled with shoppers. They would race down the steps to reach the street, cross the busy thoroughfare carefully, and proceed to walk to this world-famous shopping street. On one such visit, they stopped at the Silk King, a store that—as its name indicates—designs, makes, and sells silk garments for men, women, and children. Sasha and her father started looking for silk pajamas, and in the process, the Chinese sales ladies discovered that Sasha understood Mandarin. While they were fitting and selling the two pair of silk pajamas, they talked to Sasha in Chinese. "Where is your family from? How old are you? What brings you to Shanghai and China?" they asked. Sasha responded and returned their inquiry similarly and even translated it for her father. Being able to make connections with people this way made Sasha glad she was learning this foreign language.

ON DAYS WHEN SASHA DIDN'T HAVE SCHOOL, she and her father took several trips outside of the Shanghai city limits. The first was to visit an old Catholic monastery on the side of a huge hill about one and a half hours' drive from their hotel. Because it was still cold in China on the day of their visit, there were few blooming flowers, but they could tell that after the air warmed in the coming months, many trees would be in bloom.

The climb up the mountain to the monastery was testing, and it took most of Sasha's determination to reach the summit. Along the way, she was asked to have her picture taken with many of the other children who were also climbing the mountain, and as much as the requests still befuddled her, Sasha appreciated the momentary rest. On the very top of the mountain was an ancient observatory that had been converted into a space museum. It housed the first space telescope that was employed in this region of China dating back more than two hundred years. Sasha studied the interesting and historic pictures of famous people and far-away stars seen from this telescope. When she finished looking at the pictures, she and her father continued on in search of the monastery. After several false starts down empty trails, they finally found the old, abandoned church. But the building was locked, and thus Sasha never got to see the beautiful gothic architecture it was reputed to have.

On a second school holiday, Sasha and her father took another trip outside of Shanghai to visit an old water village. It was also about ninety minutes south of downtown Puxi. The water village was extremely crowded especially for a midday, midweek visit. Many visitors were eating at the tiny stands that lined the narrow alleyways, and although they were numerous, they were dominated by many fast-food restaurants throughout the village. As Sasha and her father walked through the crowded village, they found little of interest to see or to purchase other than fast food. Because of the extremely crowded conditions and narrow corridors, it was also impossible to avoid being bumped into and ingloriously wearing someone else's snack. Sasha was not impressed with the food or the smells of deep-frying oil that filled the air. The river was also a total misnomer; at best the village was built around narrow canals that were highly polluted, judging from the color and the smells emanating from the water as they approached each bridge. After an unpleasant hour, Sasha and her father returned to the car and proceeded back to Xintiandi, where they settled into one of the less crowded open-air restaurants to enjoy a quieter lunch.

Restaurants in Shanghai were another high point. The quality and diversity of offerings rivaled any major city. Of course, Chinese food dominated, and there was as much choice among the various styles of Chinese, Tibetan, and Mongolian foods as there was among international varieties. The most memorable dinner Sasha experienced and one of her favorites had to be the dinner show at the Ye Shanghai restaurant. Dinner was served in a large, old-fashioned building with heavy, ornately carved wood everywhere. The show began with a blend of athletic magic and operatic dance. The dancers' costumes were colorful, authentic early Chinese, and highly decorative. Sasha, as an eager gymnast, was fascinated by the dancers' movements and flexibility. She was also surprised and thoroughly entertained by the tricks performed by the various magicians.

Another night, Sasha went to a Chinese restaurant in a nearby commercial building that had been recommended to her father. This restaurant was reputed to make the best dumplings in Shanghai. Both Sasha and her dad ordered shrimp-filled soup dumplings, which burst inside their mouths with hot spicy soup at the first bite. They were indeed scrumptious. Sasha also ordered a tasty beef dish, followed by a dessert of the best mango sago she ever had. This restaurant soon became a regular favorite of Sasha's.

Another night, after completing the day's homework assignments, Sasha chose simpler fare and went to a small restaurant in a nearby commercial building for some popcorn chicken and French fries. Unfortunately, the service at that restaurant was abysmal. As Sasha and her father waited and waited for their food, other patrons were equally frustrated by the poor service and complained loudly. Sasha passed the time by translating for her father the vile comments being made by the irate Chinese patrons at the surrounding tables. The long wait became a marvelous opportunity for Sasha to realize just how many Chinese words she was learning. Finally, she and her father finished dinner and agreed that they would never return. Shanghai, however, will always hold a special place in Sasha's heart as one of the most dynamic, cosmopolitan cities she has had the privilege of living in.

6

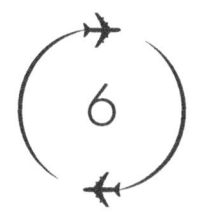

New Year's in Australia

AFTER OPENING AND ENJOYING a cornucopia of Christmas presents piled high under the family Christmas tree, Sasha left her home in Singapore for a New Year's visit to Australia. Her journey started in Melbourne, Australia's most European-like major city. Some Melbourne highlights are its spacious and attractive public parks, which are scattered throughout the city; a winding river running through it leading to extensive docklands; and most prominently, a vigorous commitment to world-class sports facilities located throughout the city. The Australian tennis open was soon to be held in Melbourne's spacious tennis complex shortly after Sasha and her parents were scheduled to leave.

When Sasha arrived in Melbourne two days before New Year's Day, Australia was in the middle of its summer since it is deep in the southern hemisphere. But it felt like anything but summer; temperatures were in the low single digits and near freezing at night. Sasha felt the bite of the cool air as soon as she stepped off the plane. She and her family hadn't thought to bring appropriate cold weather clothing, so on her first night in Melbourne, while walking along the banks of the Ybarra river following a fine dinner, Sasha shivered all the way to her hotel.

Her first morning in Melbourne started bright and sunny but very cool—excellent weather for walking around the city and visiting its many parks. After securing tickets for a New Year's Eve performance at Hamer Hall, Sasha went for a horse-and-carriage ride through downtown Melbourne. The two large horses that pulled the decorated black carriage were named Ben and Bow, perhaps in memory of the infamous pirate Ben Bow from the book *Treasure Island*, one of Sasha's favorite bedtime-story books. Sasha sat up front with the horses and their driver as the carriage drove through Chinatown and along Collins Street, Melbourne's most prominent shopping strip.

After concluding the carriage ride and having her picture taken with both horses, Sasha decided she wanted to see the famous Melbourne aquarium. She was mesmerized by the enormous shark tanks and followed these large dangerous creatures from the other side of the glass as they swam around and above her head. The only thing more exciting than the sharks were the penguins, which Sasha found adorable. She enjoyed taking pictures with them in their icy habitat.

Inspired by her visit with the penguins at the aquarium, Sasha was curious to see wild penguins in the only place they could be found on mainland Australia: Phillip Island. The visit to Phillip Island required a long bus ride to the southernmost point on Australia's mainland. As the bus drove through the flat, fertile plain, Sasha looked out the window at the huge farms where farmers grew wheat, corn, and vegetables—and where roving kangaroos munched on the farmers' produce. It was Sasha's first time seeing kangaroos except in pictures in the many story books about Australia her father had read to her before taking this trip. It was no comparison to seeing them in real life!

Once on Phillip Island, Sasha had to pull on several sweaters as well as a new hoodie purchased at the souvenir store, as the cold came with dusk. She then settled in on the outdoor stands along with everyone else, waiting until darkness to see the penguins. Their guide had informed Sasha that once the sun set behind the clouds, the cautious penguins would begin to form groups in the water before swimming through the waves and scampering ashore. Once onshore, they had to navigate an arduous climb up the cliff to their nests. They were terrified of predators such as hawks and foxes and therefore would only travel in small groups, never alone.

After a spine-chilling wait, the penguins finally appeared. First it was just a black head bobbing in the waves, then more joined, and finally they came surfing through the waves and clambering ashore, swept in by the power of the surging sea. Some lost their footing and were carried back out by the receding waves. Those then had to mount another attack, riding the next oncoming wave until their little feet found purchase on the shore.

At first Sasha watched from a seat high up in the stands. But after many of the spectators below decided to follow the penguins up the cliffs, Sasha was able to jump down from level to level until she reached the beach, and then she crawled until she came within a few feet of the little penguins waddling past. She followed their progress with rapt interest. The small penguins cautiously trod over the sand and up through the tall grasses and mosses that covered the hills.

It was difficult for Sasha to follow the penguins because of the other spectators lining the boardwalk. The thick ferns that grew over the hills and contained the birds' nests also obscured most of their movements. In the morning, these birds of the sea would make their way down the cliffs and slip back into the ocean, safe from the predatory birds and animals that hunted them.

By the time Sasha crawled back into the bus to go back to Melbourne, it was well past her bedtime, and she fell asleep almost instantly. The next morning, Sasha still could not get over the special experience of seeing the penguins in their natural habitat. It made a much bigger impression on her than simply seeing them in an enclosure and taking pictures with them at the aquarium. This experience stayed with her. The memories have been savored and relived many times since.

New Year's Eve broke bright and clear, offering perfect conditions for observing the evening's fireworks display. Following a hearty breakfast, Sasha made her way over to St. Patrick's Cathedral, the largest Catholic church in Australia. The church is a model of gothic architecture, and it is very reminiscent of St. Patrick's Cathedral in New York City, except with fewer visitors. Sasha lit a candle in honor of the end of 2013 and then ventured into Fitzroy Gardens a short distance away from the church. Inside the park, she came across a fascinating sight: English explorer Captain Cook's original house reconstructed in painstaking detail. The house was transported by ship in its entirety from its original location on the west coast of England. Inside, it was styled with real antiques and furnishings from the period. It offered Sasha a reminder of how small and cramped the Spartan lifestyle was back in the early eighteenth century, even for professional families such as Captain Cook's. No wonder men chose to sail the seas to unknown ports to break from the closures of life at home. The rest of the park itself was splendid and in full summer bloom.

That afternoon, Sasha attended a New Year's Eve program at Hamer Hall starring several of Australia's biggest musical stars. It was beautiful and acoustically perfect. Sasha happily sang or clapped her hands to several crowd-pleasing pop tunes that are played at every New Year's performance, and she attentively listened to the slower pieces. After the show, it was time for her to dress for dinner and fireworks later in the evening. Dinner was at the Sofitel Melbourne hotel that night, and it featured several French music troupes that paraded around the tables and entertained the diners with familiar French street tunes. They even sang in several different languages. Next were the fireworks displays. There were two: one a children's program at the reasonable hour of nine-thirty in the evening, and the traditional but larger one at midnight to usher in the New Year. Sasha stayed awake to enjoy both.

On New Year's Day, Sasha and her parents headed off for a long drive down to the famous Great Ocean Road. Their destination was the

Twelve Apostles, a famous series of massive rock stacks along the shore of Port Campbell National Park in Victoria, about a four-hour drive from Melbourne. After they left the city behind, the highway wound through mostly farmlands until arriving at the Great Southern Ocean. What would have been a breathtaking drive by the sea turned out to be a big disappointment on this first day of 2014; it was cold, dark, and rainy. Everyone was bundled up in sweaters and jackets, and it never stopped raining throughout the day. Occasionally Sasha and her parents stopped to get out of the car and view the long stretches of yellow beach and surging waves below. But the rain pelted down on Sasha, making the view difficult to enjoy, and the thought of visiting the surf sounded miserable. After many hours of driving along the coast through the rain, they finally decided to give up the quest to see the Twelve Apostles and reluctantly headed back toward Melbourne.

Sasha's parents chose to go back on a different route through the interior of the peninsula because of the heavy traffic on the main road leading to Melbourne. This decision proved to be a big mistake. They started traveling away from the coast on Wild Dog Road, probably the most precarious and outright dangerous single-lane dirt road in existence. It led them up and over a mountain, twisting and turning over fallen leaves and branches that had been knocked down by the storms that day. Sasha became scared and a little carsick, but she tried to keep quiet as she could tell her parents were stressed too. They finally emerged from that tortuous road and began driving on a two-lane road that went through the middle of the farm country. Feeling a little better and safer now, Sasha began searching the wheat fields for kangaroos but saw none out in the cold and rain. She did spy hundreds of rabbits crossing the road in front of a picturesque yellow farmhouse that stood out prominently against the green fields that were filled with jet black cows. Sasha's unplanned adventure ended safely back in Melbourne without any lasting regrets of not having seen the Twelve Apostles.

The next morning, January 2, Sasha and her parents headed off for Cairns and the Great Barrier Reef. When they arrived and Sasha caught a glimpse of the clear blue waters, there was nothing she wanted more than to go for a swim. The only odd thing was no one else was swimming in the Coral Sea. She later learned that there were jellyfish warnings over the entire length of the beach. Moreover, swimming in the sea was only permissible within the confines of close-netted areas scattered along the beach. The nets provided protection for swimmers from the stings of box jellyfish, which carry a strong toxin.

Instead of swimming in the ocean, the next morning Sasha dove into each of the Angsana Hotel's three swimming pools. The weather in northern Australia was a great improvement to southern Australia. It was warm, dry, and sunny all the days she was there, with a slight cooling breeze by the beach under clear blue skies. After resting for a short while on the beach, Sasha brought out a boomerang she had purchased from a local shop. She threw it along the shore, but it did not return to her as it was designed to, and she soon grew frustrated. One of the native Australian beach attendants noticed and stopped his work to walk over to Sasha and demonstrate the proper technique to make the boomerang return. It took Sasha a while to master the throwing technique, but she eventually learned to throw it properly and thanked the helpful lad. She then proceeded to show off her new skill for the rest of the day.

The beach at Palm Cove was postcard-perfect, shaded by a straight line of palm trees. Sasha took long walks searching for shells along the shore of the beautiful, long, crescent-shaped beach. It was delightful because there was absolutely no debris anywhere and the crystal-clear, warm water came rushing toward shore to cool her tired feet. The sea tempted Sasha in spite of the jellyfish warning, and she might have risked it and gone for a swim except that she learned the real danger in the northern Australia surf was the saltwater crocodiles. They grow very large, up to five meters in length, and they are quick and agile enough to leap out of the surf and capture prey. There were many stories circulating among the locals about crocs rushing on shore, snatching up dogs in their massive jaws, and dragging them into the sea. One crocodile lived in the creek that ran alongside the hotel where Sasha was staying. This one was only one and a half meters long, and the naturalists in the area decided not to capture it and transport it elsewhere for fear that a much larger crocodile would then replace it in the creek. It was a very frustrating circumstance for Sasha, since the sea looked so inviting.

Sasha's first adventure in Cairns was a trip to the rainforest. She and her parents started out early in the morning, catching a taxi to the railroad station where an old-fashioned train waited to take them up the mountain. The railroad tracks were laid nearly a century before, though the station around it was much newer and quite modern. The old train climbed the large mountain in front of Sasha slowly, cutting a big, wide path up the slope. The views from the train of the trees and foliage along the mountainside were wonderful. The train stopped a couple of times so passengers could take pictures of the impressive scenery and a large waterfall that in a few weeks, once the rainy season hit, would send a deluge of water cascading over the its edge. Finally, more than two hours later, Sasha arrived at the top to a rainforest town called Kuranda.

Sasha chose to begin her rainforest adventure by taking a boat ride along the river that eventually fed into the waterfall. The river was filled with fish, turtles, and freshwater crocodiles, which were smaller than their saltwater cousins. Numerous different types of birds filled the air and chirped from the tops of the towering trees. Sasha was intent on discovering most of the feathered species and took many pictures of the flora and fauna along the riverbank. As Sasha floated down the river, the boat captain informed her that 90 percent of all life in the rainforest lives near the tops of the trees where abundant sunlight produces most of the fruit and flowers that nearly all the rainforest species feed on.

After the boat ride, Sasha wandered along the main street of Kuranda perusing all the tourist shops. On the same street, she found a small zoo that specialized in local animals. The highlight of her rainforest adventure was getting to hold a three-year-old koala bear and having her picture taken with it. She learned that Suzy, the koala bear, was not a bear at all, but another marsupial like the kangaroos, which were in the next enclosure. She also saw a wombat, a medium-sized wooly creature that scampered along the ground whenever he suspected someone was coming. The final treat at the zoo was the tropical bird aviary, which proved to be a photographer's bonanza. It gave Sasha close-up views of an amazing assortment of colorful tropical birds. Some had harsh, throaty calls and others, like the parrots and macaws, sounded almost human. Sasha enjoyed taking many pictures of the birds and energetically tried to get them to speak to her.

Sasha holding a koala in Australia

Soon it was time to leave Kuranda. Sasha chose to take a long cable car ride down the mountain that took her over the tops of all the tall trees. From up high, she saw the waterfall from a different angle and watched it feed into a river at the bottom of the mountain that eventually flowed directly into the sea. She also saw the huge fields of sugarcane that dominated the plains below and learned that sugarcane is the principal money crop of northern Australia. The fields were bright green and provided a brilliant contrast to the deep blue of the sea beyond.

Sasha decided to make the next day a beach day, one that would offer plenty of time and space to practice throwing her boomerang again. Of course, Sasha had to keep a watchful eye on the creek just in case the resident crocodile became interested in her boomerang game. The day passed quickly as Sasha was torn between remembering the cute koala she'd met the previous day and thinking about her next adventure: the Great Barrier Reef.

Sasha woke up early and anxiously waited for the bus that would take her north along the Captain Cook Highway to Port Douglas, a sleepy tourist town that had once been wiped out by a vicious cyclone. The reconstructed Port Douglas was the jump-off port for boats headed to the Great Barrier Reef. Sasha boarded a huge catamaran that powered her very quickly out to a large pontoon anchored at the outer edge of the Great Barrier Reef.

Once aboard the pontoon, Sasha quickly changed into a full-body Lycra suit specifically designed to prevent any jellyfish contact from developing a serious infection. She then added a mask, fins, and snorkel to her ensemble before lowering herself into the warm water over the most beautiful coral formations on earth. The coral formed a multicolored panorama of various shapes and sizes and in turn housed a cornucopia of small, medium, and large reef fish. The reef to which the stationary pontoon was anchored proved to be as spectacular as Sasha had read it would be from her mom's travel books. Off in the distance, Sasha could see and faintly hear the huge waves breaking onto the outer fringe of the reef. At that point, the ocean's depth dropped immediately down to one thousand feet and contained all of the large pelagic predators that make the waters dangerous for divers. On the reef, the predators were limited to schools of relatively small whitetip sharks, although to Sasha's relief, she saw none on this trip.

After her first snorkel, Sasha decided to take a ride on a ten-person, semi-submersible vessel that glided over the reefs. Sasha was very lucky to have come to the barrier reef on a full-moon day when the tide was unusually high, allowing the submersible to glide over the entire area. The guided tour was terrific. Many fish, including a huge parrotfish, swam right up to the windows of the submersible. The highlight was a wonderfully close and lengthy view of a huge hawk-beaked turtle that was feeding on some algae just to the side of the catamaran that Sasha had ridden in on.

Sasha in a submersible in the Great Barrier Reef in Australia

Back on the pontoon, Sasha quickly grabbed some lunch, ate it hurriedly, and then squeezed back into her black Lycra suit, which seemed even tighter than before. She donned her mask, fins, and snorkel and jumped into the sea again. On her second snorkel, the tide was running away from the pontoon at a rapid pace and quickly carried Sasha all the way to the outer boundaries of the huge reef. Because of the strength of the tide, the lifeguards who were patrolling the area from the pontoon became concerned about Sasha's safety and came after her in their inflatable craft. On the swim back to the pontoon, Sasha floated over a group of divers a mere twenty-five feet below and later over a large school of small Pacific barracudas. Finally, she watched a school of large black rockfish swim over a massive coral head that hosted an abundance of algae for them to feed on. The whistle from the pontoon blew too soon, signaling all to return to base.

The next day came quickly, and Sasha was disappointed to have to leave Palm Cove. This day, too, was sunny and warm, and it made her last visit to the palm-lined beach that much more inviting and difficult to leave. Though she never got to dip in the waves, Sasha's final action before gathering her things and climbing into the taxi that would take her to the airport was to go for one last swim in all three hotel pools.

Late that evening, Sasha and her parents arrived in Sydney, the last port of call on their trip to Australia. After Cairns, and even Melbourne, Sydney looked enormous, and it is. Sydney is a large metropolis with a population well over five million. Huge skyscrapers filled the sky and spread along the inner harbor of what all experts agree is the biggest and best natural port in the world. It is a truly global city as some of the world's biggest corporations have their names attached to the tops of the skyscrapers along the inner harbor, interspaced with the names of a few of Australia's largest companies.

It was chilly that week in Sydney, especially after the warm temperatures Sasha enjoyed in Cairns. After her family arrived at their hotel, they immediately sat down to a typical Sydney dinner: fresh oysters on the half shell, grilled lamb, and a finale that included an imaginative combination of fruit and flavorful ice cream. This soon became Sasha's standard dinner menu in Sydney. For lunch, she typically chose to eat a more humble menu of pasta or hamburgers surrounded by golden French fries.

Sasha's first day in Sydney started with a ride on a hop-on-hop-off bus tour of the city. The first hop off the bus was at the famous Sydney Opera House. After Sasha and her parents walked around it and learned about the building's history from some brochures, they hopped back aboard and stopped next at the Star casino complex. After some more wandering and exploring, the family took the bus back to Circular Quay and finished the day with a ferryboat ride to Lunar Park. The park offered great views of Sydney's central business district and contained an assortment of amusement rides.

Sasha started with a ride on the Ferris wheel. Although it was much smaller than the Singapore Flyer, it still provided some wonderful views of Sydney Harbour. Then she was on a bone-jarring drive on the bumper cars and a screaming tearful ride on the small but quick roller coaster. Sasha also won three small prizes at the games along the concourse, but her most memorable moment at Lunar Park was the twirly—a high-speed circular motion machine that pinned Sasha to the sides and eventually the centrifugal force built up and lifted her several feet off the ground. She felt like a vegetable in a bladeless food processor.

The highlight of the next day was a morning ferryboat ride across the harbor to the Taronga Zoo. The ferryboat passed the great opera house, giving Sasha wonderful views of it from the water, and also a massive Carnival cruise ship that had docked along one of the long piers and was being prepared for its next port of call. The Taronga Zoo meandered up a large hill on the other side of the harbor and provided more gorgeous views of downtown Sydney.

The day eventually turned milder as Sasha and her parents climbed to the top of the hill to visit the zoo. There she saw many native

Australian animals such as platypuses and Tasmanian devils, which she learned were being bedeviled by a lethal cancer that was thinning out the packs in the wilds of Tasmania. Of course, there were plenty of kangaroos, wallabies, and koalas. The zoo also kept an assortment of African and Asian wildlife, which Sasha found fascinating. Perhaps the funniest was the huge giraffe that rolled its tongue from one side of its mouth to the other as it looked at Sasha. She rolled her tongue right back at the giraffe as though they were having a silent conversation. Sasha left the giraffe exhibit just in time to catch the afternoon seal show, and she and her parents quickly grabbed seats.

The Atlantic and Pacific seals were large and well-trained performers, and obviously very smart. Sasha truly enjoyed the show and learned a few things about seals as well. And, the memory of the seals made Sasha smile on the ferry for the entire ride back to Circular Quay. Meanwhile, her parents were imagining what her conversation with the giant giraffe was about.

Back on shore, as Sasha walked along the quay with her parents, they soon spotted an aboriginal art store and entered to see the graphic and brilliantly colored designs. While her parents studied one of the paintings, Sasha became fascinated by the ornately designed didgeridoos. The aborigines use these two-meter-long instruments for communication as well as for ceremonies. The shopkeeper noticed Sasha's interest and decided to demonstrate his talent on one of the longest didgeridoos in his store. The one he picked had a cockatoo painted on one of its sides and he played for her a long tune known only to the Australian natives. Very impressed with the sound and his accomplishment with this unique instrument, Sasha considered that one day she, too, might study the art of playing a didgeridoo.

The sun peaked through the clouds on Friday, enticing Sasha to visit one of Australia's most famous beaches: Bondi beach. *Bondi*, in the aboriginal language, means "long wave break," and the beach is certainly well named. When Sasha arrived at Bondi, she was surprised by how long the beach was and how many people were either on the sand sunning themselves or in the water swimming and riding the big waves on long boards. There were huge waves breaking about thirty meters offshore and each wave had about a dozen black, wetsuit clad surfers jostling for the best position to ride the crest. Sasha and her parents quickly changed into their bathing suits and headed down to join the other beachgoers. As soon as they found a spot and deposited their things, Sasha ran down to the water's edge. Immediately she realized this wasn't the Palm Cove. The water was freezing! She knew then why the surfers wore rubberized wet suits, for buoyancy and warmth.

Nevertheless, the sand was warm and inviting, and Sasha and her parents enjoyed gazing at the sun worshippers and surfers. The only thing that broke this idyllic setting was the constant hum of a hovering helicopter, which flew up and down the length of the beach just beyond the breaking surf. It didn't take long for Sasha's family to realize why its presence was constant: it was on shark patrol. The beaches along this coast are known to harbor the great white shark.

The next day was again sunny and warm, so Sasha decided that she wanted to see Sydney's other famous beach, Manly Beach. To get there, the family needed to take a ferry from Circular Quay and it again provided fresh breezes and a wonderful view of the inner harbor. On this morning, it was filled with sailboats of all sizes with their colorful sails unfurled. Manly beach was huge, with even more swimmers, sunbathers, and surfers than Sasha had seen on Bondi beach. Manly was a touch smaller than Bondi, though, and it had its own feel. The several streets leading down to the sand were crowded with retail clothes stores, and one side street even had a mini bazaar. Sasha enjoyed exploring the beachside shopping as much as she enjoyed playing in the sand.

When Sasha's family left Manly, next on the itinerary was Watsons Bay. Once there, Sasha and her parents paused to enjoy a typical Australian picnic of oysters on the half shell. With their stomachs full, they summoned enough energy to climb a steep slope on the far side of the bay that led to a beautiful panorama of the deep blue Pacific ocean from a ledge about a hundred meters above the waves. It provided Sasha with a spectacular view of sailboats cavorting up and down the Australian coast, their colorful sails full with the fresh breeze. If there was one thing Sasha would always remember about the Australian coast: the fresh smell of the ocean on a warm, breezy day.

Sasha's final day in Australia again began with sunny skies and warm temperatures. She had exciting plans for her last day, anchored by a seaplane ride over the quays and inlets of Sydney Harbour and beyond, and she couldn't have asked for better weather conditions. Sasha and her parents arrived at the bay to find a small six-seat seaplane tied to its dock waiting for guests. The best seat in the house with the best views and perfect for picture taking was next to the pilot in the cockpit of the plane. This is where Sasha eagerly sat, in the copilot's chair. After the rest of the seating arrangements were sorted out, the plane was ready to depart.

After a brief slow taxi on the water, the little plane accelerated and, following a full minute of rapid cruising, it began to rise above the water and soon was flying over all the famous landmarks of Sydney Harbour. They flew over a huge pleasure cruiser that was heading out on its way to other exotic destinations. They flew north up the coast past many beautiful beaches, some crowded and others empty and inviting. They flew over a national park that was all green below before finally finding their destination: a broad, slow-moving river with an inn nestled along one of its quiet shores. The plane dropped Sasha and her parents at this quaint location, where they enjoyed simple but delicious food and soaked in the quiet views from the riverside restaurant. A few large sailboats slowly floated by, blown toward the sea. The scene was mesmerizingly serene and peaceful, and Sasha thought she could live there forever.

The views from the seaplane on the ride back to Sydney were just as spectacular as they were on the flight out, but clouds were rapidly forming in the west, threatening rain. At the end of the seaplane ride,

Sasha said goodbye to Frank, the pilot, who had provided a running commentary on the beaches and scenes they passed below and politely answered all of Sasha's questions.

The remainder of Sasha's stay in Sydney included more rides on the hop-on-hop-off bus, a visit to Hyde Park where she played in the amusement park and jumped on the trampoline until she was sweaty and exhausted, more walks along the harbor and down the long pier, and some final spectacular views of the bridge, the opera house, and the inner harbor. As Sasha sat in the airport waiting for her flight back to Singapore, she recounted to her parents all of the wonderful sights and her adventures during the first two weeks of 2014. She smiled broadly at her memories of the great land down under and promised to return someday.

7

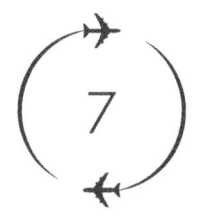

Bintan Island, Indonesia

WHILE LIVING IN SINGAPORE, Sasha and her family frequently traveled to Bintan in nearby Indonesia to enjoy a brief moment on the beach. Bintan is only one hour away from Singapore by high-speed hydrofoil boat. At first, it surprised Sasha and her parents that they could enjoy such pristine beach conditions so close to their home in urban Singapore, and it soon became the perfect easy getaway for birthdays, weekends, or when guests such as Sasha's grandmother came to visit.

Sasha had been to many other beautiful beach locations in Asia with her family, but that only helped them realize how wonderful the beach was at the Angsana hotel in Bintan. It was a perfect beach for families with young children. The pure, fine, nearly white sand gently sloped into the South China Sea. Small- to medium-sized waves poured ashore with a murmur instead of a crash. There were a few rocks on one side of the mile-long beach but no coral or spiny sea urchins underfoot or any other danger to feet or limbs when riding to shore on the occasional medium-crested wave. Best of all, there was no discernable undertow to carry careless swimmers offshore and no sharks or crocodiles to threaten wayward swimmers. In other words, the beach in this little cove was ideal. The safety of this crescent-shaped beach was thanks to the large boulders at each end; the strength of the waves on the opposite sides of each rock pile increased several times over, as that side faced the open sea.

The beach beckoned all to take leisurely strolls in search of the odd seashell or wade deeply into the froth-capped, green-blue surf. Its calm waters encouraged body surfing in those modest waves. And the coral reefs about 150 meters offshore beckoned snorkelers to swim out from the beach and explore the tropical sea life.

Sasha and her family always stayed at the Angsana hotel, one of two hotels that bordered this peaceful stretch of sand. The other was its sister hotel, the Banyan Tree, just a short walk along the beach or accessible by a longer ride in the hotel limousine from the boat dock. Once at the Banyan Tree's main lobby, it was necessary to take a buggy to navigate the steep hills against which the hotel was set.

The family's usual plan for these trips was to relax on the beach, soak up some sun, frolic in the gentle waves, and read some undemanding literature. Sasha usually began her vacation by jumping right into the Angsana's pool. But the sea was so calm and warm that it soon beckoned. Sasha was hesitant to approach the waves on her first visits, but she grew more comfortable with each passing year and each return trip to Bintan. At six or seven, she would jump up as the gentle waves passed underneath her. She soon became more daring, plunging headfirst into them while holding her father's hand. By the time she turned eight, Sasha was determined to test her nerves against the strength of the surf.

Sasha eventually started to truly enjoy playing in the waves, and she attempted to body surf in the wake of most of them. This was the first time Sasha enjoyed riding the waves, and with each ride she slowly gained confidence in her swimming ability. She soon began to swim farther offshore to capture bigger waves before they broke and lost most of their energy.

When Sasha eventually tired of playing in the waves, she would start for shore. She and her father would play soccer along the beach and often encouraged other children to join them. One time they played a very spirited game with some boys from Germany and some of the local beach activities people. Sasha enjoyed the game, but quickly discovered the young boys were very talented soccer players. On another day, the beach soccer match started with the German boys against a group of teenage French girls. Then more young people joined, and the goals had to be moved farther apart to accommodate all the players. These casual matches were Sasha's first real experience of playing competitive soccer.

On another sandy, sunny afternoon, Sasha began a very ambitious project to build a large castle with a moat around it in the sand. With the help of her parents, she built it high up on the beach so the incoming tide wouldn't wash it away. Sasha became so fond of her accomplishment that she left a message next to it asking people not to destroy it. The next morning, Sasha and her parents ran down to the beach to secure their favorite lounges and to check whether the tide destroyed their sandy masterpiece. It was still there, untouched by tide or people. Its survival overnight motivated Sasha to extend her original creation in two directions. On one side she constructed a huge house and on the other side a school. Both were surrounded by individual moats and connected by intricate bridges. Each area had two guardhouses to control entry and protect against imaginary vandals.

Soccer, sandcastles, and swimming always left Sasha with quite an appetite come dinnertime. While she typically enjoyed a breakfast of island fruits, eggs, and fresh-baked cakes at the Angsana, the restaurants at the Banyan Tree Bintan just up the beach that served dinner were better and more refined. Saffron, their best restaurant, offered a menu of excellent Thai food in an exotically Asian ambiance. Other nights, they ate at the outdoors mixed-menu restaurant, Terrace, under a plentiful blanket of stars. Most of the restaurant's selections were Indonesian, and the setting was divine. Tables were perched on a deck high above the

South China Sea. The breeze blew in from the sea, cooling the deck, and at night it required a sweater to be comfortable. Dinners at the Terrace were delicious: crab, duck, shrimp-filled spring rolls, spicy beef, and a wonderful coconut crème brûlée.

Sasha and her family always left feeling relaxed and rejuvenated. The boat ride home from Bintan was not as depressing for Sasha as returning from other resorts usually was, because she realized that such a wonderful golden beach lay only one hour away.

8

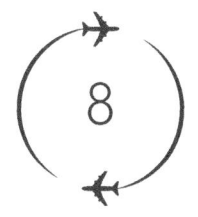

A Visit with Friends to Angkor Wat

WHEN SASHA AND HER FRIEND Philip Ohm learned that their parents were planning on taking another trip without them, they both began to complain loudly. Their parents' first trip without children was to visit Myanmar (formerly known as Burma) to view the country's famous colorful Buddhist pagodas. The photos and stories their parents shared from that trip created an intense desire in Sasha and Philip to take part in the next adventure with their parents. The parents eagerly agreed to their children's demands and soon planned another trip to see another one of the marvels of Southeast Asia, the Angkor Wat temple complex in Cambodia.

The flight to Siem Reap, Cambodia, was just two hours straight north from Singapore, but arriving at the local airport after leaving the outstanding world-class one Sasha departed from made it seem as though she and her friends were traveling back in time. It was also a signal of what was in store for all of them as they began their trek through Cambodia. Cambodia is one of the world's poorest countries, ranked as 101st by the World Bank in 2023, with a per capita annual income of

$1,800. Poverty was apparent everywhere Sasha looked. There were no swift, gleaming rail systems to take visitors from the airport to the main streets of Siem Reap, no well-paved highways to take visitors to see the massive Buddhist temple, one of the eight world heritage sites.

Cambodia today is a dramatic contrast to the relative wealth that must have existed in the twelfth century to support the construction of such a monumental edifice. The past seventy-five years especially have been difficult for Cambodians, and many still remember the trials committed in their recent past and feel the economic legacy it left for them. First, the Khmer Rouge razed most of the wealth in Cambodia to the ground, and then the fanatical Rouge were beaten down by the Vietnamese army after the Americans left Vietnam. Nevertheless, most Cambodians today have great reverence for their storied, historic past.

The massive temple complex was originally built as a Hindu temple in the first half of the twelfth century by Khmer people and later converted into a Buddhist temple by a rival regime that also moved the capital of the region from Angkor Wat (*Angkor* means "capital") to the north. The change in political power put in motion the long decline in usage, both religious and political, of the former capital. When Angkor was constructed (of sandstone and wood), it was a city with thousands of residents, a temple, and the emperor's palace. It also featured a moat and a fifteen-foot wall designed to guard it and keep attackers at bay. Today, only the wall and the temple remain. Nevertheless, there was plenty for Sasha and Philip to see and explore among the ruins of this magnificent site.

The Grand Hotel in Siem Reap, where the two families stayed, was originally built as an embassy. It was an enormous colonial-style building with a large swimming pool that Sasha and Philip loved to jump in to cool off after hot walks through the immense expanse of the temple. The first night in Siem Reap, Sasha and her companions attended a performance by a local acrobatics troupe in a rudimentary theater. Sasha was thrilled by the stunts the artists performed and enjoyed the ending best when she and Philip were carried out of the arena by two of the performers.

The next day Sasha and Philip would visit the famous temple. The numbers of visitors to the ruins were inestimable. As they walked through the crowds to the main entrance, they were jostled by young Cambodians selling all types of souvenirs. What struck them most were the massive sandstone blocks that were piled high on top of one another in a happenstance manner, some neatly lodged and some precariously balanced between others. Sasha began to wonder what happened to them since they were not uniformly built. Once inside, it became clear that the jungle surrounding the site was slowly taking over the entire monument. Huge trees were everywhere in the confines of the temple, and the entire facility was encompassed in a forest except for the front entrance where the moat separated the temple from a flat plain with sparse vegetation. Presumably the sparseness of this front area was due to the throngs of visitors that walked to the temple over the centuries. Everywhere else, the big trees pushed their roots and branches through every crevice among the sandstone blocks and over time moved the blocks farther apart.

Sasha at Angkor Wat in Cambodia

Of course, while the children walked through the main parts of the temple, there was much jumping from block to block and running down secret passageways playing hide-and-seek. The temple walls contained many magnificent murals; some were faded and others retained their colors. Many had religious meaning, others were historical representations of battles fought on the site, and yet others depicted urban life within the city of Angkor Wat in its heyday. Practically all of the exposed exterior walls had carvings of dancers or soldiers, and the spires had carvings of deities. There were panoramic sculpted scenes of actual battles that had been fought with bows and arrows, spears and swords. Some had enormous carvings of maned animals, perhaps lions used to frighten away evil spirits. There were also a few standing altars with stone statues of religious deities with umbrellas and silk garments around their shoulders and a plant-filled pot at their side or pieces of ornate foliage indicating that these altars were still being used for religious purposes. Fortunately, Sasha's parents had hired a guide who was there to explain and teach Sasha and Philip about the signs, pictures, and sculptures. As the game of hide-and-seek grew more adventuresome, Sasha was startled when she turned a corner of the monastery and noticed a troupe of visiting monks walking in their dusty sandals and dressed in their saffron-colored tunics. It added a sense of drama for her and a historical reference to the temple visit.

On Sasha's second day visiting the temple site, she was told that she had to awaken early in the morning to catch a van that would take them to the far side of the moat to observe the sunrise over the temple spires. It was cold at 6:00 a.m. as they waited for the sun to make its appearance, and Sasha and Philip were full of complaints. The sun finally arose, satisfying the thousands of tourists who were patiently (or impatiently) waiting for its arrival. Sasha noticed that most of the visitors were Asian with a few Europeans thrown in. However, she was disappointed because she could not hear many speaking Chinese.

As the sun rose overhead and the temperature climbed higher,

Sasha and Philip made their way to the wall's perimeter. As they were looking into the forest, they noticed a small band of young boys running in their flip-flops under the trees. They were armed with slingshots, which they used to hunt the squirrels that were jumping from tree branch to tree branch. Sasha didn't see any successful shots, but she knew the boys must eventually succeed since they were so determined and the squirrels were indeed afraid. As Sasha and Philip stood in the forest of trees, they found it very unusual that there were no flowering trees or shrubs, in contrast to home in Singapore where it seemed every bush or tree had a flower. They also met several Cambodian families with children around their age, but there was little contact among them.

Outside of the great temple attraction were rows upon rows of open-air stalls where the local people were selling mostly inexpensive, colorful clothes, some of which attracted Sasha's attention.

On the way home from the temple, the group stopped along the Siem Reap River to board colorful, elaborately designed flat-bottomed boats, which were propelled by long poles from the rear. Each boat had a large carved figurehead of a lion with a golden mane on its bow. Sasha and Philip had fun sitting together in one boat and posing for pictures their parents were taking from a second boat. Everything was peaceful until they heard a large crash of water and turned to see several large black buffaloes jumping into the river. Then the families knew it was time to go. It was time to cram back into the van for the drive back to the hotel and the enticing pool to cool off. In contrast to the temple area, the hotel had many flowering trees and bushes flaunting their white and red flowers. Dinner at the hotel was mainly fried shrimp and chicken, always served with a colorful flower and small bowl of spicy hot sauce.

After a third day of climbing over the boulders and stepping over tree roots, Sasha and Philip thought they had seen enough of Angkor Wat. So the next day, the two families climbed into the van to take a drive through the countryside of Cambodia and see how people outside the tourist areas lived. Most of the rural houses and farms Sasha saw were constructed of unpainted wood and corrugated metal, and most had only three covered sides. They were constructed on stilts, in case of floods, and the land in front of and around the houses was rough and natural with some farm animals poking about. Clothing was hung on tree branches to dry. Some of the buildings had tables in front with farm produce or other simple packaged goods for sale. The villages they passed through were equally simple, just with more stores adjacent to one another and more people standing around.

The van drove to another village built along the side of a narrow stream of light-brown water. All the buildings were built on high stilts, implying that the narrow stream turned into a much wider and higher-flowing river during the rainy season. Everyone seemed to live about twenty feet above the ground, with large ladders leading to the open-air structures.

Life in poverty in Cambodia

The people of the village fished or netted anything that moved through the water past the village.

In this water town, Sasha, Philip, and their families boarded two wide, flat-bottomed boats, far more rustic than the remarkable boats they had taken the day before with their gold-crowned figureheads. Sasha's and Philip's families were anxious about the safety of these boats, but all were seated in them as they floated slowly down the river of the stilt village to a large lake that was seasonally low. The crude boats passed by several small groups of children who were swimming in the brown water and a few adults who were sorting through the produce that had been collected earlier from their nets to distribute to the community for food. On the way back to the boat dock, Sasha and Philip were lucky to watch several villagers casting their nets into the narrow brown river hoping to land some haul. Most of the children they saw in the stilt village wore little or no clothing, and they all stared at Sasha and Philip as they passed by. It was a vivid portrait for Sasha and Philip to see how rural life in Asia is still being lived by many in the twenty-first century.

Later that day, Sasha and Philip visited a silk factory to see how this fine fabric is made. First, they saw the silk worms inching around on green leaves in large straw baskets. When they reached maturity, the worms would weave a cocoon of raw silk, enclosing themselves in these bead-like capsules. These cocoons were converted into white strands by women who processed them by hand on antiquated machines into threads, and then other women added color to the threads. Sasha and Philip found the worms the most interesting part of the whole process, but all of it was new and intriguing to them. Finally, it was time for a last jump into the hotel pool before heading home to Singapore.

(9)

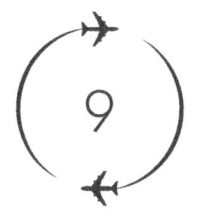

St. Petersburg, Russia

Sasha usually made an annual summer visit to Russia to spend some time with her Russian grandmother. Sasha's maternal grandmother came to America when Sasha was born to help care for her while her parents were attending to their demanding jobs. Since her grandma spoke only a couple of words in English, most of the first words Sasha heard as an infant were in Russian. Thus, Russian became her first language. Each summer trip to St. Petersburg, where her grandmother lived, would become an opportunity to improve her Russian language skills and observe Russian culture in this magnificent city.

Sasha's grandmother also often visited Sasha in all the places she lived and accompanied the family on other travel excursions from time to time. She came to visit Sasha and her parents several times when they were living in Singapore, often toward the end of the school year so the two of them could fly back to St. Petersburg together at the start of Sasha's summer break. The summers of 2014 and 2015 started this way. Sasha said goodbye to schoolmates, especially those leaving Singapore to travel to new homes scattered throughout the world, and then quietly boarded a Singapore Airlines flight with her grandmother and flew to St. Petersburg to begin her summer.

Walking past the Hermitage Museum in St. Petersburg

Sasha's grandmother lived in an apartment located in the heart of St. Petersburg. Someday Sasha would inherit this apartment to return to whenever she travels to Russia. She usually stayed for two weeks with her grandmother to enjoy the cooler weather—a relief after Singapore's high heat and humidity—and experience life in this northern city. Because it was mid-June, Sasha was able to experience the pleasure of seeing "white nights," when the sun sets in the wee hours of the morning and returns maybe one or two hours later. The normally frozen rivers would be flowing freely, and residents would be starting to eat their dinners hours later than people typically did in Singapore.

Dinners for Sasha in St. Petersburg typically consisted of Grandma's wonderful cooking or an outing to one of several Russian restaurants of very different styles. Some offered traditional northern Russian food, while others were Georgian and Uzbek with significantly different, more Middle Eastern tastes. Sasha wasn't partial to any of it, but she still appreciated the food that made up her cultural heritage.

While living with Grandma in St. Petersburg, Sasha had to quickly redevelop her Russian speaking skills, which had lapsed in between her visits. She had little occasion to practice her Russian in Singapore, or anywhere in Southeastern Asia, but the words quickly returned to her each summer. Apart from improving her speaking skills, Sasha also began to learn the Russian alphabet and to read Russian text. Earlier in her life, Sasha's grandmother taught Russian language in schools in Tashkent, Uzbekistan, and she was more than qualified to help her granddaughter acquire this challenging but beautiful language.

Aside from her language lessons, Sasha's grandma took her everywhere in the city to visit the many huge and internationally respected historic museums and iconic churches, attend ballet performances, and even see several circuses, which are prevalent in St. Petersburg during the summer. To arrive at these destinations, Sasha and her grandmother had to travel on the beautifully maintained and very efficient underground system in St. Petersburg. This subway system had been dug deeper than similar systems in other major cities in the world because it was used as a bomb shelter during Russia's European wars.

Sasha's favorite attraction to go to in St. Petersburg was the Dolphinarium to watch the circus on the water. The performances included trained dolphins, sea lions, and even a huge white orca. The Russian handlers were extremely careful in feeding and riding these potentially lethal ocean mammals. Sasha also liked the big playgrounds where she could run freely and drive miniature cars within a circumscribed arena. She and her grandmother also took a trip to the St. Petersburg amusement park, which was at least an hour's travel from the center city. They had to take two different buses that were filled with families from all over Russia. The park was both an amusement park with traditional rides and a small zoo filled with mainly Russian animals, some of which were conditioned to be friendly with children.

Her grandmother also took her to several performances, including a famous Russian play with puppets, which Sasha liked so much more than the Cinderella ballet they went to on another night. Most of the audience came to the theater dressed in their finest clothes, and it looked like they really enjoyed the performance, but their enthusiasm didn't affect Sasha, who said she had seen and read too many versions of this classic Disney tale for her to enjoy this version.

Sasha's mom or dad would sometimes join her in St. Petersburg during the summer when their work schedules allowed. Her father made the trip there a couple weeks after Sasha in the summer of 2015, and together they visited several new attractions. First, they climbed the 230 steps up to the midlevel of the famous Kazan Cathedral in St. Petersburg to view the city on a cold, cloudy day. On another day, they took a long bus ride to the famous and beautiful summer palace of the tzars and enjoyed seeing the extraordinary fountains that were scattered over this huge property. In the fall and winter, the fountains morphed into exquisite individual ice sculptures.

The trip through the palace's vast museum of historic pictures and highly ornamental, even gilded, furniture and living quarters was less exciting for Sasha than the stroll through the gardens. Sasha preferred admiring the many spectacular fountains and occasionally taking pictures from within the tall ones that were designed to be viewed from inside the curtains of falling water. Because it was summer, they were able to take a cold boat ride back to the central city from the dock at the tzar's palace and museum. Boats didn't run in the winter because of the ice.

Sasha had mixed emotions about her visits to Russia. Naturally a vacation away from her demanding parents was always welcome; however, she grew less keen on visiting Russia as she grew older. One factor was the lack of any friends her age. Despite her natural ability to make friends, she was unable to integrate with the children she encountered on the local playgrounds. She also missed the friends she left behind in Singapore, making trips to Russia feel somewhat lonely.

And while St. Petersburg is home to a host of grand architecture in the world-famous churches and palaces, as well as the monuments to World War II and to Yuri Gagarin, the first cosmonaut, Sasha was too young to appreciate most of it. She was happy to visit the blue St. Nicholas Naval Cathedral in St. Petersburg, the beautiful orthodox cathedral where her parents were married, but more as a piece of her family history than to appreciate the ornate beauty of this working church. Her trips walking through the enormous, tourist-clogged museums that dominated the center of St. Petersburg and were filled with irreplaceable art quickly became boring. She loved the boat rides, bus trips, and subway stations with their rich colorful designs, and most of all the challenge to improve her language skills, but she was always happy to see her father and lapse back into English. Still, she would return here to visit with her grandmother and to maintain her Russian passport and heritage.

10

Summer in Switzerland

NEUCHÂTEL IS A LOVELY, small, French-speaking town, something between a village and a city, lying on the western shore of Lake Neuchâtel. The lake is the largest in Switzerland, spanning twenty-eight miles in length with a depth of 211 feet. This little town became home for Sasha during the summers of 2014 and 2015, in between her family's usual life in Singapore. In Neuchâtel, she lived in a very modern apartment high above the quaint town with a marvelous view of the old city and the harbor where the ferryboats blew their whistles at ear-splitting volume when they entered and left the port. The spectacular view seen from the windows and small balcony off the living room extended across the lake to the mountains beyond. At the end of a long day, the light from the falling sun illuminated the ski trails that had been cut through the trees in the distant mountains to the east.

There were many new things for Sasha to see and experience in this historic city during the first summer she was there. Perhaps most apparent was the language, which is French, since Neuchâtel is located in the heart of Switzerland's French quarter. All communication was written and spoken in French, which was new and foreign to Sasha. A corollary novel experience for Sasha was coping with the money: Swiss francs. She had only lately become acquainted with prices in Singapore dollars and recently Russian rubles, and now she had to think about Swiss francs. Unfortunately, she was much too young to have learned the concept of translating US dollars into these different currencies, but the exposure to all of them continued to widen her view of the world.

The weather in Neuchâtel was also very different from what Sasha knew in Singapore, albeit it was quite fine. Most summer days were blessed with clear blue skies, plenty of sunshine, and far less humidity than in Singapore. Although the view of Lake Neuchâtel from the apartment was lovely, the water was quite cold to swim in. Ask Sasha—she tried on several occasions.

The trip from the family's apartment to the center of town could be made several ways: by climbing down hundreds of steps, driving a car down narrow winding roads, or riding the nearby funicular. The funicular was Sasha's favorite means of transport. She loved seeing the city from almost straight above as the tram descended on rails so extremely steep that they seemed nearly certain to crash on some building's roof. It was the most fun and fortunately also the most convenient method of passage.

The stores in Neuchâtel were stocked with many fresh and delicious food products, but the most amazing experience for Sasha was attending the Saturday morning farmers' markets. All of the local farmers brought their produce to the center of the town square, which magically turned into a thriving market overnight. The plethora of fresh vegetables and fruit made the farmers' market an incredibly difficult place to make choices—everything was fresh, and it all looked so good. There were mounds of fresh berries and currants, local fruits, vegetables, mushrooms, cheeses of all descriptions, freshly baked breads, and sausages.

On Sasha's first visit to this market, she and her parents filled three huge shopping bags with fresh produce before clambering aboard the waiting funicular to head back up the mountain to their apartment. They sampled some of their treasure for breakfast that morning and were astounded by the taste of the locally grown fruit and tomatoes. Their intense sweetness and fullness of flavor made the produce they were used to eating back in Singapore seem very dull in comparison. Sasha asked why this was the case, and her father had to keep reminding her that Singapore didn't grow any crops locally and had to import all produce from other countries.

On summer days in Neuchâtel, Sasha would ride her rented bike with great enthusiasm and the intense concentration of someone learning a new trick. Her parents later bought Sasha a scooter, since every child in Neuchâtel seemed to have one. Initially, the scooter resulted in many painful bruises, which she stoically accepted as part of the learning curve, but before long Sasha was riding her new scooter on the hilly paths of Neuchâtel and scooting very easily on the flat terrain surrounding Lake Leman. Most days, she would scooter or bike up to the big public pool that was located next to the lake for a cold swim and a fun plunge from the high-diving boards. On the way back, she and her parents would always stop at the miniature golf course for an intensely competitive game. Sasha had to win—otherwise there would be enough tears to flood the lake.

Sasha quickly grew accustomed to life in Neuchâtel, and by her second summer, she was familiar with the town and the surroundings. She helped her grandmother, who came from St. Petersburg to visit Switzerland for the first time, discover all the important places in Neuchâtel and figure out where to go and how. The first place she brought her grandmother was the central marketplace to shop for berries and then have dinner in the square, which was usually filled with summertime tourists.

There were several other places in Neuchâtel that Sasha considered key: the park that stretched along the shores of the lake; the swimming pool and diving boards north of the lakeside park; the beautiful botanic gardens with their exotic flowers, in addition to flora of the realm to the east of the lake; and, of course, the central square. Sasha knew that all life somehow revolved around the central square. Most days Sasha would take her grandma on the funicular, descend to the town square, and then start walking to the lake, or to see the old Christian cathedrals and their art and architecture, or the elegant Beau Rivage hotel located right at lakeside.

SASHA SPENT THESE SUMMERS away from her Singapore school friends, who traveled far and wide to various summer destinations of their own around the world. She was far from lonely, though, as she quickly made friends among the young people in Neuchâtel. One bright morning, as Sasha was returning from a trip to the farmers' market in the center of town, a friendly voice called out to her. Minutes later two blonde-haired young girls appeared in the garden below her apartment. As luck would have it, they had just moved into the building after the previous tenants, students from Neuchâtel University, graduated and moved out. Sasha was delighted to realize that she would have two English-speaking friends living in the same building. Their English sounded slightly different to Sasha but was always correct, as they had come from Birmingham, England. Sasha spent most of the rest of that summer in Neuchâtel getting to know her new friends and playing badminton in the building's garden or traveling to the lake or pool for quick swimming contests.

When her new friends were busy with their parents' agendas, Sasha had the good fortune to travel throughout the region, mostly with her father. Her mother was usually busy working (her firm's European headquarters were located in Neuchâtel) and therefore didn't have the time to make all of the day trips with Sasha. Her father was eager to show Sasha that Switzerland was like a mini version of the European Union with its twenty-six cantons, each with its own customs and ethnicity—while all sharing one central government and a common currency.

Most people think of Switzerland as a world of high, snowcapped mountains. It does have plenty of mountains, but in the wide valleys between the mountains and along the plentiful lakes and rivers that wound their way through them, the industrious Swiss created a bountiful palette of agriculture. The hills leading up to the mountains were planted with vines for cultivating grapes, ultimately producing excellent, reasonably priced wine. Above the hills, on verdant pastures high above the valley floor, wandered cows that produced the milk, cheese, and ice cream that made Switzerland famous. As Sasha was slowly discovering as she ventured outside of Neuchâtel, there was so much more of Switzerland to see, especially on the German side.

Bern and Murten

One of the first outings Sasha and her family took after they comfortably settled into their apartment was a day trip to Bern, a German-speaking city in a different canton. Bern is much larger than Neuchâtel and is situated along a tiny river that meanders through the entire city. The city's residents constructed many elaborate bridges to traverse it. Sasha would notice as her travels continued that almost every city she visited in Switzerland was located along a river or at the end of a lake.

Since Bern is a German-speaking city, Sasha had the chance to hear another language and to explore a different culture. Bern is a beautiful and wealthy city with impressive architecture in a very old, classical European style. Its buildings sit on grassy slopes overlooking the river below, and most are no more than three or four stories high.

Sasha's first lunch in Bern was superb: German-style sandwiches followed by the richest ice cream she had ever tasted. After lunch,

Sasha crossed the longest bridge spanning the river to visit the bear pit, which was located at the water's edge. This was one of the most unique attractions in the city and a highly unusual method for displaying these wild animals. Several large adult European brown bears were chained to stakes inserted deep into the ground. They had sufficient freedom to amble to the river's edge and to display typical bear behavior. Visitors to the enclosure were high above the bears so they could look down on the bears without intruding on their activity. Needless to say, this was a very captivating moment for Sasha, although scary at first—especially when the bears began running toward the lookout spot she was standing on. Later that day, she climbed up the highest hill in Bern to see the famous rose garden that was planted on a hilltop over the river. There were hundreds of rose bushes blooming with flowers of nearly every color imaginable.

Sasha's next day trip was to another German-speaking town approximately an hour's drive away from Neuchâtel. The medieval village of Murten, founded in the twelfth century and conquered many times thereafter by Austrian, French, and German armies, is located high on a hill above Lake Murten, one of the three lakes in the region by that name. There Sasha discovered that it was possible to sail from Lake Neuchâtel to Lake Murten and return by boat through all three lakes. The village was old, quaint, and home to the ruins of a castle erected several hundred years ago. Most of its walls were still standing. The major attractions that Sasha visited were a cathedral built in the sixteenth century and the remaining walls of the centuries-old fort that had been continuously attacked.

By the time Sasha and her parents started their drive back to Neuchâtel, it was evening, and the setting sun was casting golden streams of light through the beautiful Swiss countryside. Most of the landscape consisted of a flat valley filled with neatly spaced farms of wheat, corn, sunflowers, green vegetables of all kinds, and fields of flowers that were grown to be distributed to local stores and sold as cut flowers. Flowers were omnipresent throughout Switzerland, and this was one of the most noticeable cultural factors that distinguished life in Europe from life in Asia.

Lausanne

Sasha's next adventure took her through the French region to Lausanne, her father's favorite location in Switzerland and one the family would often revisit. It took almost two hours to drive there through the Swiss French countryside, past the grape arbors that lined the hills through much of the journey. Lausanne is a beautiful, hilly city by the shores of Lake Geneva. It sits between France and Switzerland and boasts a twelfth-century gothic cathedral in good functioning order. The lake is filled with snow-white swans and bordered by some very high mountains from both countries. Sasha's parents walked along the lake, while Sasha rode her rented scooter and observed the various boats cruising by and the people stopping to take pictures of the French Alps across the lake. It was Sasha's first experience seeing the Alps, the oldest and tallest mountain chain in Europe. The mountains had ski trails cut in between the evergreen trees, which kindled fun-filled thoughts of skiing in Hokkaido in Sasha's mind.

The view was even better from the balcony patio of the fancy hotel on the far side of a broad avenue that parallels the lake where Sasha's family stopped for lunch. The day was sunny and bright, and Sasha had a full view of the clear lake water, which reflected the huge mountains on its far side. As she sat on the patio enjoying the sun and the chilly air, Sasha couldn't stop looking across the lake at the high French mountains. She did not realize it, but she was also looking at the French village of Evian, where the famous water originates.

Lunch was superb, fancier than all that she ate before because Lausanne was a very popular vacation destination that had attracted wealthy Europeans for decades. It is also the home of the International

Olympic Committee headquarters as well as the Olympic museum. Sasha followed lunch with a vigorous scoot along the lake through Olympic Park. As she zipped through the park, she rode past many statues of great gold medal Olympians from the nineteenth century to the present and throughout the games' history. Each one was a reminder to Sasha of the glory of athletic prowess, and she wondered if one day she might reach such heights in her own sports, such as gymnastics.

Montreux

Montreux is one of the most storied cities in Switzerland, famous for its annual jazz festivals, and Sasha and her father decided it was a must-see for them. It was raining lightly the day they set out from Neuchâtel to drive to Montreux, which should have been a warning of what they would face later that day. As the pair approached Montreux, the sky was dark, filled with heavy, gray clouds. They were climbing higher with every kilometer they drove and suddenly extremely tall mountains were filling every window of the car. Their soaring gray peaks, framed by the darkening clouds, appeared menacing to Sasha, who had never experienced such majestic mountains up close, and they made her feel very uneasy.

Montreux was another Swiss city nestled next to a cold, clear lake, only this famous city was built closer to the imposing Alps in all their grandeur than any Sasha had seen thus far. The view from the lakeside was unsurpassed, as it comprised snowcapped mountains as far as the eye can see on the other side of the lake. The darkness of the afternoon, caused by the heavy cloud cover, obscured the mountain peaks, adding a sense of mystery to the magnificent views.

Sasha began her visit to Montreux with a walk through the Château de Chillon, an ancient stone castle and monastery on the shores of Lake Geneva that has a stormy past. Its exterior resembled a fort, with places cut out for archers to defend its walls. Its tortuous history included several rounds of conquests by nearly all the indigenous peoples of Western Europe. After visiting the castle along with hundreds of Chinese tourists (which conveniently gave Sasha a chance to brush up on her Chinese), Sasha and her father made their way back to the city center and decided on lunch at another lakefront hotel. The hotel restaurant provided very good food, a fine view of the lake and distant mountains, and great opportunities to people watch. The city's music festival attracted young and old, rich and bedraggled, many of whom sported a most amusing cornucopia of attire and hairstyles. The city center was also heavily populated by large groups of Chinese tourists, possibly attracted by the heavily advertised music festival.

From the crowds in the streets to the other guests dining at the restaurant alongside Sasha, Montreux had a festive and grand but chaotic feel to it. The geographic setting was more thrilling and dramatic than Lausanne, but its character and ambience was far less desirable. Sasha preferred the lower-key ambiance of Lausanne and its quiet, elegant setting beside the lake with less dramatically steep mountains and the quieter character of the people and buildings.

Auburn

Sasha's next stop in her exploration of Switzerland took her back to the German-speaking parts of the country. She and her father took a short drive to Auburn, a tiny village in between Neuchâtel and Bern. The journey there took them over a usable, but very old, wood-covered bridge spanning a mountain stream that fed into the three lakes. This sturdy bridge was built more than one hundred years ago and had been designed to accommodate horse-drawn carriages; therefore, it could permit only one car to pass through at a time. It was Sasha's first experience passing under a covered bridge.

The central square in Auburn was small, but every summer it was used to host famous guest performers from around the world who entertained customers as they sipped their aperitifs in the small restaurants and cafes surrounding the square. Auburn was picturesque and quaint, a quintessential German Swiss village, but it was too small to make a large impression on Sasha.

Gruyere

Sasha's next trip was quite memorable since it took her to the most authentically Heidi-like setting in Switzerland. All along the way, she was treated to a landscape of large green pastures in between patches of trees growing high on the gently upward-sloping mountains. The famous village Sasha came to high up in the mountains was Gruyere, the cheese capital of Switzerland. The village was perched on a hilltop, and the town's authorities prohibited automobile traffic. Thus, Sasha and the many cheese-loving tourists had to trek up the hill from the parking fields below to reach this magically quaint village. The hike proved to be a healthy blessing for everyone who had visited the Gruyere cheese factory at the bottom of the mountain and tasted a few too many cheese treats in the factory restaurant.

Sasha really enjoyed the tour through the factory, learning how cheese was made, reading what the cows consumed on a large diorama, and smelling the cheese at different stages of its development. Switzerland is full of cheese factories, and Sasha toured them on more than one occasion. Farmers bring liters of fresh milk to the factories from the herds of cows that dot the Swiss landscape. The milk is then processed and heated, and the curds and whey are separated in huge copper drums. Sasha and her father watched from a balcony above as the milk was continuously stirred. Afterward, Sasha had an opportunity to sample the freshly made Gruyere cheese the factory produced. They gave her eight different samples, which varied mostly by the storage age of the cheese. Eighteen months was the longest-aged cheese Sasha tried, and its taste proved to be most flavorful. Sasha however, preferred a milder, less-aged sample.

The village of Gruyere was full of fascinating history and sights. It was elevated high above the valley floor and offered a panoramic view of the valley and factory below and the mountains above. Its buildings were unique: mostly stone, with steeply peaked roofs to prevent snow from piling up during big winter storms. It had a bizarre macabre museum and an adjacent bar next to it with a similar gruesome décor that matched the museum's very odd and strangely sinister displays. Sasha was both fascinated and frightened by what she was looking at and said she couldn't understand what it represented, or what it was designed to inspire besides terror. A tiny church with a severely peaked roof was perched at the end of the main street of Gruyere, well above the rest of the village. It was entirely gothic in design and dark and foreboding inside—a remarkable complement to the macabre museum down below.

On the trip back from Gruyere, Sasha and her father drove past the town of Bulle, where the largest chocolate factory in Switzerland, the world-famous Nestle company, was located. It was a sweet reward for having visited the bitter sights of Gruyere. Sasha begged to stop, and she was able to watch as the factory's machines churned out all shapes and colors of chocolate. As she watched the machines swirling through the masses of milk and cocoa beans, Sasha realized the potent smell of the chocolate was the thing that struck her most, powerfully stimulating her memory and making her mouth water. Unfortunately, the factory store had just closed when Sasha and her father arrived, and therefore they couldn't purchase samples of chocolate, but they promised each other they would return and visit the factory the next time they traveled to Gruyere. Chocolate is one of Switzerland's greatest and most popular products, and the extremely high quality of Swiss chocolate is acknowledged worldwide. Chocolate factories in Neuchâtel have the reputation of manufacturing the highest quality of chocolate in all of Switzerland.

Basel

In between scooting around the center of Neuchâtel and visits to the lake for quick, cold plunges into the icy water among the tame ducks and the white swans, Sasha and her parents took a day trip to Basel. This is a large, bustling city set close to the borders of France and Germany with the beautiful Rhine River running through the middle of it.

This was an important visit for a young student interested in history, as the city is home to a few very beautiful and famous churches that had been erected during the beginning of the Reformation, when the Protestants split from the Roman Catholic Church. Here Sasha was able to visit the church where John Calvin made his famous speech that led to the Great Schism. Seeing European history alive this way was very different from just learning about these events in a classroom.

Basel also boasted a few historic buildings erected in the late Middle Ages and constructed with the indigenous red stone blocks that are found throughout this region. All of these historic buildings had traditional sloped roofs and gothic architectural styles. The city wisely protected and preserved these buildings as landmarks, and they are now used primarily to attract tourists to visit the town.

Sasha took advantage of being in this historic environment and strolled through the grounds surrounding one of the most beautiful and well-preserved red stone churches. There she heard its massive organ performing from inside the church. Unfortunately, the church keeps its doors locked when there is no service, and consequently Sasha could not see inside this church, but the soaring music was nonetheless inspiring.

After a fair amount of walking, Sasha stopped for a rest and enjoyed a superb German-style lunch in a café facing the main city square, which was bustling with residents and visitors alike. After lunch she wandered into a wonderfully large music store, which turned out to be one of the highlights of this visit. Sasha immediately found a set of drums and began banging on them after she refused all requests from her parents and one of the shopkeepers to play a tune on the store's grand piano. Sasha had been taking piano lessons for two years in Singapore and could play several songs from memory, but she found the drum set much more novel and engaging. Sasha also visited a local bakery, where she bought a few loaves of delicious bread baked in a traditional German style that she and her parents would enjoy over the next few days.

Auvernier

Sasha made a couple stops at Auvernier, a tiny Swiss village to the west of Lake Neuchâtel, to visit the first-class wine caves there and learn about Swiss-style wine making. Grape arbors dominated the hilly landscape throughout this region. They surrounded the caves' main buildings and flowed down to the lake. These arbors were mainly planted with pinot noir grapes that the vineyard made into an excellent rosé wine called *oeil de perdrix* (eye of the partridge), and a very high-quality red pinot noir, which only in the past year or two was aged in oak barrels for two years. The quality of this château's output has been improving each year since they began a process of restricting the number of grapes grown on each of its vines.

The knowledgeable and friendly staff at the winery contributed eagerly to teach Sasha about wine making and marketing. Perhaps the most amusing lesson Sasha learned was the wine makers' decision not to age most of the wine as the French do to improve its quality because the local Swiss consume almost all of it as soon as it is ready for sale. This also meant there was no wine left over to export out of Switzerland, so this was the one place in the world where one could taste the flavorful wine from these grapes. Sasha wasn't ready to taste their latest vintage, but she certainly did inhale the aromas from the wine cave and choose her favorite vat by its fruity smell—a connoisseur in the making.

Geneva

The next weekend, Sasha and her family drove to Geneva. Internationally renowned for its beauty, Geneva is a French-oriented city situated at the southern end of Lake Geneva and at the foothills of the Swiss and French Alps. Gracious mansions built one or two centuries ago line both sides of the lake and stretch for several hundred kilometers north. Some of the best views of Mont Blanc can be seen from the center of this city.

Sasha brought her scooter and scooted along the paths that bordered the lake. When she needed to replenish her energy, she ate huge scoops of ice cream and gelato and wore some of the evidence of a well-enjoyed snack on her dress. That afternoon, Sasha and her family boarded a sightseeing boat to view the city from the lake and have a closer view of Mont Blanc. Sasha loved the giant fountain at the mouth of the lake. The *jet d'eau* (water jet) spurted five hundred liters of water per second 140 meters into the sky. The fountain sits on an extended jetty that stretches well out into the lake and marks the entrance to the inner harbor. The sightseeing boat passed very close to the giant fountain, causing Sasha to duck unnecessarily. Once she realized the water wouldn't hit her, she stood up to appreciate the rainbows created by the brilliant sunshine as it refracted off the plumes of water.

Along the lake's edge were many small marinas filled with sailboats of all sizes. Also along the shore on both sides of the lake were historic mansions, many of which had been turned into museums. These beautiful structures claimed everyone's attention, including Sasha's. She pointed eagerly and said, "Let's go see that one," as their boat sailed by a spectacularly ornate mansion. These mansions are the lasting symbols of the wealthy who lived in and around Geneva in times past.

After debarking from the boat, Sasha and her parents left the harbor and began wandering up the hills of Geneva's old town quarter. Sasha marveled at the churches and ogled the restaurants that spilled outside onto the sidewalks of the steeply inclined streets, some with their own patios. She even spotted a gold-domed Russian church perched high above the lake, which for the sake of her cultural education, Sasha had to visit to remember that the orthodox religion is spread throughout Europe. As the sun began to set behind them, the family clamored down the steep, hilly streets to their hotel, the Grand Geneva Resort and Spa, which stood on the shores of Lake Geneva. They decided to eat dinner in the hotel's restaurant, and it turned out to be a very good decision. It was at this restaurant that Sasha encountered her namesake Fabbri olive oil, which she enthusiastically and gleefully consumed in large quantities with her French baguette and salad.

Le Locle

The first destination Sasha visited during her second summer in Neuchâtel was Le Locle, a tiny village set well up in the mountains that separated France from French-speaking Switzerland. The area was well known as a mecca for watchmakers, and the village supported a famous and beautiful eighteenth-century mansion that had been turned into a watch museum, honoring many of the most famous old watch designers who had lived, studied, or worked in this region of Switzerland.

The inside of the museum was fascinating—it displayed watches spanning three centuries. There were grandfather clocks and elaborate mantle clocks, ones with birds, others with flowers, and more with every style of ornate decoration you could imagine. There were two movies devoted to early watchmaking that were fascinating as well. Sasha had never seen such displays of fine craftsmanship before, and she walked from one elegant, elaborately decorated room to the next until her tired feet implored her to stop.

This region on the French border was replete with historic relics. Sasha's next stop was a historic bakery. It was not the usual kind of bakery, and you couldn't buy any bread there today, but 150 years ago, bread was the principle source of nutrition for the region. This bakery was below the ground in a freezing cold cave. It had an underground stream running through it to drive the giant gears that turned the enormous millstones that ground the local millet and barley into flour for bread. It didn't run in the winter because of the extreme cold, so the locals had to store the bread that was made in warmer times in their homes. The cave went several stories below ground. It required steel ladders and occasionally a flashlight to see the machinery at the bottom. Building and maintaining this mill must have been a true engineering feat when it was in operation. Sasha couldn't believe that men brought these gigantic gears down into this small, cramped site.

Today, it is a challenge just to maneuver in the tight quarters to observe the mill's workings and see the underground river flow. The extreme cold was also challenging, but the proprietors of the site distributed heavy jackets to all the visitors to keep them warm while they climbed down to visit the mill. The pure brutality of this underground mill was a sharp contrast to the highly refined, exquisite perfection of the watchmaking museum Sasha had seen just prior. Though Sasha enjoyed the activity of climbing through the ancient mill and found this unique piece of history fascinating, she still preferred the warm smells and delicious offerings of modern European bakeries to the cold, wet environment of the processing cave.

Annecy

Sasha decided she wanted to see some sights in France, so on a local friend's advice, the family drove across the border into neighboring France to the small city of Annecy. It is a picturesque town situated along a glacier-created lake with some tall mountains on the far side, an old castle that had been turned into a museum, and some exceptionally good food.

After a delicious local lunch, Sasha visited the museum in Annecy and saw some early motion picture photography along with its permanent collection of eighteenth-century and older furniture and weapons. Sasha was fascinated by the clothing women wore back then: long, ruffled, lacy garments that dragged along the floor. She was also intrigued by the display of large old swords and tried to pick one up, but she was immediately stopped by the guards. It was probably too heavy for her to lift or use anyway.

Following the tour of the castle museum, Sasha and her parents decided to take a boat ride on the lake. She remembers the beauty of the lake and the surrounding mountains, but not as much as she remembers being stranded in the middle of Lake Annecy after the boat's motor stopped working. This unfortunate development left the family and the other passengers at the mercy of the wake from every passing boat, and Sasha became quite worried and annoyed. Eventually a cell phone call was made to the dock staff, who soon brought a towboat to the location and rescued all by towing the stalled boat back to the dock. The passengers were immediately transferred to another boat and promptly headed back out on the water to visit two communities on the lake's other side. These villages were tiny and very isolated, situated underneath some very tall mountains. Sasha was bemused by their quaintness and separation from the rest of the world and kept asking, "Do people really live here?" Her travels were opening her eyes to the fact that many people in this world live in places and ways very different from what she was used to in her everyday life.

Crans-Montana and the European Masters

One of the much-anticipated trips for Sasha and her parents was a weekend visit to Crans-Montana to watch the European Masters.

Crans-Montana, a golf resort and country club perched high in the Alps, is host to the European Masters, an annual tournament that draws the best professional golfers in Europe. The event is sponsored by Omega, the large Swiss watchmaker, and is attended by thousands of golf fans. A lovely resort town has been built up around the club with first-class hotels, restaurants, and shops. The region offers great hiking, mountain biking, and skiing in the winter for the adventurous. For the less adventurous, it provides a wonderful venue for gazing at the snow-capped mountains and enjoying very fresh Swiss food and drink.

Sasha's hotel room came with a balcony that provided a glimpse of the glaciers on the distant mountains and the villages that dotted the countryside on both sides of the valley below. The day after she arrived, Sasha demanded to see the golf course she had heard so much about. She had been taking golf instruction in Singapore for the past two years and thought maybe she would be able to test her new skill. The golf course was as picturesque as any of the advertising postcards made it out to be. It was beautiful, laid out on perfect grass with little or no heavy rough, but it had plenty of ups and downs along the mountaintop and incredibly difficult, undulating greens to read for putting. Sasha was able to follow the professionals and watch them strike their ball from tee box to green as she observed the different aspects of their game.

As she ate her lunch on the terrace at the front of the main hotel, she could watch the golfers hitting approach shots to the sixteenth green and perform their putting. Lunch included raclette, a very unusual cheese specialty of Switzerland.

Sasha's favorite thing to do at the golf tournament was to take part in the golf games that corporate sponsors of the tournament had set up for visitors. She participated in nearly all of the events and happily won a few golf tees, some ball markers, a few logoed golf balls, and a golf hat with the club's unique trademark design. However, the highlight of the day for Sasha was something that happened while she was following several groups of professional golfers as they played from hole to hole. One of them, a Welshman by the name of Jamie Donaldson, saw Sasha and tossed her one of his personalized golf balls. She caught it and tucked it safely away as a wonderful memory of this beautiful place and the pro golfer's kind gesture.

Watching the professional golfers inspired Sasha to have a golf lesson from the teaching pro at the golf club of family friends, Hans and Dinette Koolhaas, back in Neuchâtel. On a chilly afternoon, Sasha walked off with rented clubs and followed the teaching pro to play five holes at the Neuchâtel golf and country club. The lesson proved to be less than she expected because the coach did not provide her any advice or try to improve her technique. Truth be told, his English was very rudimentary. Better golf for Sasha would have to wait for another opportunity.

Lyon

Sasha wanted to visit France again after one of her friends told her about the wonderful candy stores in Lyon, so she and her parents drove there one cloudy, chilly day. Lyon is a large, beautiful city, often considered the heart of French cuisine and perhaps best known for its tasty sausages and elegant Rhône wines. The city straddles two rivers, the Rhône and the Seine, and possesses several magnificent cathedrals, including one perched high on a cliff overlooking the Rhône River. The family parked their car close to the historic city center of Lyon and walked to the first church, which was partially under restoration. It was dark and gothic in design, with beautiful stained-glass windows. After a brief look around, they took the funicular to the top of the hill to visit the famous cathedral dedicated to St. John the Baptist. It was the seat of the archbishop of Lyon and a truly spectacular building. It was also gothic in design and had elaborate carvings, magnificent murals, beautiful colorful stained-glass windows, and many side altars. The artworks that adorned most of the interior walls of the cathedral could have been placed in any museum in France or anywhere else. It was one of the critical reasons Sasha's parents stopped to explore this fifteenth-century cathedral, as a clever way to induce Sasha to look at and study some of the great paintings from the Renaissance without having to convince her to walk through a French museum.

Sasha left the summit impressed and hungry, so the family traveled down the slope by the funicular (primarily because Sasha did not want to walk down the "hill of prayer," as the hill is locally described). From there, they had lunch at a small open-air restaurant in Lyon's old quarter followed by dessert at another local café. By chance, Sasha found an ice cream store close by and indulged in some delicious ice cream and sorbet while battering her father with questions about the paintings of the famous saints she had observed in the cathedral. As she left the ice cream parlor, Sasha discovered a large candy store—possibly the one her friends from Neuchâtel recommended—and begged to purchase a dozen different types of candy, which she placed in a bag and was forbidden to eat until after dinner. Walking a little farther through the old city, she and her parents came to a bakery that sold all types of cookies and purchased another broad sampling to try later that evening. Lyon was easily living up to its reputation as the culinary capital of France. The city's many delicious offerings left a favorable impression on Sasha, and she certainly wanted to return one day.

Gstaad

Sasha's next adventure took her to Gstaad, one of Switzerland's most storied and expensive towns, for another prime athletic event in Europe. Gstaad is perched on top of another mountain not far from Crans-Montana and slightly more than two hour's drive from Neuchâtel. Gstaad is as elegant as Crans-Montana is rustic. It has several five-star hotels and a shopping district with every well-known, high-end brand retail store in the world on display. Gstaad is also the traditional site of the Swiss Open tennis championship.

The year of Sasha's visit, 2015, was a special year at Gstaad because it was the one hundredth annual tennis tournament. Large signs adorning the town's buildings and sign boards featured pictures of all the famous tennis tournament winners of the past one hundred years, including Roger Federer and the previous year's winner, Stan Wawrinka, who was one of Sasha's favorite players. Sasha was well primed for the event since she was taking weekly tennis lessons in Singapore and had watched many important tennis contests on television. She beamed when she saw how immaculate the clay courts at the tennis arena were, as they were constantly swept, and she couldn't wait to see the contestants begin their final match.

By big-city stadium standards, Gstaad's stadium was tiny and quite intimate. Fans could hear and see the players' emotions and watch the matches happen up close. Although Sasha had been to the US Open when she was very small, this was her first real experience seeing competitive professional tennis this close. Having played some tennis herself, Sasha was all the more impressed at some of the shots the professionals took. Between matches, she had a grand time sampling the ice cream vendors' products and perusing the logo items for sale at the various sponsors' tents.

Gstaad has several world-class hotels and enumerable famous restaurants. Sasha and her parents tried one for lunch and another for dinner. Lunch was in the center of town and dinner was at a hotel situated high above the city on one of the local mountains. Sasha had to change from her tennis attire into something more formal to sit for dinner. At the tables around her, men wore jackets and ties, and women were in splendid dresses complete with dazzling jewels. Seeing everyone so dressed up, Sasha wondered if she was dressed well enough. She asked her parents if this was a holiday in Switzerland for people to be so elegantly dressed. She had never encountered formal dining before in

Singapore, Shanghai, or even in Neuchâtel, so to Sasha, it seemed her fellow patrons put on quite a show.

Dinner was delicious, and the view from the table alone was well worth the effort of dressing up. The setting was as picturesque and quintessentially Swiss as one could imagine. There were three different mountain peaks in view, all boasting spectacular ski trails and the wonderful sights of the many glaciers that capped the alpine mountains, along with a few farmhouses built high in the mountains. Sasha eagerly drank in the spectacular view and asked her parents how soon they could return to Gstaad to go skiing.

The Birthday Trip through the Alps

The crowning jewel of Sasha and her family's travels through Switzerland was an extended adventure through the Swiss Alps. They packed their travel bags relatively lightly since they would have to carry them on and off a myriad of trains during the journey. The clouds were forming and threatening rain as they climbed aboard a bus to go to the local *gare* and board the first train of their long trip. This train trip was a short one to Bern through the Swiss farmland. In mountainous Switzerland, relatively flat land is scarce and very precious, requiring farmers to plant their crops as efficiently as possible. The train afforded beautiful views of these carefully designed farms.

In Bern, the family changed trains to begin the second leg of their journey, which would take them to Zermatt. The weather improved slightly as this second train traveled through the three lakes region and headed south toward the promise of very high mountains.

The train gradually began to climb to a high altitude above the valley floor. Sasha could tell the temperature was dropping rapidly by the thick clothes the farmers and bikers outside her window wore. As the train progressed higher toward Zermatt, it passed through many tunnels dug through the foothills. The villages along the way became noticeably smaller, with fewer houses and people. The farms shrank from the broad fields of the lake region to tiny, terraced plots of grape vines, and the architecture looked more and more Alpine and classically Swiss. The rooftops were now more steeply sloped, made of large pieces of slate lapped over one another in an effort to prevent heavy snowfalls from accumulating on the houses. These tiny villages built along the sides of the very steep mountains shocked Sasha as she tried to imagine how they could be constructed so high up on the mountain and how dangerous and difficult life was on these steep slopes.

The train finally approached Zermatt. As it exited the final tunnel and traveled around the last curve of the mountain, Sasha came upon a breathtaking view of the Matterhorn, the steepest tooth-shaped peak in this part of the Swiss Alps. This magnificent mass of granite has long been a target for climbers and mountaineers, and seeing it in person, one could easily understand why it has attracted so much attention over the centuries and why it is so dangerous. The first three men who successfully reached the top died on their decent.

Having arrived at their destination, Sasha and her parents left the train and walked to the small, very quaint town of Zermatt. Sasha's eyes took in the main street lined with all kinds of professional ski and hiking stores, Swiss restaurants, and bakeries. This was a mountaineering mecca, and Sasha got a thrill at the thought of climbing the great mountain someday when she grew older and stronger.

Sasha stopped at one café for a quick slice of pizza and consumed it while sitting on the restaurant's second-story veranda. This gave her a perfect view of the hikers and bikers in their mud-splattered boots as they marched through the main street of town. However, the most memorable sighting came a few minutes later when the sound of low-pitched bells called everyone's attention to a procession of big-horned mountain goats walking up the main thoroughfare of Zermatt. Their shaggy black-and-tan coats were long, suited to life in the high mountains. The main group of goats was led by one young herdsman, but they were

The Matterhorn in Switzerland

mainly controlled by a large lead goat that kept all the others in line by aggressively bullying and butting with his horns any goat who strayed. This incredible event happens only once a year when the mountain goats are paraded through the center of the city to drive them to summer pastures higher up in the mountains. What a thrill for Sasha to happen to be in Zermatt on that day to witness it!

That first day in Zermatt also happened to be Swiss National Day, the annual Swiss celebration of nationhood. August 1 is the official date of the Swiss Confederation of 1891, which replaced the original Swiss confederacy of 1291, and this date has been celebrated by all of the twenty-six cantons ever since.

Soon after the goats passed through, Sasha was greeted by another sound of the annual celebration: the blowing of the mountain horns. These large wooden horns, with several-meters-long necks and cup-shaped mouths, produce a deep sound that resonates across the mountains, echoing from one village to the next, signaling to one another across vast distances long before the advent of modern communication devices. This evening, seven horns were being blown by performers dressed in ancient Swiss costumes in the center of the town's squarew, and they played a simple rendition of a classical piece of music in honor of National Day. The sounds of these horns reminded Sasha of the didgeridoos that she saw and heard in Sydney, Australia. The observation impressed on her the similarities and common ground one finds across the world's cultures, and she felt lucky to have observed so many in her young life.

The annual migration of goats through Zermatt

Later that night, Zermatt capped off its National Day celebration with an impressive fireworks display. Sasha and her family hurried up the side of the mountain to their hotel because it afforded a perfect view across the narrow valley to where the town was shooting off the fireworks. Halfway up the other mountainside, they could see the fireworks soaring skyward and exploding over the town below. From Sasha's vantage point on the hotel's veranda, the scene before her looked like a battlefield, and it almost seemed like the explosions were aimed directly at her! As impressive as the fireworks display was, it was not the highlight of the night. The most impressive moment came in the midst of the fireworks show when a giant bolt of lightning lit up the canyon, followed by a resounding clap of thunder that echoed off the surrounding mountains at such a high decibel that Sasha jumped in surprise. It was as though God wanted to participate in the celebration in His colossal manner.

Unfortunately, the storm that followed the atmospheric pyrotechnics meant that gray clouds would dominate the next day, obscuring the Matterhorn and the tops of the other mountains. It also chilled the air and caused Sasha's family to don hats, sweaters, and jackets for their ascent to the top of Matterhorn mountain via a chain-linked train that climbed from the valley floor all the way to the top, an ascent of about 1,800 meters. The train dropped Sasha at the mountain's peak, well above the natural tree line and 3,800 meters above sea level. Vegetation of any kind was sparse at this elevation. It looked very much like how one might imagine a lunar landscape: cold and barren, with deep gullies leading down the mountainside into massive valleys far below. Sasha was amazed to discover some very athletic hikers and bikers clambering over the steep trails and massive rocks along the way. She found it hard to imagine having the stamina to endure the freezing temperatures, thin air, and bleak topography, but she had deep admiration for those hardy individuals who chose to engage in such exercise.

On the trip back down the mountain, Sasha saw a small herd of rare ibex searching for something to eat from the hardscrabble ground on the tops of the mountains. When she and her parents reached the town, it was drizzling and cold, making a warm dinner and a dip in the hotel's heated pool seem even more inviting. Every hotel in the mountains needed a sauna and a heated pool to soothe tired muscles from a day of hiking, biking, or skiing in the mountains.

Sasha loved the authentic, rustic character of the hotel. Their room even featured a real fireplace, which went unused, but Sasha kept imagining how it would have provided everyone with light and warmth on cold winter's days. Sasha liked the hotel so much that she made her parents promise to return one winter to experience the snow, cold, and skiing in the picturesque Swiss Alps.

The next morning, after a hearty Alpine breakfast of yogurt, cheese, and croissants, Sasha reluctantly repacked her bags and headed for the train station. This time she boarded a special train, the Glacier Express, which would take her through the mountains to St. Moritz in slightly more than eight hours. Unfortunately, the weather remained overcast for most of those hours, obscuring views of the tall Alpine mountaintops. Sasha did enjoy seeing the quaint Swiss villages dotting the hillsides with their steeply pitched slate roofs, and they inspired her to think that life in these mountains probably hadn't changed for hundreds of years.

The village of St. Moritz was larger and much more glamorous than Zermatt. Its streets were broader and most of the buildings were modern, filled with all the upscale, brand-name retail stores seen in the world's biggest cities. One massive hotel, the Grand Hotel, dominated the city. It was perched on the cliff overlooking Lake St. Moritz and offered magnificent views of the surrounding mountains, the ski runs, the glacier, and the village itself. In spite of its idyllic setting, St. Moritz lacked the rustic charm and the energetic ambiance that permeated Zermatt. However, what it lacked in athletic energy it more than made up for in elegance and wealth. Rather than outdoorsmen seeking mountaineering equipment and an après-ski aperitif, the town center was dedicated to well-heeled shoppers from around the world looking for other glamorous people to mingle with, extravagant parties to attend, and multiple-star restaurants to enjoy.

After hours of sitting on the Glacier Express, Sasha needed some exercise. She began by walking along the lakefront and then climbed the multiple stairs that led back to the village high above the lake and eventually to the Hotel Steffani in the middle of St. Moritz, where she and her parents were staying. They enjoyed dinner at the hotel restaurant. Although residing in the French side of Switzerland, the meal had a very heavy Italian influence and provided Sasha an early clue to what she would encounter on the next leg of her journey when they traveled to Italy.

The next morning was a bright, clear, brilliantly sunny day which provided spectacular views of the Alpine scenery. Sasha and her parents walked through St. Moritz to the train station and boarded the Bernina Express, which took them through more than four thousand kilometers of mountainous terrain and offered spectacular views of the huge Bernina glacier. The train also wrapped itself around many bridges and tunnels to pass through the mountains and across rivers along its steep descent to Tirano, a town on the Swiss-Italian border in Italy.

This was Sasha's first time in Italy, the home of some of her ancestors, and it gave her a first opportunity to sample authentic Italian pizza. As soon as the train arrived in Tirano, Sasha sprinted across the small piazza to a tiny outdoor restaurant so she could be first to order a Margarita pizza. She sat with a simple smile caressing her face as she gazed across the warm, sunny Italian piazza. The pizza was different from what she was used to eating in Singapore, but she thought it was delicious. She had to consume it quickly because she had to catch the last bus leaving Tirano that day—it would take her all the way to Lugano, which was back across the Swiss border.

The three-hour bus ride through northern Italy took Sasha past many scenic villages and small cities along the way. The Italian cities they passed were clearly more densely populated and situated on flatter terrain than the Swiss villages Sasha had seen earlier nestled in the

Swiss mountains. The larger population in Italy also meant more clutter and much more evidence of commerce and industry. Shopping centers and factories were scattered about everywhere in a helter-skelter fashion, and the farms seemed untidy by comparison to the well-kept Swiss countryside. The bus did traverse nearly the entire length of beautiful Lake Como and passed the many colorful holiday resorts and amber-hued homes along its shores. Sasha dreamed of taking a vacation on this watery paradise some year in the not-too-distant future.

Lugano proved to be a much bigger Swiss city than all the others Sasha had visited thus far. It was also the southernmost city of her journey, and its warmer climate permitted a wider selection of foliage to grow alongside the usual stately mountain pines, including many types of palm trees. Lugano is situated on the west side of Lake Lugano, a large glacial lake that harbored commercial as well as pleasure craft, in the Italian-speaking canton of Switzerland. Lugano is big, surrounded by mountains, and hosts a large population of Middle Easterners who could be seen walking along the lakeshore, some wearing strict Muslim attire. Sasha, at first, was very confused in Lugano, thinking she was still in Italy instead of across the Swiss border in the Italian-speaking canton. Italian was spoken everywhere, and dinner that night was quintessentially Italian.

The next morning, Sasha headed back toward the train station to board the William Tell Express, named for the famous Swiss folk hero and legendary archer who lived in these mountains. This was another magnificent, comfortable train with panoramic windows providing a full view of the mountains on either side. Evergreen trees covered these mountains, dotted with an occasional village, and a river ran along side of the train tracks for most of the journey to Flüelen. This tiny Swiss village on the southern shore of Lake Lucerne was where Sasha and her parents left the William Tell Express and stepped aboard the Uri, a large white paddle steamer that would take them on a five-hour boat ride up Lake Lucerne to the city of Lucerne.

Lucerne was one of the most beautiful cities among the many Sasha visited on this spectacular trip. Situated on the north side of beautiful Lake Lucerne and surrounded by high mountains, it is significantly bigger than Lugano and clearly a full-service commercial city. The town boasts four ancient bell towers, and it has enough clocks sounding the hour throughout the town to keep even William Tell abreast of the time. It is located in a German-speaking canton, and its architecture reflects traditional German gothic style. This was most evident in the old quarter of town, which was filled with narrow streets, gabled roofs with red tiles, quaint restaurants, two wood-covered bridges that crossed the river Reuss with medieval art hanging from the rafters, an ancient water tower, and several seventeenth-century Baroque churches. The city possessed an architectural vibrancy that spanned many centuries, marking it as unique among all the other cities Sasha visited along the incredible train journey through the Swiss alps.

Lucerne hosted a fleet of paddle wheel vessels, some almost one hundred years old, that plied Lake Lucerne, promising great adventures in the multitude of tiny villages and hotels situated up and down both shores. A family could spend a decade of vacations sampling the villages, each with their unique character, riding the funiculars to the tops of the tall mountains and lounging in the hotel pools that were featured at each stop along the lake.

Sasha walked across one of the ancient covered bridges to the old quarter of the town and wished that she had brought her scooter. She then decided to climb to the top of the Zytturm clock tower. This thirty-one-meter tower was erected in 1442. It was a long, arduous climb, but it eventually led to a very rewarding view from its summit and an instructive sight of the longest weight-suspended clock in Switzerland. Sasha was told by one of the maintenance staff at the tower that it strikes the hour one minute before all of the other clocks in Lucerne, but she couldn't understand why. After climbing down the hundreds of steps to reach the bottom, Sasha's legs began to ache, and she eventually had to walk backward down the hill to the center of the old quarter to relieve the pain in her muscles.

The next day was the last of this trip. Sasha and her parents woke early and took a local train fifty kilometers away from the center of Lucerne to Mount Pilatus. There they had to wait in the piazza for the funicular that would takes them to the top of this mountain. The piazza was filled with tourists from all corners of the earth and hikers all waiting to ride to the top. It was there Sasha learned that a bottle of mineral water cost the same as a bottle of Swiss beer.

"So why drink water?" she asked.

When it was finally Sasha's turn to ride the funicular, she clambered in, eager for an aerial view of Lucerne, the lake, and the surrounding countryside. But clouds formed about one-third of the way to the top of the mountain, obscuring all these sights. Sasha learned later that she would have had to stay days rather than hours to have an unobstructed view of the city, lake, and opposite mountain range, as the clouds were persistent and clear days were rare.

Sasha and her parents returned to Lucerne by the same local train and then headed to another train station to take one final train home to Neuchâtel. Sasha watched sadly as the tall mountains slowly faded into the background. She regretted having to say goodbye to them, but she wouldn't soon forget this wonderful adventure through some of the world's highest mountains, past glaciers and crystal-clear lakes, all made possible through awe-inspiring feats of Swiss rail engineering.

11

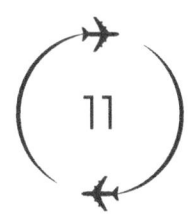

Boracay Island, the Philippines

Sasha started 2015 with a trip to Boracay, one of the 1,780 islands in the Philippine archipelago. She stayed with her parents in the most luxurious hotel in the islands, the Shangri-La, situated at Boracay's northern tip. The journey there from Singapore wasn't easy. Sasha and her parents arrived at Kalibo International Airport on Panay Island in the Philippines after a three-and-a-half-hour flight. They then climbed into a van for a ninety-minute drive to the end of this island, where they had to wait for a speedboat that would take them across the straits to Boracay. Caticlan was a very poor, largely undeveloped island, and the car ride provided Sasha a good opportunity to gain some insight into the normal lives of the Philippine people. All the islanders were dressed modestly, and there were no buildings above two stories. In fact, most of the land was devoted to rice farming and agriculture, and all forms of livestock ran loose along the roads. Even the houses were widely scattered once the van left the few towns and tiny villages that dotted the island.

The wind was up, and it created large waves in the straits between the islands. Sasha's planned boat ride to the Shangri-La hotel's private dock had to be canceled because of the dangerous sea conditions.

Consequently, the family took a smaller but faster boat to the public dock on the south side of Boracay. The passage between the islands was rocky, and everyone on the boat had to wear life jackets for their safety. When Sasha arrived on the island of Boracay, she jumped onto the sandy beach and then climbed aboard another van for the trek across the island to the hotel. This van ride added another forty-five minutes to the already lengthy journey, but it offered Sasha a glimpse of life across the entire island. They drove past crowded shops at the White Beach area and many small hotels and stores along the way. Aside from the areas dedicated to tourist shops, the rest of the island looked even poorer than Caticlan, since it seemed to have no visible industry apart from tourism. Boracay is widely regarded as the prime destination for tourists in the Philippine islands, and it became evident to Sasha as she traveled across the island how much tourism had shaped the landscape and the lives of locals living there.

Finally, after a grueling day of travel, Sasha arrived at the Shangri-La hotel, unpacked her things, enjoyed a pleasant dinner, and jumped into bed with great expectations for enjoying the beach when she awoke in the morning.

Breakfast the next morning was served on a large open balcony off the hotel lobby. Its doors and windows were flung wide open to encourage the fresh sea breeze to blow through and keep everything cool. It was refreshing and added to everyone's appetite. Breakfast was hearty, and since very few people chose to eat on this balcony, it made Sasha feel special and grateful. The views through the open doors and windows provided her with a bird's-eye view of the extensive resort.

The air in Boracay was much cooler and drier than in warm, sunny Singapore, and the wind was still very strong that day. The seas were brimming with white caps and the surf was pounding along the shore with at least five-foot waves. Sasha ran down to the beach after breakfast to secure beach chairs for her family, and everyone then settled into chaise lounges along the shore to enjoy the wild, thrashing sea views on this cloudy, windy day. The temperature of the sea was also a big surprise to Sasha, especially compared to the sea at Bintan, Indonesia, which was the last beach she'd visited. It was cold. It took real determination to get into the cold water, and the rapid slope of the beach made entry and exit from the surf arduous. The beach had very coarse sand filled with broken shells and particles of coral from the offshore reefs that extended nearly to the surf line. The coral and shells were constantly being washed ashore by the tide and broken up by the plunging waves. Before venturing into the sea, Sasha had to learn to do some reconnaissance to discover where the sandy lanes between the coral reefs lay.

Nevertheless, Sasha did not enjoy the cold water and even refrained from venturing into the resort's huge pool. The pool was a real feat of aquatic architecture. It had multiple islands with towering palm trees in its middle, and it was highly configured into myriad shapes offering bathers quiet coves to settle into, or large open spaces for swimming. Sasha looked achingly at the pool and dipped her toes in a few times, but she always exited quickly.

She ended her first full day on Boracay Island looking at the sunset over the South China Sea and watching the hotel's South Seas dancers perform along the beach. The dancers were dressed in black with wild bird feathers in their headdresses, and they carried spears and shields to resemble not-so-ancient Polynesian warriors from a century past. Sasha loved watching the dancers twirl their fiery spears into the air and shift rhythmically along the beach, and she observed their performance with rapt attention every night she was there.

The sun broke through the clouds on Sunday, the wind abated, and the waves grew more moderate. It was easier to enter the ocean now, and all the hotel tourists did so for as long as they could withstand the cold. Sasha and her parents played sharks and frogs in the surf, and then Sasha started to build an extensive sand structure. Inspired by her adventures in Switzerland the previous summer, she built a sandy version of her vision of the Swiss Alps with winding highways going in all directions and mountains with tunnels dug underneath just like she saw on the great train trip. Her parents watched the parade of single-hulled blue sailboats blow past the beach on the fresh breeze that prevailed all day. There was also a flotilla of motorboats, mostly carrying snorkelers and scuba divers from the down-island beaches of Boracay to some well-known dive sites on the island's northern side.

Sasha and her parents planned to stay at the resort a full week, and in that time there were many restaurants to try, beach and pool days to be had, and pictures to take of the surroundings, the sea, the fauna and flora, one another, and the sundown dancers on the beach. The best pictures were of the magnificent sunsets—the most spectacular of which occurred on Wednesday evening at the end of another lovely sunny day with just enough clouds in the sky to catch the sun's last rays. It was a beautiful pink and red display, a gift from nature to all those lucky enough to have seen it. Sasha listened intently to the staff of the Rima restaurant as they described that night's sunset as the

Evening entertainment in Boracay in the Philippines

sunset of the year for its intensity of color, brilliance, and long-lasting afterglow.

That Wednesday was memorable for Sasha for other reasons too. In the afternoon, just before the magnificent sunset, she had played tennis with her parents and proved to them that her tennis lessons were beginning to click as she hit backhands, forehands, volleys, and overheads with impressive form.

Russian Christmas also happened on Wednesday. In the morning, Sasha and her family exchanged a few small gifts to commemorate the Russian holiday and then had dinner that night at Rima, their favorite Italian restaurant at the resort. Though it is only a holiday according to the Julian calendar, which the Eastern Orthodox Church follows, to Sasha's surprise, they weren't alone in celebrating Christmas on that day at the hotel. Boracay was clearly a popular destination for Russian tourists, many of whom celebrated their Christmas at the large hotel buffet that evening. Sasha heard Russian being spoken everywhere—along the beach, in restaurants, and even in the very well-equipped hotel gym where Sasha watched several muscular Russians work out every morning. By Thursday, the day after Russian Christmas, the composition of guests at the hotel started to change. The Russians began to leave, and more Taiwanese and European tourists arrived.

Sasha's trip to Boracay also included a visit to the highly publicized White Beach. It is advertised as the whitest sand beach in the world. The beach itself was a long strip of land stretching well into the sea like a giant sand bar, and every inch of it was crowded with sunbathers and backpackers. The shallow water at this beach was very warm as the sun was able to heat it much more efficiently than the deeper water by the hotel beach. Even the water farther out beyond the sand at White Beach was littered with bathers and boats for hire.

The land side of the beach was filled with bars, restaurants, dive shops, tattoo parlors, souvenir stores, and junk shops. The most interesting attraction Sasha discovered was in the big shopping mall. It was a vertical climbing wall, and Sasha just had to try it out. She climbed the wall twice and went much higher on her second attempt after she overcame her nervousness. The climb helped Sasha understand the value of experience and knowledge gained from doing something more than once.

The road back from White Beach was the same one they had taken the first night going to the hotel through the heart of Boracay. The views from the van, as Sasha and her parents headed back to the Shangri-La, provided an up-close view of a very poor community. The spaces between the run-down, squalid shacks that lined the island's main road were filled with junk and garbage. The side roads that jutted off perpendicularly from the main road were lined with even more humble living quarters and open storefronts. Boracay was indeed a very poor island, and after observing it firsthand, Sasha understood why so many English-speaking Philippine women chose to emigrate and work as domestics in more affluent cities in the orient such as Singapore and Hong Kong.

The weather turned bad on Friday; the sky was dark and foreboding. The wind wasn't strong, but it was enough to spoil Sasha's plans for a day of sailing on one of those blue sailboats. She instead sat on the beach for most of this day until it started raining and she moved with her father to the hotel's game room. Though they missed observing sunset on the beach on this final night because of the constant rain, Sasha and her parents dressed for dinner early and headed out to experience a Philippine buffet that included native dancers and a full menu of novel food selections Sasha had never heard of before. Pork was the main ingredient in most of the dishes, including a huge suckling pig that was roasted and carved right before the diners. The desserts were also new to Sasha, being unique to the Philippines and very sweet.

The best part of the dinner, however, was the dancers. The entertainment included a trio of guitar players and several singers who accompanied them. Sasha was fascinated by the Philippine dancers, and she was thrilled when they invited her and the other diners to join them on the dance floor. Sasha jumped up from the table and followed along, performed all of their moves, and thoroughly enjoyed herself.

The last activity Sasha and her family squeezed in before leaving Boracay on Saturday was to go on a much-anticipated sailboat ride. The weather had cleared, and conditions were perfect as Sasha walked down the beach to the dock, where her parents hired a white-hulled, narrow-beamed sailboat with outriggers on both sides and a red genoa sail. The boat was named *The Scorpions*, and it took two sailors to sail it.

Sasha was initially scared of being in the boat and didn't want to go, but finally she relented and climbed aboard—wearing an orange life vest, plenty of sunscreen, and a deep frown. She and her parents took their seats on either side of the main hull on top of the netting that stretched from the hull to the two outriggers, and then they were off. The ride was delightful. They caught the prevailing breeze as they sailed up and down the coastline. Time quickly ran out, and they all wished the ride could go on for much longer. Once again, Sasha was sad to say goodbye to the beautiful beach and hotel on Boracay Island.

12

Da Nang, Vietnam

DURING SPRING SCHOOL BREAK, Sasha and her family took a short trip to Vietnam hosted by the Young Presidents' Organization (YPO), a global leadership community of business executives of which Sasha's mother was a member. Sasha left Singapore on a gray, rainy day in the middle of spring, hoping for a reprieve from the monsoons. The weather in Vietnam was exactly the same as in Singapore even though it is two-and-a-half hours to the northwest. Their plane landed in Da Nang, a destination chosen by the trip organizers because it is the closest main city to the cultural center of Vietnam.

The trip happened to fall close to April 30, Unification Day, which is celebrated throughout Vietnam as a national holiday. It was the day the North won reunification with the South as the last of the American forces left the country in 1973. Of course, many South Vietnamese followed the Americans and similarly left the country in search of more political stability and economic opportunity. Unfortunately, the reigning Communist government proceeded to lead the country into forty years of poverty. Throughout the trip, Sasha would see many reminders of Vietnam's war-torn history.

On the ride from the airport to the hotel, Sasha immediately noticed that the roads were filled with motorbikes. As they drove, she observed sections of typically poor Asian urban dwellings crammed together along with small shops selling everything. Nearly adjacent to the slums were tall, modern high-rises, which represented the potential future commercial success of Vietnam. These tall commercial buildings lie on the old border between South and North Vietnam. Da Nang was being built up at a very rapid pace; massive construction sites were evident everywhere. Property developers undoubtedly believed this area would soon become a hot tourist destination.

The hotel Sasha and her family stayed in, the Hyatt Regency, was very large, very new, and very low to the ground. It sprawled along a dark-brown sandy beach by the edges of the South China Sea. The YPO group had arranged a barbecue by the main pool for the first night's entertainment. Sasha and her family joined the group around the pool, and Sasha was introduced to many of the members who were milling around the tables under a brilliant set of stars. The night sky was clear here because there was no serious industry, and the area had a very low population density. From the poolside, Sasha listened for the faint sounds of waves quietly lapping along the beach. The barbecue included food choices from the West and traditional Vietnamese specialties such as pho and wonderful fried and fresh spring rolls. Sasha went Western and chose lamb chops, rice, and several types of dessert.

Perhaps the most important reason behind the YPO family retreat was to kindle friendship, and that's exactly what was happening that evening at the edges of the beach. Sasha was seated next to Alba, the daughter of another YPO family from Spain. They began talking and soon found out that they went to the same school in Singapore. They played on the beach and decided to meet at the pool the next morning for an early swim.

After swimming together in the pool and eating breakfast the next day, Sasha, Alba, and their parents got ready for a trip to Hue, the old capital city of Vietnam and the center of the Cham kingdom from AD 300 to 1400. The Cham people originally came from India and traveled across all of southeast Asia before settling in Hue. They built elaborate temples in Myanmar, Cambodia, and central Vietnam. Unfortunately, time, weather, earthquakes, and war have taken a destructive toll on these structures.

The road north to Hue was long and arduous. The bus drove over mountains and down into flat river basins as it lugubriously traveled north. From the top of the mountain several kilometers north of Da Nang, Sasha caught some incredibly magnificent views of the city and the sea. The bus stopped at the top of the mountain to permit everyone an opportunity to take photographs of these spectacular views. At a souvenir stand by the bus stop, Sasha bought a tiny marble bracelet for herself and one for Alba. A friendship was developing.

After the bus left this high mountain perch, it descended into Lăng Cô, a small fishing village situated right at the mouth of a beautiful, brackish-water bay where the local fishermen farmed oysters. The rest of the road to Hue was long, hot, and dangerous. It wound through poor, small villages, many large rice paddies, and past an occasional stream or river flowing underneath very narrow, old, apparently fragile bridges. If traffic were coming from the opposite direction, the bus would have to stop before entering the bridge to let the traffic pass.

Sasha finally arrived in Hue after a long and thirsty three-and-a-half hours of driving. The group immediately stepped off their large tour bus and clambered aboard smaller buses that would take them across the narrow confines of a set of bridges that crossed the Perfume River and into the old Cham palace grounds.

During the Cham's period one side of the river was for the royalty, and the other side was for everyone else. The palace grounds consisted of three concentric sections, each enclosed by a wall and a surrounding moat to protect against invaders. The palace was very reminiscent of the Imperial Palace grounds in the Forbidden City in Beijing. Eventually, Sasha entered the middle ground, which was set up like a courtyard.

Sasha wandered the 1,500-year-old palace grounds with great interest. Somehow the ancient palace survived the multiple wars that occurred over the centuries, although some of the buildings she saw were rebuilt with the help of UNESCO, as these palace grounds were designated as a national heritage sight.

On the way back to Da Nang, Sasha and Alba happily sang *Mama Mia* songs together, entertaining all the adults on the bus. That night, as everyone enjoyed a generous and delicious dinner at a Vietnamese restaurant and the parents talked over wine, the girls made a new friend, Mischa, who was eleven, one year older than Alba and three years older than Sasha. She was attending United World College in Singapore, another highly rated school, so the girls were able to compare their studies, teachers, and homework at the two schools. They enjoyed their time together by themselves without their parents telling them what they should be eating.

The next morning, Mischa joined Sasha and Alba for breakfast and an early morning dip in the pool, where they competed to see who could go down the long water slide the most times. The entire group met again at noon and hopped aboard a bus to Hội An, a lovely, quaint city next to a tiny river that flowed into the gulf of Cua Dai before emptying into the sea. Hội An has a very intriguing cultural history. Initially, it served as a port city for cargo and passenger ships departing from other Asian ports on their way to Saigon. This former port city's cultural history is richly reflected in its unique contrast of Asian and Western architecture. Mixed in among Hội An's simple wooden Chinese shophouses and temples are elaborate French colonial buildings with balustrades on their balconies and elaborately tiled roofs. Sasha was attracted by the many colorful buildings and intrigued by the disparate styles and materials all mixed together in their construction. When her father told her of the many different people and cultures that contributed to the creation of this city, she began to search for the different shapes of the buildings, especially the indigenous ornate Vietnamese houses.

And, like most tourists visiting Hội An, she, too, was fascinated by the eye-catching Japanese Covered Bridge with a temple at the top. Again her father added to the picture by telling Sasha it was built by the Japanese in the sixteenth century to connect their quarter with the Chinese quarter across a tributary of the Thu Bồn River.

Hội An today has both a Chinese and a Japanese section, and unlike Hue, it was mainly spared during the many wars fought in Vietnam over the twentieth century. Hue, being on the border between North and South Vietnam, became a major target for both combatants during the many wars and, most notably, was the scene for the 1968 Tet Offensive when the North stormed through the South's defenses.

The old city of Hội An is filled with many small shops peddling clothes, leather goods, art, and souvenirs. It also has many restaurants, bars, and cafés that compete with the retailers for tourists' attention and money. This lovely city south of Da Nang is a mecca for tourists, and on the day Sasha visited, there were multiple tour groups visiting the city from all over Asia. Sasha's friends' group had lunch in a restaurant a slight distance away from Hội An's main tourist center. The restaurant was located in a magnificent French colonial building directly in front of a Cam Nam Island bay, which was fed by a tiny tributary from the main river. The large grounds were filled with lush, flowering trees, all kinds of beautiful foliage, and many small pools surrounding the main building. These tiny pools were filled with frogs and small fish, and they became an immediate draw for Sasha and her friends. They enjoyed searching out and capturing frogs from the ponds while the adults enjoyed the best Vietnamese food any of them had ever tasted.

The group spent the rest of the afternoon wandering through the quaint old town, shopping, sightseeing, and being surprised by the authenticity of this very touristy place. The small streets were dotted with many sights of everyday life in Vietnam, and while the buildings that housed the small shops were very old and most were in need of serious repair, this only added to the charm of this old city.

That night before going to bed, Sasha took a moment to gaze up at the sky, wondering how different the same stars looked from all the different places she had been. The night sky in the middle of Vietnam is extremely clear and cloudless because there aren't any major cities or sources of industrial light pollution nearby. There was a full moon this night that lit up the sky and cast giant shadows on the South China Sea. The many scattered stars shone brightly against a cobalt blue sky, but were isolated from one another. It was incredibly different from the blank, often cloudy, starless sky Sasha saw most nights in Singapore.

On the final day of the YPO retreat, everyone was asked to choose an activity. Options included golf, Vietnamese cooking classes, relaxing by the pool, or venturing to My Son. Adventure sounded like the most fun to Sasha, so she hopped aboard the bus. My Son lies about sixty kilometers west of Hội An, high up in the mountains that separate Vietnam from Cambodia. It is a historic ceremonial place built by members of the Cham kingdom, and it's said that some ethnically Cham people continue to live in the nearby mountains, living quite apart from everyday Vietnamese life. These religious structures were built in a style highly reminiscent of Angkor Wat in Cambodia, though the buildings at My Son are less well preserved and lie in the midst of a jungle next to a small river that floods the area every monsoon season. As a result, large trees had overgrown the buildings and knocked down walls over time. My Son was also the scene of some of the heaviest fighting during the US war in Vietnam. Bullet holes could be found in the walls of the temples everywhere, and land mines still exploded forty years after the conclusion of the war.

My Son lies between two very tall mountains and is only twenty-two kilometers from the Ho Chi Minh trail on the border of Cambodia. During the war, My Son's temples were used as a base by the Viet Cong to store food and munitions as they carried out raids on nearby villages. When the Americans discovered this, they began to heavily bomb the area in an effort to drive out the Viet Cong. Some of the ancient temples were destroyed in the process. In response, the Viet Cong mined the surrounding area quite extensively. As recently as one year prior to Sasha's visit, two people had their legs blown off by mines as they were walking around the area. Sasha was worried when she learned this and made an effort to tread lightly that day.

She listened attentively to the tour guides who were recounting stories from the war and its effect on the local historic buildings. They repeatedly called the war "the American War," which puzzled Sasha. She had no knowledge of this war that ended more than thirty years before she was born, and she was intrigued by the detritus left from that long-ago fighting that marked the buildings and the land. She asked many naive questions, such as "Why was America here, since it is so far away?" She would be reading about this war in history classes later in her education. Then she would have some insight into how the battles were fought and how they affected the land and the people, even if she never did learn the answer to her childlike question that day.

The ride to and from My Son was much more rugged than the roads lined with tourist shops Sasha had seen earlier in the trip on her way north along the coast road to Hue. The passing landscape was much less scenic, with no views of the South China Sea, but it gave Sasha much more insight into everyday Vietnamese life. This road wound through rice paddies that stretched as far as the horizon, with huge horned water buffalo scattered throughout and a host of very creatively constructed scarecrows to ward off the ever-present predatory black birds. These sights of everyday life in rural Vietnam became her vision of what the countryside looked like before the bombs fell. It seemed peaceful and lush, a dramatic contrast with what she saw at My Son.

The buildings in the villages that Sasha saw amid the rice paddies appeared much poorer than the ones that existed along the major coast road. These shacks housed the farmers and were open to the elements on nearly all sides. They also had little or no furniture. These were agricultural communities, and in front of each house that lined the sometimes-bumpy dirt road, Sasha saw rice drying on mats. Every third house or so, she would spy long red chilies drying on the same mats alongside the rice. She later learned that the government owned the land, and the farmers must pay the government a large portion of their produce to rent the acres they tend.

Sasha was very glad she had chosen to take the adventure to My Son and was able to learn so much about the real Vietnam. Another thing that always made Sasha happy was making new friends on her travels, so, of course, she vowed to remain close to Alba when they returned home to Singapore and school at SAS.

13

Algarve, Portugal

SASHA VISITED PORTUGAL IN the summer of 2015. Specifically, her family arranged to fly from Neuchâtel for a vacation in the Algarve, the southernmost part of Portugal, bordering the Atlantic Ocean and southern Spain. It has a sunny, very dry climate with cool ocean breezes. The flora is unusually varied with palm trees, cacti, pine trees, and deciduous trees that were still in full green foliage. The ocean temperature was nineteen degrees Celsius, about the same as the land temperature, making the water very difficult to get into and quite easy to leave.

Sasha stayed in a resort called Pine Cliffs, perched high above the ocean with an elevator running alongside several flights of stairs to transport bathers down to the sea. She spent many fun days riding the elevator and climbing the stairs to and from the ocean. The resort had everything: multiple pools, bicycles, children's playgrounds, miniature golf, tennis courts, and a nine-hole golf course.

Sasha and her family rented bicycles immediately and used them exhaustively to travel to the beach, tennis, golf, and virtually everything, including dinner on most nights. Dinners were delectable, ranging from fresh-caught ocean fish to thick, mouthwatering steaks imported from the United States. Vegetables and fruits were local and very fresh and tasty.

Each morning Sasha started her day in the big resort pool, spending most of her time riding on colorful floats. That was often followed by daily tennis lessons after she watched her parents play on the resort's immaculately rolled red clay courts on their first day there. Her instructor was a young English coach whom she liked very much. The only thing she objected to was that he used soft compression tennis balls instead of the regular yellow ones. She was offended by this choice because she thought that they were for younger, less experienced players.

On her third day in Portugal, Sasha decided that she and her parents should play golf. It proved to be a very eventful decision, as Sasha accidentally hit her mother in the mouth with her golf club on her backstroke on the third hole. The accident quickly ended the family golf match and required that the entire family go to the local hospital so her mother could receive five stitches. The hospital personnel spoke mainly Portuguese, making communication and treatment complicated. The staff kept asking how this wound happened, thinking maybe it was due to family violence. Sasha quickly acknowledged that learning many languages was a real advantage in life, as she realized that the misunderstanding at the hospital caused so much wasted time and confusion.

This unfortunate accident did not end the family's golf experience, however. They played again on Monday without any additional mishaps, though it was miniature golf this time. Miniature golf was much less stressful than playing actual golf, and the course was much simpler than the miniature golf course in Neuchâtel that Sasha often played and enjoyed.

After the first few days, Sasha began to spend more time on the beach than at the pool. It was easy to build sandcastles on this beach because the sand was constantly wet from the enormous tide that daily swept in and out of this part of the Atlantic Ocean. The water was very clean as there was no commercial boat traffic and few pleasure boats or fishing boats in the area. However, Sasha was not the only one enjoying these pleasant conditions. There were hundreds of people on the beach, stretching as far as the eye could see. Competition for the lounges along the beach was intense, even if they were reserved for hotel patrons. There were simply far more guests at the hotel than there were lounges. Sasha and her parents often had to wait for guests to depart before they were able to secure a couple of lounges.

There was a restaurant right on the beach, barely a meter or two above high tide. It was very informal and served only fresh fish and vegetables. Sasha ate there for lunch several times and for dinner once. Sasha had more fun running along the beach in between meals and after dinner, and she loved taking the tram up to the hotel after dinner for a very bumpy but fun ride when the family did not bring their bicycles.

Sasha left Portugal early on a Wednesday morning wishing she had had more time to play in the waves and on the clay tennis courts. Summer was drawing to a close for Sasha, and she would soon have to turn her attention back to school and all her extracurricular activities at home in Singapore.

14

Jimbaran Bay, Bali, Indonesia

SASHA AND HER FAMILY arrived in Bali on a Friday in mid-October to celebrate her upcoming birthday. In just three days, Sasha would turn nine years old. As they drove into the main building of the Four Seasons Hotel in Jimbaran Bay, Sasha marveled at everything in what was arguably the most luxurious resort she had ever stayed in. The hotel was spread out across a hill overlooking Jimbaran Bay to the east. It had a spectacular design of old-fashioned Balinese architecture. All the villas and main buildings, including the lobby, had thatched roofs and were open-air. Upon check-in, Sasha and her parents were immediately greeted with cold towels and a refreshing lime and ginger cooler. It was a great beginning for Sasha's birthday, and the resort continued to greatly impress her for the rest of the trip.

Staff members took the family to their villa—a private, walled enclosure with two buildings. The first had a dining area and a living room, and the second had a bedroom and bathroom. It, too, had a thatched roof with intricate poles holding the palm thatching together. There were two showers—one in a marble-tiled bathroom and the other an outside shower fed by a cane pipe situated behind the ten-foot-tall cement walls of the villa compound. The outdoor shower was the only one everyone used.

Sasha's favorite feature of the villa was a delightful, private plunge pool decorated with a stone-cut, medium-height, lion-headed creature spitting water into the center. It took mere minutes for Sasha to jump into the cool, refreshing pool. The water's temperature was the same as the air, and this made entry to the pool very comforting. She later learned that the temperature was colder in the early morning from the overnight rains, which dropped fresh water into it. By lunchtime, the sun heated the water to a wonderfully warm, jump-right-in temperature. Sasha thoroughly enjoyed the plunge pool and used it every day.

In addition to the private pool inside this luxurious villa, Sasha soon discovered the resort's main infinity pool facilities. She quickly dropped her beach things on a nearby chaise lounge and began jumping in and out of the big pool as well as the three additional swimming pools close by. One was a hot pool, a second was a cold pool, and a third had a tall, powerful waterfall at its back that was fed from the infinity pool located high above on the resort's main terrace. The waterfall was extremely useful for massages and playing hide and seek. After testing out all three smaller pools, Sasha climbed up the slope and jumped back in the resort's main pool. It was long and deep and beautifully shaped, and it offered an incredible view of Jimbaran Bay below.

The weather pattern Sasha experienced in Bali went from partial clouds in the morning to bright blue skies in the afternoon. For the first few days, she and her parents quickly secured two very private lounges situated at the edge of the cliff overlooking the bay, providing Sasha with a spectacular view of the long, white sand beach below. A large white umbrella covered the lounges and provided shade during the morning. By afternoon, the sun passed overhead and bathed the lounges in warm sunshine.

Lunch and dinner were both served by the pool, and the area was lit by Balinese-style lamps and torches, making it a very romantic setting.

Sasha chose from an assortment of Asian foods for lunch, and dinner had a different theme each night. Friday's was a seafood barbecue with several types of crustaceans and local fish cooked to order. Saturday was Thai night, and dinner was served inside the main dining room.

The property's main beach was down the hill and to the right of the villa, directly in the mouth of the beautiful circular bay. It featured a very large tidal change every six hours. The waves poured ashore in long, straight lines but dispersed by the time they reached the beach, making it a very safe swimming place for children. The sand was hard and compact from the retreating tide, and it was filled with millions of tiny crabs laboriously digging new holes in the sand. They frightened Sasha, although they were totally harmless. The entry into the surf was flat, and the sand shelf extended well out into the bay. There were very few pieces of coral or shells lying on the sand that would impede entry into the surf.

Though Sasha readily took to the pool, she approached the beach and its waves with more apprehension. After much convincing and some hesitation, she slowly walked and then jumped into the bay. The waves were mild and created just enough lift to make everyone consider jumping in the waves. Wave-jumping finally made Sasha enjoy this beach, and in just a few minutes she learned how to ride the gentle swells. It was Sasha's last day as an eight-year-old, and having conquered one more little fear, she was going into the coming year full of anticipation and delight.

When Sasha finally tired of playing in the surf, her family decided to take a complementary ride on a thirteen-foot catamaran. The bosun launched the sailboat from the surf, everyone jumped aboard, and Sasha sat eagerly on its edge. The breeze was gentle and pleasurable, and so was the day's ride around the bay. The sailboat's bosun was a kindly local Balinese man, and he even jumped off the boat while it was sailing to retrieve Sasha's hat, which had blown off. Everyone enjoyed the ride so much that Sasha's family decided to do it again on another day.

The sun was beginning to set as the boat returned to shore, and as Sasha walked along the beach to go back to the hotel, she noticed that hundreds of locals were converging along the shore to swim, play soccer, and take long walks along the hard-packed sand. Seeing the many locals enjoying their evenings on the beach reminded Sasha that though she was there on vacation, this bay was home to many people who seemed to love it just as much as she did.

The next day was Sasha's birthday. The big day had finally arrived. Sasha received several telephone calls wishing her well from places as far away as New York and St. Petersburg, Russia. She had presents from loved ones in Florida, New York, and Switzerland. She awoke early, eager to celebrate her special day.

Because all the hotel staff knew it was her birthday, they had prepared a surprise for her: a birthday cake with a big "Happy Birthday" sign on it. The staff also sang "Happy Birthday" to her as soon as she sat down for breakfast.

Sasha's birthday in Jimbaran Bay, Bali, Indonesia

Sasha's birthday continued with more surprises. She enjoyed a spa treatment in a gazebo by the ocean with a Balinese massage followed by a romp in their hot tub, sauna, and steam room. She became so relaxed she fell asleep, lulled by the sound of the waves gently folding on the ground-coral-crusted sandy shore and the tweeting of hundreds of colored birds. At the conclusion of her treatment, the spa staff brought her a lighted candle and some chocolate, and then sang "Happy Birthday" to her while presenting her with a beautiful garland of flowers for her hair.

Dinner was another special occasion. Sasha had dinner with her parents in the restaurant by the beach. From the corner table perched at the end of the veranda high above the beach, she could hear but barely see the long rows of waves breaking along the shore. Green laser lights sparkled from across the bay. Once Sasha and her family settled into their chairs, the staff came to their table carrying a bouquet of roses and presented her with another garland for her hair. Then they sang "Happy Birthday" to her.

Dinner was a unique experience. The food at this restaurant was served family-style, and all the choices were modern Asian. Sasha's family chose crab, pork ribs, and duck, and all were delicious. Dessert was a specially ordered birthday cake, and the waiters once again sang "Happy Birthday" to Sasha. She smiled throughout the dinner in her new blue dress, the flower garland in her hair. It was quite a memorable day for Sasha. She received long-wanted gifts and greetings from all her family, listened to three "Happy Birthday" concerts from the staff, ate two birthday cakes, and wore two different flower garlands.

The next day was Sasha's un-birthday. There were no new presents, no birthday parties, and she wasn't feeling well, either. Nevertheless, she had another filling breakfast, played games in the four different pools, ventured down the beach, and took a sail on a small trimaran with her parents. They then left the beach for the tennis court.

The court had very efficient lighting (the sun sets early in Bali), but its surface was not good. It was artificial grass, and it needed to be sanded to prevent contestants from sliding. The reaction of the tennis balls was also quite unpredictable; at times the surface slowed the pace of the balls, at other times it caused a very high bounce, and sometimes the ball would skid past the opponent. None of this stopped Sasha from playing tennis there throughout the trip. She even had a couple of tennis lessons with a young Chinese coach from Hong Kong, who proved to be very strict. Her lesson for Sasha was to train her footwork to improve her strokes. They also had an opportunity to speak in Mandarin to each other. After the tennis lesson, the coach said that Sasha had a good foundation for tennis at her young age.

On Sasha's final day in Bali, she had the opportunity to learn another exciting sport: surfing. Sasha had always wanted to learn to surf, and she took to it immediately. After just a short lesson, Sasha's natural athletic ability and balance enabled her to jump on the board in the sea and ride it to shore. Her Australian surfing coach told Sasha that her gymnastics training was a key to her quick success in surfing and all of her athletic activities. She spent the next hour riding the waves under the watchful gaze of her coach. It was the fulfillment of a great dream of Sasha's, and she left the beach and Bali giddy with joy.

This trip had to be Sasha's most memorable birthday yet, filled with sunny days, a beautiful beach and pools, and many happy moments with her parents.

15

India: The Golden Triangle

IT WAS CHINESE NEW YEAR 2016, and Sasha and her parents decided to spend her school break on a trip to India. The entire trip was arranged by their family friend, Tatiana Ohm. Philip, sister Julia, and the Ohm family would join Sasha and her parents for their second Asian adventure together, this time to explore the mysteries of India.

Sasha, Philip, and their parents arrived at the Delhi airport on a Friday night and were immediately greeted with the typical Indian administrative inefficiency—it took an entire hour to pass through immigration. By the time Sasha finally collected her luggage and everyone made it to the hotel, they were very late for dinner and ready to fall right into bed.

Sasha's first full day in India started early, as did all her subsequent days on this trip. At breakfast, the grown-ups warned Sasha to avoid all fruits and water, which weren't purified to the same standards as she was used to. Sasha even had to be very careful when washing herself and brushing her teeth to make sure she never swallowed any water. When she finished eating that first morning, Sasha and her companions climbed aboard the moderate-sized bus that would take them over the next several days on their trip around India. They were joined by a guide named Ruti. She was born in New Delhi, spoke English very properly, and had attended college in Delhi. The bus was roomy and moved relatively slowly as it bounced along the potholed roads and streets of central India.

Even the mid-sized bus couldn't manage the tiny streets of Old Delhi, so to see local life in that historic part of the city, Sasha and Philip had to clamber onto a bicycle-drawn rickshaw. As Sasha rode through the old city, a terrible stench permeated the air. Garbage had not been picked up in Delhi for more than a week because of a worker's strike. Piles of refuse were scattered everywhere, and the smell wafted through the air like in the unflattering stories of India past. The garbage smells were unpleasant, but Sasha and her companions were met with more pleasant ones as they entered a marketplace in Old Delhi. Huge, heaping sacks of spices lined the pathways. Each one had its own color and aroma. Some were pungent, greeting Sasha's senses immediately. Others required her to lean in close to detect their more subtle scents. In other parts of the marketplace, stores concentrated on leather crafts, mainly camel leather shoes. Yet another section of the marketplace sold cloth that was principally used to make elaborate, colorful Indian saris.

The shops in the marketplace were packed on top of one another and crammed with products. There was no space to spare, as if it would be a sacrilege to waste any useable area. It would be a management nightmare to account for inventory in these stores. Sasha noticed that all the stores were owned and run by men. No Indian women were present except their guide, Ruti, and the only other women were Western and Chinese tourists. Ruti loved shopping in the traditional way: looking through the packed market stands of Old Dehli for produce and purchasing the ground spices she found there. Sasha's family, too, took some time to purchase a few spices and some tea to bring back with them to Singapore.

After leaving the marketplace, the group drove around the crowded, noisy, smelly streets of Old Delhi for a few more hours. They also visited several temples in the old quarter. There are four main religions in Old Delhi: Hinduism, Sikhism, Jainism, and the Muslim religion. Sasha noticed how the temples differed according to the religion they represented. The Muslim mosque was the largest temple in Old Dehli, and Sasha saw that all the Muslim women had to wear a large cloth that covered their entire bodies. In contrast, the smallest was the Jain temple; it was also the most elaborate. It featured colored-glass murals that adorned every wall on the top floor of the building. The temples and religious cites attracted many poor and homeless people, as the temple staff often provided them with food and some shelter.

Once out of Old Delhi, the bus quickly drove Sasha and her hungry companions to a very modern shopping center recently built in New Delhi, where they stopped for lunch. Their repast consisted of a cornucopia of Indian treats. It started with a curry lentil dish from northern India accompanied with four different sauces, each with its own distinct color and "intensity," which is an Indian euphemism for hotness. More dishes then followed, each with a different heavy curry. All were filled to the brim with chicken, lamb, cheese, and vegetables. Accompanying these entries was naan, buttered and laced with garlic, and rice. Everyone ate too much because the food was tasty, spicy, and novel. Sasha tried to enjoy these new tastes, but filled up mostly with chicken and rice. They finished their meal with a cup of masala chai flavored with spices.

The next stop was Jaipur. The road there was long and tedious, and Sasha soon grew restless. She passed the time by looking out the bus window and playing games on her laptop with Philip. The flat Indian countryside was barren of trees and foliage. The roads were dotted with crumbling brick buildings and small villages, populated mostly by men sitting indolently in front of storefronts or local restaurants. Houses were low, one-story buildings constructed of sand-colored brick or thatched together with any discarded material. They did not have any floors, only the earth on which they stood. Cows, goats, and dogs wandered freely throughout these buildings, even entering the living quarters. It was an eye-opening experience for Sasha to see all types of animals move about so freely among the people and houses.

Sasha and her family finally arrived at their hotel in Jaipur too late for dinner again, and Sasha quickly fell into bed. Breakfast came fast and early, and then Sasha and her companions climbed back aboard the bus to head toward the Pink City, which is Jaipur's old quarter. The thick pink walls of the old city were constructed with sandstone and made this city truly memorable.

Across the main street of the old city was a large pink sandstone façade, five stories high, elaborately festooned with overhanging balconies, curved roofs, spires, and at least fifty windows, which were used by the Indian women to observe the many happenings on the street below. Sasha couldn't believe that all the buildings in Jaipur were pink; it is truly a distinctly different city from anywhere else.

Inside the walls, the streets were lined with small shops selling every conceivable item. As Sasha explored these streets, she passed turban-clad men with long, elaborate mustaches blowing their pipes in front of covered baskets. She soon learned that inside these baskets were coiled cobras. The snakes were large, black, and hooded. The men and their snakes made for a very curious, colorful partnership that was truly foreboding. Sasha was intrigued and at the same time frightened by the snakes and the bearded men, but inquisitive enough to walk up to the nearest basket and wait for the cobra to appear.

After watching the snake charmers for several minutes, barely blinking the whole time, Sasha and her companions left to make their way on foot to see the giant castle perched on top of a nearby hill. The castle appeared to be well fortified against attacks, which occurred frequently during the sixteenth century when local maharajahs warred constantly for more territory. The last master of the castle was a mogul who had many wives. Sasha walked through the castle's public and private spaces, marveling at the beautiful arches, observing the distinct architecture of the building, and thrilling at the marvelous views from the many arched windows to the fields and city below.

Snake charmer in Jaipur, India

The next stop on the tour took Sasha up another steep hill just on the city limit of Jaipur to an impressive red castle. To climb the hill, everyone was herded into groups of four to step up onto the backs of huge black Indian elephants. They provided a very rocky ride—everyone swayed from side to side as the elephants walked up the steep slope of the hill to the red castle. The swaying was great fun for Sasha and Philip once they became accustomed to the motion. On their way down the mountain, the group declined another ride on the elephants and instead jammed themselves into a jeep, which made its way slowly and carefully through the maze of people, motorbikes, and elephants. It was a much scarier ride than the one on the elephant's back because of the enumerable opportunities for accidents this descent created. When the jeep finally came to a stop at the bottom of the large hill, everyone was grateful to file back into their roomy tour bus.

After Sasha and her companions finished another delicious lunch of Indian specialties and settled their overloaded stomachs with cardamon-and-ginger-infused chai, the bus drove them to another famous castle, the amber castle. This castle was located in the new part

Elephant ride in Jaipur, India

of Jaipur, and Sasha was awed by the immense scope of it. Next to it was Jantar Mantar, an open-air astrological observatory built in 1724 and refurbished in 1901. Today, it is a UNESCO-designated world site of astronomy. This outdoor museum showcased many different mechanisms to measure time and the movements of the sun, moon, and stars. Sasha reveled in trying out various sundials and telling everyone in earshot what time it was. The museum was fascinating and provoked in Sasha a great deal of admiration for the genius that built it so many years ago.

That evening, Sasha and her parents dressed for dinner in red and gold to commemorate the Chinese New Year. Living in Singapore made her whole family more aware of Asian traditions and the events on the lunar calendar. Unfortunately, the Chinese restaurant in India did not serve Sasha's favorite New Year dish, lo mein, but she did have spring rolls and fish. Dinner was much less elaborate than lunch, in keeping with the family's habit of eating less heavy Indian food later in the day, but it was enjoyable nonetheless. Sleep came early for all that night.

The next morning the group awoke early, dressed quickly, and ate breakfast at a breakneck pace to set out as early as possible on the next long bus trip, this time to Agra. As the bus drove out of the modern city of Jaipur, Sasha observed the slums on the city's outskirts. They were dirty, crowded, and stacked with stores and carts selling food.

Conditions were not much better in the flat countryside between Jaipur and Agra. The soil looked to be poor quality, as though it had been farmed out long ago. The only agricultural products to be seen growing were mustard seeds with their pale-yellow flowers. The land was dotted with very small villages and occasionally a town. Most of the houses were in shambles with either the roof or walls missing. Animals were everywhere. Dogs were lying along the sides of every store, and cows wandered freely. Occasionally a troop of monkeys could be seen around rivers and large pools of water. Wild pigs were seen rooting for something to eat, and an occasional camel could be seen pulling a heavily laden cart. Poverty was evident in every village. Sasha had trouble reconciling the living conditions of people in rural India with the life she saw in modern Indian cities such as Jaipur. She asked her friends on the bus to explain why the young didn't move to the cities. None of the parents had a well-conceived opinion. Sasha believed there was every reason for the young to leave this life, if they had any place to go.

There were many buildings along the way that were partially completed and totally deserted. Eventually Sasha asked the bus driver, VJ, why so many buildings were started but not finished. VJ speculated that the reason was that the builders did not obtain all of the necessary licenses and that perhaps while waiting for the long administrative process to obtain those licenses, the builders ran out of funds.

The final observation Sasha and her companions found curious was that there were no women visible in all of these towns. Groups of men were seen everywhere—talking, standing, sitting, and playing cards. The only women Sasha saw were those watching over small herds of sheep and goats in the distant fields.

Sasha's main reason for journeying to Agra was to visit the Taj Mahal, particularly to see it at sunset. This spectacular site drew visitors from all over the world. The Taj was constructed in the seventeenth century by the Mughal emperor Shah Jahan as a tomb for his wife, who died in childbirth. The Taj is considered the jewel of the Mughal world since it is a blend of Indian, Persian, and Islamic styles. At first glance, Sasha was struck by its magnificent symmetry; the view of the Taj was designed to be the same from every side, and Sasha decided she had to test whether this description was true.

The Taj, and the smaller mosque and convention center built adjacent to it, were all constructed along the sides of the Yamuna River. Its white marble sides radiated and reflected the last warm rays of the sun as it set behind the river. Each piece of white marble was intricately curved and colored with dyes made of ground stones.

The next day, Sasha and her travel group visited the humongous red sandstone castle in the center of Agra. It was built after the Taj Mahal by the son of the king who had built the Taj. The son, Aurangzeb, a strict Muslim, became king after leading a revolt against the father and butchering all of his brothers. He then locked his father in a special quarter of the great sandstone fort in Agra, which surrounded the castle and was built with the same white marble as the Taj. This elaborate jail faced the Taj so the old king could always see his creation. He was a captive there without visitors until he died.

Sasha wandered around the fort and the castle for a while before leaving Agra a little dustier than she'd arrived. Sasha's impression was that Agra was poorer than Jaipur, and its streets were dirtier and laden with dust. The crowds of tourists and residents were everywhere, from the stores on the main streets to the side streets that led to the locals' living quarters, which, if possible, were even dirtier than the main thoroughfares. Once again, the only women to be seen were on the buildings' rooftops, viewing the scene from above while remaining mostly out of sight.

Sasha at the Taj Mahal in India

Sasha and her friends shook the dust from their shoes, climbed aboard the bus, and headed back to Delhi to complete their tour of the golden triangle of India. As the bus left Agra, Sasha could see some women washing clothes in the nearby river below the highway. It was her second view of women working in the rural parts of India apart from those who could be seen on the balconies of Jaipur and Agra. The road from Agra to Delhi was completely different from the road they took to Agra from Jaipur. The landscape was much greener, and the rich farmland was dotted with a few farmhouses, but no villages.

Occasionally, there were small herds of sheep and a few groups of cattle but hardly any people. And this time, instead of the rough road they traveled on the way from Jaipur, the bus took the Yamuna Expressway, a modern highway. It was a true highway and is considered the best one in India. Sasha was surprised that it was completely elevated, and she asked VJ why. He replied that it was constructed above the land to prevent the rural locals from erecting shops along the sides of the roadway and to prevent their animals from venturing across the highway and slowing traffic.

The journey took Sasha past the brickyards containing long fields of drying bricks. They were piled about three feet high and were the traditional sand color that one saw on most of the buildings in Agra. Once dried, these bricks were fired to develop their distinctive red color. Occasionally, Sasha and her friends passed a group of thatched conical houses that stood beside the green fields. The fields were primarily empty of people aside from an occasional solitary person walking through them. This sole person, maybe a farmer working in the field, was a very long distance from any observable shelter they could see. Another quirky mystery began to bother Sasha and her friends as they drove through these large fields: There was no evidence of any farm equipment that could be used to work these massive fields. Sasha began to speculate if the produce was real or artificial. She never found an answer.

All along this lengthy drive and the next day as their flight departed Delhi for Singapore, Sasha thought about the architectural wonders that were created hundreds of years ago in India and contrasted it with the congestion, pollution, inefficiencies, poverty, and poor hygiene she saw in India in the present day. India, soon to become the most populous country on earth, was still a bundle of mysteries. It celebrated its exit from colonial captivity a mere seventy years ago, and in that time, economic development has happened in a socialist yet uneven manner, leaving many poor Indians to live by the roadside. Sasha's father filled in some of this history for her throughout their trip, but the nuances of India's culture and economy still left many questions for Sasha to explore as she grew older.

16

Langkawi: The Beach in the Rainforest

FOR THE ANNUAL MAY DAY celebration in Singapore, Sasha's family decided to travel to Langkawi, Malaysia, on the Andaman Sea. This is one of the most highly recommended vacation destinations in Asia, and Sasha was excited to see it for the first time. It was situated within a national park, a five-thousand-hectare rainforest that sprawled down to the Andaman Sea. There were only two hotels—sister hotels—built within the rainforest, and both were hidden in the dense foliage and could barely be seen from the sea or the highway. One, called Datai, was a beautiful, adult-oriented facility perched high on the mountain adjacent to a picturesque stream that began higher up on the same mountain with a natural trail through the forest that leads down the mountain to the beach. The other hotel, the Andaman, was more family-friendly.

No other property was permitted in the national park aside from a golf course that was built contemporaneously with the sister hotels. The golf course provided a clue as to why these two hotels were permitted to be constructed within the national park. Before their trip to Langkawi was complete, Sasha and her dad visited the golf shop at the golf course. However, before they were permitted to enter, they had to wait for a contingent of police and security guards to usher out the prime minister and his guests, who had just finished their round of golf.

Sasha and her parents stayed in the more family-friendly of the two hotels, the Andaman, located closer to the sea. It had a large, sprawling pool and easy access to a very long beach. There were easily more than one hundred chaise lounges spread along the entire length of the beachfront, many tucked under the trees for shade.

As Sasha walked in, she felt like she was entering a grand tree house. The ceiling of the lobby was constructed in a traditional Malaysian style in local hardwoods. It peaked four stories above the lobby floor. There was a beautiful wooden pagoda made with rare ironwood, which never deteriorates, in the center of the lobby. The far side of the lobby offered a magnificent view of the pool set in a wild array of jungle flowers. The building was surrounded on all sides by thick rainforest, obscuring the view of Datai Bay.

Sasha's family chose to come to Langkawi to meet up with her new friend Leah, whom she'd met in Bintan, Indonesia, earlier that year. Leah's family lived in Tokyo, and when they decided to visit Langkawi during Japan's Golden Week break, Sasha's parents agreed to join them there. Both families got along splendidly on these trips. Leah's father was Greek and her mother Austrian, and both spoke German, Greek, French, and English very well.

Leah and her family wouldn't arrive until the next day, but Sasha was always making new friends on her travels. Her first day in Langkawi, Sasha immediately made a new friend, Sophia, a nine-year-old who lived in Malaysia and whose family came from Norway and Scotland. This new friendship kept Sasha in the pool playing the whole afternoon. She would find more friends there the next day when she met Summer and Kiowa. They were seven and ten years old, and like Sasha, loved to play in the pool. When Leah's family finally arrived, Sasha introduced Leah to her new friends, and the girls quickly jumped into the pool together. The pool was enormous, with several islands and a huge slide, and the water temperature was perfect. Sasha would stay at the pool all day while her parents sought out chaise lounges on the beach beneath the trees.

The water in Datai Bay was just as warm as the water in the hotel's pool, and it stretched all the way toward the Thai islands on the horizon. The sand on the beach was nearly white and littered with crab holes, pieces of coral, and tiny shells. The beach sloped gently into the Andaman Sea, and swimmers could wade well out into the bay at low tide. The coral reefs that protected the beach were only a few meters away, making it a very safe sea environment, but they limited how far out one could wade. After a lengthy swim in the sea, everyone gathered at the beach restaurant for lunch and to observe the beautiful view across the bay toward Thailand.

Dinner on the first night was in the hotel's Japanese teppanyaki restaurant, where Sasha was thoroughly entertained by the chef as he swiftly chopped up eggs, vegetables, meat, shrimp, and chicken at the large grill top right in front of her table.

Another night, the families went to a famous restaurant in the Datai, an Indian restaurant called the Gulai House. It was a totally open-air restaurant in the middle of the rainforest. The space was roughly constructed of local wood, and thatching was used for the ceiling. A few ceiling fans moved the generally still, humid air. The food was authentic and delicious, and it reminded Sasha of her trip to India not long ago. As night drew near, the rainforest around them came alive with sounds of life. Sasha and her companions were told that there were numerous types of lizards in the area—including sea-going monitor lizards—hundreds of different birds, thousands of insects, many snakes, and two types of monkeys. One was an aggressive gray type and the other a more timid black monkey with white markings on its head.

Monkeys were plentiful throughout Malaysia. Sasha saw many troops of the aggressive gray monkeys along the highway from the airport, and both varieties frequently appeared around the hotel. The two types of monkeys would fight if they came close to one another.

One evening while Sasha and her parents were getting dressed to go to dinner, several gray monkeys climbed up to their third-floor room and looked at them from the balcony. Sasha howled with fright and then amusement when she discovered them. Her parents had to quickly close the balcony doors to keep them out of the room. They had been warned by the hotel's staff that the monkeys would enter hotel rooms and look for food.

Sasha, Leah, and their new friends never tired of splashing in the large pool, and most afternoons found them there among the tropical flowers, racing down the water slide. They did interrupt their time in the pool one afternoon to venture down to the beach for an evening sail on the hotel's catamaran just before sunset.

The girls also enjoyed taking kayaks out from the beach and did so several times during Sasha's stay. Once they paddled out to a nearby island to explore what was on it. When Sasha returned, she reported that there was nothing there, just more beach and some refuse, probably left by other kayakers.

When Sasha's final day in Langkawi arrived, the girls decided to take paddleboards out on the calm waters of the sea and paddle along the shore. They quickly learned to balance and maneuver themselves with the long paddle. Meanwhile, their parents tried snorkeling in the sea but, unable to see much, soon switched to kayaking instead. The water was murky, and the coral was mostly devastated by the tsunami that hit the coast in 2004. There were very few fish to see.

At midday, everyone quit paddling and snorkeling and headed along the beach to the Datai Langkawi for lunch by the pool. They would return to the same beach club restaurant for their final dinner that night. When dinner was over, Sasha's family said goodbye to Leah and her parents and wished everyone a safe passage home. Sasha said goodbye to all the monkeys that were sitting in the trees watching her and her parents walk back to their lodging to pick up their luggage and prepare to leave this beautiful and still largely undiscovered spot in Malaysia.

17

Tuscany and Rome

THIS IMPORTANT SUMMER TRIP started and ended in Rome—that is, after Sasha and her parents boarded their flight from Singapore to Rome and before returning to their home in Asia the same way. The stated purpose of this trip was to show Sasha the picturesque rolling hills of central Italy on a bicycle. Before the great expedition started, however, Sasha had the opportunity to visit Rome, one of the ancient cradles of Western civilization. Sasha was anxious to see what was left of some of the Roman monuments that she had seen pictures of in her European history textbooks. She was also overjoyed to be able to taste authentic pasta and pizza at its source.

Sasha had to wait patiently before sampling authentic Roman cuisine, though. After dressing for dinner, her parents first took her to the rooftop of the hotel where they were staying to view the ancient city from above. The hotel was conveniently perched on the peak of one of Rome's seven famous hills and therefore offered an extraordinary bird's-eye view of the city. With aperitifs in hand, Sasha and her parents watched the setting sun decline behind the other Roman hills farther west. The view was spectacular, encompassing green bands of trees around brown- and ocher-colored buildings and then up to more verdant green bands of the next hill. Finally, it was time to order and sample some of Sasha's favorite foods. She wasn't disappointed.

The next morning came quickly, and Sasha had to gather her things, put on her athletic clothes, and take a taxi to the train station. There she boarded a train that would take her to Florence. It was a simple one-hour trip with some magnificent natural scenery along the way. Once in Florence, she and her parents took a taxi to the St. Regis hotel (on a bank of the Arno River) to meet the other YPO members from around the world who had come to Italy to engage in this bike tour of Tuscany. Everyone boarded the buses that took the group to their launching spot, a bike tour office nestled among the verdant hills. There, Sasha was introduced to her bike, which she would ride for the next seven days. To ease the expected initial physical exhaustion, Sasha's parents had reserved an electric bike for her. There were several other children around Sasha's age who would also join their parents on this tour.

The tour's riding plan was to begin the first day with a twelve-kilometer ride and then to gradually increase the riding distance to thirty kilometers by the end of the week. Early mornings would offer the fittest an opportunity to ride an additional ten kilometers before everyone else arose. Each day would end at a local inn or country hotel where dinner would be served. The day's riding would break for lunch, which was usually held at a château or winery, where the long history of the vineyard would be told by the owner or chief winemaker. Most of the châteaus were hundreds of years old, and all had undergone the horrors and destruction of the many wars Italy had been involved in. Some owners revealed the secret passages that led to hidden shelters that had been built for the château's previous owners and their families to protect them from the invading armies that came marching through their property. These tales of war and hiding were of keen interest to Sasha, who couldn't comprehend why foreign armies would be trampling on the beautiful properties and destroying vines and the ancient buildings. Lunches were the best part of Sasha's day, since they consisted of authentic Tuscan cuisine.

After the first day of biking, Sasha's legs were aching, but the prospect of helping make pizza at the local inn that first night was more than enough to keep her awake and interested. This is when she began to make friends with some of the other children who were on the bike tour. Her parents couldn't tell which gave her more pleasure, eating her pizza or making it. Her wide smile encompassed both.

Each day, the riding became more arduous and tiring. Sasha listened to the bike leaders of the tour who kept telling everyone that biking would become easier as their legs built up strength by the end of the week. She hoped they were right. The bike tour did provide a van that followed the bikers and was available for those who became exhausted. Sasha's promise to her parents on the second day as the bike distance lengthened was that she would not use this safety reprieve. Several young and old people did—every day at least one person made use of it.

The third day's ride ended at a slightly larger hotel that had a pool. To everyone's delight, the water was cool and refreshing, and all the children happily jumped in almost immediately upon seeing it.

The bike tour took the group through the most beautiful countryside of Tuscany: over rolling hills—some of which were quite challenging to bike up—past huge châteaus, across enormous acres of vineyards, and through some delightfully quaint villages. The tour stopped at every one of the villages, and each was more picturesque than the last. All had the look of time, with cobblestone streets and brick houses attached to one another. Some were constructed with sun-colored painted bricks. One day, it made Sasha very happy to watch a tradesman make gelato in a huge drum of a container and then serve large scoops to the children and adults who wanted some. Sasha had become friendly with two girls on the trip who lived in Los Angeles. One was older and the other a year younger than Sasha. They shared their love of gelato and compared their chosen flavors, screaming that their choice was more delicious than all the rest.

The next day, the bike tour stopped at an olive grove for lunch, and after a good meal, there was a demonstration of how virgin olive oil was created from the olives grown on the property. It was not a long, laborious process, but the oil was crafted under very strict guidelines so each bottle was appropriately labeled and dated to authenticate its quality and freshness. Sasha and her new friends had very little interest in hearing about extracting oil from olives, and instead sat together outside the oil mill sharing stories.

That night was special because the tour stopped for dinner at the home of one of the bike tour guides. It was a large old stone-walled house with an immense yard framed by ancient hazelnut trees, which provided welcome shade from the setting sun. All the children were very excited because they were expected to help prepare and serve the homemade food. The delicious salad came from the neighbors' gardens, and the pasta was made from scratch by the guide's grandmother. The children helped her prepare and roll out the dough and then watched as she folded it into popular shapes. The pesto sauce to accompany the pasta also had to be made from scratch, and the children ran under the trees to collect hazelnuts, pine nuts, and fresh basil from the garden. Sasha and her friends used the family blender to combine the ingredients into an appetizing green pesto sauce to spoon over the hot pasta shapes as they emerged from the oven. Sasha truly had a good time helping prepare and eating the homemade Italian dinner, and the experience helped her appreciate authentic Italian food even more.

The villages that the group biked through were usually built around the tops of the hills or mountains and consequently offered the most magnificent views of the surrounding countryside. Besides agriculture, there were very few other sources of economic activity in the terrain the tour rode through until they came to Siena. This is the second-largest city in Tuscany and quite unique—very different in scope and design from

Florence. While Florence is famous for the centuries of art, sculpture, and architecture, Siena is smaller, lesser known, and less well traveled by tourists, in part because its attractions are less externally focused. Yet it does have its own unique history that Sasha came to appreciate.

The medieval city is divided into seventeen districts, each hosting its own district club. The districts all originate from the great piazza at the center of the city. Each club is very private and selects its own members, who must eat most of their dinners at the club meeting hall and sponsor their own horse and rider for the great annual Palio race in August. The club members all don their clubs' very specific colors for the race, and thus the square is filled with hats and cloaks reminiscent of centuries past. Much prestige is borne by the winning club, but members make more money on betting and arranging (conniving) for the victorious team. Sasha laughed as she listened to the stories of great races and the lengths of deceit and trickery to which club members would go in arranging the winner. Her father wasn't sure she understood the skullduggery club members resorted to and merely explained to her that these exploits were very Italian. Sasha's final wish as the group was leaving Siena for the last inn just outside the city was to be in the center of the ancient square with its high tower and magnificent monastery next year to witness the great medieval horse race.

That night was the final night of the bike tour, and it included some impromptu entertainment. The bike tour riders gathered at a crude stage after dinner was cleared and began singing popular songs in Italian and English. While their voices were not of professional quality, the enthusiasm they generated with the diners was genuinely thrilling. They asked the diners for volunteers to sing along with them, and a few adults did. They then asked if anyone played guitar, and Sasha raised her hand. The bike tour leader offered Sasha his guitar for her to play a song she knew. It was a moment of truth for Sasha. She hesitated a long time as parents, friends, and tour guides encouraged her to come up and play one song. Eventually, with bright red cheeks and very much embarrassed, she worked up the courage to go up to the make-do stage and play her one song, and then she quickly returned to her seat and tried to hide as cheers for her rang out through the building.

The ride on the final day was the shortest of the tour and would end around one o'clock in the afternoon. Consequently, the group of bikers for the extra early morning ride was double in size compared with prior days. Everyone's legs had become stronger with the daily riding exercise. It was a particularly clear morning, and the temperature was very cool before the sun had fully risen. The trail that day led down to a river, which was more of a stream than a proper river, and the breeze off the water increased the coolness. It seemed everyone wanted the biking days to go on, including Sasha and her friends.

The bike tour ended at a beautiful, huge old stone inn perched on a hilltop with an adjacent large stone stable. Life-sized statues, which intrigued Sasha and her friends, were scattered about the extensive garden among very old trees. Lunch was served on a massive buffet table filled with grissini, Italian breads, sheep and goat milk cheeses, tasty meats, local olives and tomatoes, and bowls of pasta, each with a different enticing sauce, all set on the sprawling, tree-lined lawn. It was a quintessential Italian setting to end Sasha's journey through Tuscany.

With some sadness but many great memories, Sasha said goodbye to her biking friends, and she and her parents picked up their luggage. A tour van took them and many of the YPO bikers to the local train station. As Sasha stepped onto the train and finally rested her weary body, she reminded her parents that she never had to use the safety van in spite of often arriving last to each stop along the tour, well after the other children who were older and more experienced bikers or younger and gave up biking the final kilometers. Sasha and her parents celebrated with a hearty high five.

They were headed back to Rome, which was less than one hour away. When their train arrived in the eternal Italian city, it didn't seem like Italy to Sasha. After her long and strenuous bike ride through the

Tuscan landscape, those green hills filled with vineyards and olive groves and quaint villages on hilltops with narrow cobblestone streets became Sasha's vision of Italy. In just one week, Rome became just another large and highly populated city to Sasha.

Sasha woke up the next day, looked out the hotel window, and surveyed the large garden surrounded by tall pine trees and dotted with the ever-present human-sized statues of famous Roman centurions, senators, cardinals, and emperors. The immense presence of the tall pines and Roman statues began to alter her thinking, helping her see once more that Rome was indeed greater than her first impressions, and she clamored to see more.

Sasha's first destination was the famous Trevi Fountain. Before she reached the celebrated fountain, her appetite was whetted by several extraordinary fountains containing massive statues of old Roman gods in spectacular poses. At every turn, she encountered another arched passageway with a statue guarding the entrance to a huge mansion. Sasha even found an occasional chair to sit on and laughingly shared an advertised pizza with the baker's statue. Finally, as she turned another street corner into the Piazza di Trevi, the enormous fountain appeared. Its reputation attracted a huge crowd of tourists taking photos, making wishes, and throwing coins. The prodigious fountain did not disappoint. Sasha followed everyone else and made a number of wishes and threw several coins into the splashing water. Throwing coins into the fountain and making a wish harkens back to ancient times, when Romans would throw a coin into a river before they crossed it to ensure safe passage.

All of this activity prompted Sasha to demand a reward, a large gelato, which she consumed as she walked down a main avenue that led to the Pantheon. On the way, she discovered a shop where a Pinocchio puppet was featured, and she wandered in to examine his long, slender nose. The ancient Pantheon was originally built before Christ by Roman Consul Agrippa as a temple to celebrate old Roman gods and emperors. Because it was built of timber, it burned down twice before

Hadrian, more than one hundred years later, built its replica with stone. The Pantheon was converted into a Catholic church centuries later. To this day, the dome thrills modern architects, who are humbled by its perfect hemisphere shape and the round opening in its crown. Sasha kept staring at the opening, which permanently permitted sunlight to enter, and asked, "Why is there a hole in the top? What if it rains?"

Before lunch, Sasha had to see the Monument of Victor Emmanuel II. He was Italy's first king and the unifier of all of the separate regions of Italy. The monument is perhaps the largest in the Eternal City, more than seventy-five meters high, and constructed of marble with a massive statue of King Emmanuel on horseback in the front. The building itself contains a museum reflecting themes encountered during the unification of Italy. Its size and the brightness of the marble dazzled Sasha, who wanted to know who this king was and why so much space and marble were devoted to him. She was too hungry to wait for answers, though, and she sat and quickly consumed her pasta at a nearby restaurant in the shadow of the monument. After lunch, Sasha resumed her walking tour, but she quickly tired of visiting Catholic churches and admiring the exquisite religious paintings adorning the ancient walls.

The next day, Sasha would visit ancient Rome and see the iconic Colosseum. She wasn't impressed with the Roman Forum and all the crumbling structures that were left—it was too early in her education for her history classes to have covered the ancient heritage of Roman government and society. She was more impressed by what was left of the Colosseum, especially when the guide who accompanied Sasha on her tour of the ancient structure began reciting the activities that went on in the Colosseum to satisfy the citizens' demand for carnal entertainment. The stories of gladiators fighting with one another and against wild beasts piqued her interest in visiting the gladiators' quarters and the rest of the physical remains of the two-thousand-year-old edifice.

The afternoon was devoted to a trip across the Tiber River to visit the Vatican and St. Peter's Cathedral. The construction of the original

St. Peter's Basilica was started by Emperor Constantine in the fourth century, but it was badly damaged by Saracens. Pope Leo IV rebuilt it a century later with a wall around it to protect the basilica and to establish the Vatican territory. After many centuries, the basilica had deteriorated, so in the sixteenth century it was demolished, and the present basilica was built. Art and statues were added over time to beautify the current church, and tombs of popes were laid in the building's cellars. Its ceilings were completely covered in Renaissance art similar to that of the Sistine Chapel, which Sasha would visit next after waiting her turn among the throngs of visitors standing in front of its doorway.

St. Peter's Cathedral in Rome

Visitors were everywhere within the confines of the Vatican. Viewing St. Peter's Basilica required not only walking through it but also climbing its stairs to view Rome and all the red tiled rooftops below and to the east. Sasha thought it was an impressive architectural masterpiece, but it was too big to remind her of the familiar churches where she worshiped. It also took much too long to get through the crowds, and she complained of the crook in her neck from looking at the painted ceilings in the Sistine Chapel. Sasha could not imagine how anyone, even Michelangelo, could have painted that elaborate and imaginative fresco while lying on his back.

On the hike back to the hotel, Sasha had to navigate the Spanish steps and suddenly the complaints stopped as she had the opportunity to visit all the retail shops along the Via dei Condotti. Sasha's mood quickly brightened as she was able to window shop on this avenue of *alto moda* Italian fashion. The end of the Condotti led Sasha to the Piazza del Popolo and another stunning and intricately carved fountain, this time of Neptune. A quick stop at a neighborhood restaurant for a bowl of pasta was needed before climbing through the green parklike gardens that led to Villa Borghese. Once there, Sasha was able to get a splendid view of Rome and the Vatican. The villa was built on another one of the seven hills of Rome and looked down on the Piazza del Popolo, the center of Rome, the gigantic monument to Victor Emmanuel II, and in the distance across the Tiber, the dome of St. Peter's Basilica.

The glorious gardens of the Villa Borghese were filled with statues and relics of ancient statues and fountains. It was such a large, hilly garden that Sasha's parents decided to hire a golf cart to traverse the property. Sasha begged to drive this small cart within the garden because it reminded her more of a toy than a proper vehicle. When they came to the lake in the center of the gardens, they ditched the cart and hired a boat to paddle across the hazel-colored water. Exiting the rowboat on the other side of the lake, Sasha and her parents climbed up to the top of the garden, where they took many pictures before finally taking a taxi back to their hotel to have their last dinner in Rome and prepare for their flight back to Singapore.

On the plane ride home, Sasha admitted that she was impressed by all the attractions in Rome, yet thought of it as though it were a different country from the rolling hills of Tuscany. She began to understand why Rome is called the Eternal City: Ancient history comes to life in its statues of people famous more than two thousand years ago, and in its centuries-old, sometimes millennia-old, buildings like the Pantheon and the Colosseum that were built before Christ and are still visible to visitors.

18

A Final Trip to Hokkaido

SASHA DIDN'T KNOW IT when she flew from Singapore to Hokkaido for another ski trip, her fifth, that this would prove to be her final winter in Japan. This time skiing in Hokkaido was different—very different. Accompanying Sasha and her dad was one of Sasha's school friends, Mia, and her father, Todd. It was a father-daughter trip. They arrived at the New Furano Prince Hotel first and waited there for Sasha and her dad. Of course, the hotel was old hat to Sasha, since she had visited it so many times in the past.

Sasha and her dad left Singapore on January 2, right after a festive New Year's Eve celebration. They took a day flight instead of their usual overnight one. They landed first in Tokyo and then took a smaller plane on to Asahikawa. It was cold and dark when Sasha and her father arrived in Hokkaido and, after they had a quick snowball fight at the airport, she begged him to book a taxi to the hotel instead of waiting for the slower lavender bus. The two arrived at the hotel after nine o'clock at night, tired and a little hungry but excited for the next day.

Dawn came, and Sasha and her dad woke up early to get a head start on the other vacationers to select boots, skis, poles, and helmets. Then it was on to breakfast, where they would meet Todd and Mia. Breakfast was finished quickly since Mia had arranged for a nine o'clock ski lesson and Sasha had one at ten o'clock with Osama, her instructor from the previous year. Osama immediately took Sasha up to the top of the mountain to begin this year's instruction.

After the lessons were over at twelve o'clock, everyone regrouped and had lunch in the main building. The girls focused on planning their afternoon and decided to ski mainly on the green run and through the adjacent trees toward the bottom of the mountain. They quit skiing early and played in the snow for a while before Sasha took Mia to the hot springs for a warm bath. Mia was quite shy at first, since she wasn't accustomed to being naked in front of strangers.

After bathing, everyone met for an early dinner in Sasha's family's favorite restaurant: the Japanese grill on the bottom floor of the hotel. The food was delicious, as usual, and everyone enjoyed it. Soon afterward, the clamor started for a snowball fight. Sasha led the group across the street to the ancient village, and all engaged in a massive snowball battle.

The sky was gray on Wednesday morning, and the temperature was unusually warm: five degrees Celsius. Of course, Sasha knew that it would be colder at the top of the mountain. On this morning there were no other coaches available for Mia to ski with, so she joined Sasha for a combined lesson with Osama, though in the end they simply enjoyed skiing together more than learning new skills.

Around midday, everyone decided to stop skiing and have lunch at the top of the mountain at one of Sasha's favorite places. Since everyone was hungry and cold, they ordered plenty of hot curry dishes. After lunch they skied down to the bottom of the mountain as a group. The girls decided to stay on the bottom of the mountain and ski among the trees again, while the dads decided to take "the rope," as the reader will recall the tram is locally known, and ski the more conventional runs at the top.

Sasha and Mia quit skiing early so they could soak in the hot springs and then still have time before dinner to visit the village across the street for some shopping and other snow-related activities. Once the sun descended, it became much colder, and their dads joined them across the street at the slides to watch as they took numerous rides down the tubing and sledding tracks. The girls also went to visit some Siberian huskies that were tied up nearby. The dogs had been brought there to pull sleds over the snow-covered fields. Sasha had never seen dogs like this before and thought they looked like wolves. Once she and Mia were convinced that most of the dogs were friendly enough, they then chose their favorite ones and competed to see which dog liked them best.

Once Sasha and Mia had their fill of tubing, sledding, and dog petting, the father-daughter duos went back across the road to have dinner at the Japanese grill restaurant. There they devoured more fresh sushi, hot miso soup, tempura, and fried chicken. The most amusing part of dinner was the location of their dining table—the hostess had put them into a private room with a service buzzer. Sasha had never seen one before; nor had Mia, and therefore they made great use of the one lying on their table. They buzzed repeatedly and competed to see how fast service would be provided.

After dinner, the group again walked back across the street to the ancient village and engaged in another heated snowball fight. The wooden boardwalk was slippery with snow and unseen ice, but it also featured several elaborately made snowmen to show people the path if they got lost. Some of the snowmen were small and cute, while others were huge, almost life-sized. By the end of the evening, Sasha was extremely tired but happy to be experiencing Hokkaido with her friend.

Thursday was Mia's last day in Furano; she had to return home on the night flight to Singapore. That morning, she and Sasha again shared a ski lesson with Osama. As portended the previous night, the temperature dropped sharply to minus twelve degrees Celsius at the bottom of the mountain, and it was even colder at the top. In spite of the cold temperature, Sasha decided to have lunch at the top of the mountain since it was her last day with her friend. After lunch, the two of them skied down to the bottom of the mountain to ski among the trees and play in the mounds of snow. They also wanted to save time so they could visit with the sled dogs at the snow park across the street again and do more tubing.

As night descended, it was brilliantly clear with many stars visible in the dark sky. It was also extremely cold, but that didn't prevent Sasha and Mia from doing more sledding. When they had finally had enough, it was time to get ready to go to dinner. On this last night, they went to the hotel's fanciest Japanese restaurant on the twelfth floor to enjoy the view and eat shabu-shabu. The restaurant also offered Hokkaido Bay scallops and sashimi, though Sasha preferred cooking the pork and vegetables in the large hot pot. Unfortunately, there was no time to have another snowball fight because Mia and her father had to catch a train that would take them to Niseko. As they left the hotel, everyone agreed that they all would return to Furano next winter for more skiing. Little did Sasha know that this would be her family's final winter trip to Hokkaido.

Fortunately, it started to snow on Thursday night and continued through Friday morning. The mountain had looked skied-out on Thursday since it had not enjoyed the normal amount of snowfall that year. The new snow provided Sasha with an opportunity to begin her snowboard lessons. Her instructor was a young Japanese girl called Yuri, and Sasha immediately liked her. The lesson finally ended after many falls, and now Sasha wanted to show her parents how much she had learned. Sasha's mother joined them that afternoon. Sasha did have more falls, but she showed good progress on her snowboard. As a reward to celebrate Sasha's progress and resilience to keep getting up after each fall and try again, the family went to the bakery for a lunch of fresh-baked pastries.

The snow kept on falling throughout Saturday, providing fresh snow over the well-skied trails. Skiing in the snowstorm on Saturday reminded Sasha of past trips to Furano when she skied in fresh snow nearly every day. This day, Sasha enjoyed the best ski conditions of the year.

The final day of this trip arrived too soon. The snow had stopped, and the sun was shining brilliantly, as it usually does following a storm. The sky was a deep shade of cobalt blue, and it framed a perfect backdrop for one last day of enjoying the mountain. Sasha's dad woke early and took an early morning ski. It was a perfect opportunity to luxuriate in skiing first tracks on all of the runs from the top of the mountain all of the way to the bottom.

Monday was also Russian Christmas, and Ded Moroz and Snegurochka had arrived during the night and left some simple presents for Sasha and her mother. With such wonderful ski conditions and it being their last day, the family could not spend time dreaming over presents and instead had to take advantage of their last ski day. Sasha had her final snowboard lesson in the morning, and her parents enjoyed skiing on the best snow conditions of the vacation. It was effortless to glide down the trails that had proved so challenging a few days ago.

Dinner on their final night was upstairs in the more formal Japanese restaurant. This time they ordered sukiyaki, which is another hot pot-style of food but fried instead of boiled as shabu-shabu is. This pot was filled with beef and vegetables instead of pork, and they enjoyed it immensely. By the time dinner was done, Sasha was very tired and ready to head back downstairs to their room.

This ended Sasha's fifth consecutive year at the New Furano Prince Hotel, and she had loved each one. As Sasha and her parents left on Tuesday, they wished they would return to Furano for more fun, skiing, and good Japanese food in another year. But it was not to be. This would be Sasha's last trip to Furano, and also her last trip to Asian destinations that Sasha took from her home in Singapore. In just a few months, she would be leaving Singapore for a new life in the United States, but she would never forget all the fabulous journeys she took throughout Asia.

19

Deer Valley, Park City, Utah

IN THE SUMMER OF 2017, Sasha's mom accepted a new job that required the family to pack up their apartment in Singapore and relocate to the United States. This time, Sasha moved to Fort Lauderdale, Florida. Sasha's new home was on the beach in Lauderdale by the Sea and very different from the dense apartment buildings she was used to in Singapore, but she had always loved the sea and quickly adjusted. When fall came around, she entered fifth grade at Pine Crest School, where she rose to the challenge of starting anew: new friends, new routines—and lots of new places to see and explore.

Sasha's first ski trip in the United States was to one of the most perfect mountain settings in the world. Although Sasha had only previously skied in Hokaiddo, where the snow conditions could not be beaten anywhere in the world, skiing in Japan could not compare to the luxurious setting she found herself in when she entered the hotel, Montage Deer Valley.

The hotel is set in the Wasatch Mountains high above Park City, Utah, and most of these ski venues were used during the 2002 Winter Olympics. The Montage is a colossal building wrapped around a mountain with ski-in-ski-out access, indoor and outdoor heated pools, and a friendly, smiling staff trained to make hotel guests feel ultra comfortable. The room Sasha and her parents had in the Montage even featured a working fireplace that kept everyone toasty warm.

When Sasha and her parents arrived in Park City, after a long airplane ride from Fort Lauderdale, where winter temperatures ranged from a comfortable seventy to eighty-five degrees during the day, they immediately confronted two ambient challenges: the temperature and the altitude. The temperature was in the thirties, relatively mild by winter mountain standards, but coming from sunny Florida, the family immediately started shivering and ran as fast as they could from the van into the hotel. The second challenge they faced as soon as they engaged in any strenuous activity was the altitude. The hotel was situated at eight thousand feet above sea level and therefore was eight thousand feet higher than their home on the beach in Fort Lauderdale. Sasha felt the effect on her breathing immediately, and it slowed all of the family's activities throughout the next several days.

But Sasha wasn't about to let that slow her down. After renting skis, boots, poles, helmets, and purchasing lift tickets on the first night there, Sasha gamely put on her ski clothes the next morning, ate a very large, satisfying breakfast, and went out to meet her first American ski instructor. His name was Lance, and she soon learned that he wasn't American. He was Swedish, and he spent his summers back home in Sweden. Their first lesson together was filled with testing Sasha's ski level, ability, and aggression, so for that lesson they stayed on green and blue runs.

The Deer Valley ski slopes span over six different mountain peaks and cover more than two thousand acres of skiable terrain. There are twenty-one different chairlifts, making this ski resort one of the largest and most complex in the United States.

Sasha split her days between private lessons with Lance and skiing at the Deer Valley ski school. The instructors all wore Kelly green and tan ski uniforms that could be readily seen all over the mountains. The sessions ran all day, and Sasha enjoyed getting to ski with her peers for a change. Her first day at the ski school, she was excited to see some schoolmates from Pine Crest who were skiing there, too.

In the coming days, Sasha started trying out some of the more challenging terrain, which profoundly tested her abilities, including moguls and black diamonds. She had one big wipeout from skiing in a black diamond mogul field called Lady Morgan's Bowl. She ended her ski school that day with a headache and a vivid memory of her ski blowup. Nevertheless, she decided she would keep going. Later that week, she made a new friend in ski school, Emily from New York City, which made a wonderful ski trip even more exciting for Sasha.

After skiing for hours each day, Sasha would soak her sore muscles in the hotel's outdoor hot tub under a bright, warm-looking sky facing the white-clad mountains. Lucky for her, the hot tub was located adjacent to a deck where the hotel offered s'mores around a bonfire each evening. After soaking in the hot tub for a while, Sasha would leap out of the pool, put on a robe, and venture up to the deck to make and eat one of her favorite treats. The cold suddenly seemed more tolerable as she sat at the edge of the barbeque pit roasting marshmallows on a long skewer.

Sasha making s'mores in Deer Valley, Utah

The morning of Sasha's second lesson with Lance, dark, ominous clouds covered the sun, promising another day of snow. It had turned much colder, and the wind blew the snow around on the tops of each mountain peak, making skiing treacherous. Despite the conditions, Lance took Sasha up to Empire Peak, and they skied all of the black runs, mogul-filled bowls, and steeper bowls. At the end of the three-hour lesson, Sasha was thrilled at having skied all of the challenging runs in the Empire region.

Valentine's Day came on a Wednesday while Sasha and her parents were in Deer Valley, and they celebrated by exchanging cards and small gifts they'd bought at the hotel. Everyone decided to dress in fancy red attire as they prepared for a festive Valentine's Day dinner at the hotel's best restaurant, Apex. They toasted each other with glasses of champagne (juice for Sasha), took pictures at the table, and ate a delicious meal of elk chops, sea bass, French chicken, and a selection of gourmet French fries. Everyone was hoping to see snow before going to bed, and the weather did not disappoint.

On several nights, Sasha and her parents decided to leave the hotel and venture down to Park City, about twelve hundred feet below, for dinner and a walk along Main Street. Sasha entertained herself with browsing through the touristy shops that lined the street. The shops were filled with everything from ski gear and clothes to souvenirs and artworks in the style of the American West. Nestled among the shops on Main Street were several local restaurants for the family to choose from to have dinner.

Friday marked the first day of the President's Day weekend, and suddenly the mountain became crowded. Skiers appeared from everywhere, and the slopes became much busier than they were earlier in the week when there were fewer skiers and most of them were skilled local skiers. The ski conditions were wonderful; however, the number of skiers made skiing difficult and sometimes hazardous. Families from all across the United States made Deer Valley their President's Day destination, and the mountain also attracted many families from Latin America. Sasha frequently heard skiers speaking Spanish among the crowded lines waiting for a lift.

On her final day of skiing in the Wasatch Mountains, Sasha decided to sign up for a NASTAR ski racing event, which would track and score her times skiing the racecourses here and across all the ski mountains in the United States. On her first attempt at downhill slalom ski racing, she was timed at 28.8 seconds. She did well, but she wasn't satisfied! After two more attempts, she improved her time to 28.03. Sasha's father skied the racecourse with her twice, and his times were 25.8 and 23.7 seconds respectively, and this only made her want to train harder and try again on her next ski vacation.

As Sasha packed her bags to head home to Fort Lauderdale, she reflected on this wonderful winter ski vacation on a fabulous mountain ski area. With skiing like this, maybe she wouldn't miss Asia so terribly after all. Deer Valley is a huge mountain territory with all types of terrain and ski run choices. It was far bigger and much more glamorous than the mountain resorts she had skied in Japan. Sasha believed that she had become a very good skier, both from an improved-technique perspective and from her attitude to rise to the challenge of facing even the most difficult and dangerous runs.

20

Eleuthera: The Bahamas' Beautiful Beaches

IMMEDIATELY AFTER GRADUATING from Pine Crest's elementary school in Fort Lauderdale, Sasha began a most fulfilling and eventful summer in 2018. In contrast to the prior summer, when moving from Singapore to Fort Lauderdale dominated all family summertime activities and precluded plans for travel and vacations, this summer was packed with adventures. Sasha managed to attend two separate weeks of gymnastics camp in the Pocono Mountains in eastern Pennsylvania; a summer STEM program at Pine Crest; and a one-week Mandarin course at the renowned Concordia Language Villages in Moorhead, Minnesota. She even hosted her friend Philip and the Ohm family from Singapore in her new Fort Lauderdale home. The families chose to visit Universal Studios theme park in Orlando, Florida. It was a quick visit for the Ohm family, who had to travel to their new home in Hamburg, Germany.

The summer of 2018 thus provided Sasha with many opportunities for adventure, travel, education, and friendship. It also offered her several opportunities to fly alone and be away from home without her parents—some important benchmarks of growing up.

To cap off the summer, Sasha and her parents boarded another airplane together to make a short flight to the island of Eleuthera in the Bahamas. The plane trip was brief and ended with a quick taxi ride to their vacation resort, the Cove, in North Eleuthera. The Cove was a simple yet elegant set of wood framed buildings, all painted white and perched high over the sea spanning two small, separate bays, or small coves as the locals called them. Each cove had its own beach and beautiful, aquamarine-colored surf. The water was incredibly clear, clean, warm, and calm. There was no evidence of pollution and no mounds of seaweed like the ones that populate the beaches Sasha knew in Fort Lauderdale. The translucent surf had hardly any movement, and there were no waves in either cove even though both faced the open Atlantic Ocean. Curiously, there were hardly any fish in either cove, except for a few that swam along the coral at the farthest points of each peninsula, where the end of land meets the Atlantic Ocean.

Sasha awoke early on her first full day in this ocean paradise to a brilliant, sun-filled morning. There was nary a cloud in the sky to block the bright sunlight from streaming down on the twin aquamarine pools below. The temperature was warm, not hot, much drier than in Florida, and luxuriant in a prevailing breeze from the ocean that was always fresh and never threatening. The biggest concern for all the lucky tourists on this island was to apply enough sunscreen to minimize the risk of sunburn. While Sasha and her parents were at the Cove, there was only one gray, cloudy day filled with showers; most of the rest of the days there featured a few black clouds that dropped rain in the afternoons north and south of the Cove, but never overhead.

In spite of the attractions of going into the lagoons at the Cove, Sasha initially preferred to stay at the long infinity pool that overlooked the north cove and swim there. In contrast, her parents chose to swim in the crystal-clear sea of the north cove and take leisurely rides on the paddleboards and kayaks. Once Sasha realized that her parents were using the beach's resources, she immediately ran down to claim the paddleboard from her mother and leaped up on it, capsizing it and her mother. Sasha then demonstrated to everyone on the beach how to successfully navigate a paddleboard around the quiet waters of the lagoon. Like most of Eleuthera, the Cove was a quaint, island-style resort perched above its twin beaches. The Cove boasted great views of the surrounding ocean, which was framed at dusk by multicolored sunsets. Rarely was there an oceangoing vessel, which probably accounted for its pristine, clear, unpolluted waters.

The best part of the resort, apart from the spectacular beaches, was the cuisine. The Cove employed a magnificent French chef who supervised the staff to provide delicious breakfasts, lunches, and dinners. The formal menu was complimented by a sushi bar, which presented fresh rolls, mainly featuring local seafood ingredients such as crayfish, conch, and local fish. All were prepared in many different and imaginative ways.

The pinnacle of Sasha's vacation in Eleuthera was the boat trips. The family hired a twenty-seven-foot open boat; its captain, named Shaw, took them to a number of smaller islands in the Bahamas island chain surrounding the northern tip of Eleuthera. The first day, they visited Pig Island, where Sasha swam and fed several large, seagoing pigs that joined her in the water. There were also several flocks of ducks that swam out among the pigs to gather whatever food was left. After leaving Pig Island, the captain took Sasha and her parents farther out to sea to visit a shipwreck whose mast extended above water and whose submerged body became a major attraction for many species of fish. Sasha had a chance to practice her snorkeling technique while observing the colorful fish life swimming around the shipwreck.

Next, they sailed to another island where there was an exquisite reef. Sasha spent some time snorkeling above it to witness the beauty below. The reef was populated with many species of tropical reef fish, both large and small, but its prime attraction was the multitude of amazing sea fans waving in the water. They existed in a multitude of colors: purple, violet, brown, and gold. Complementing the proliferation of sea fans were the many types of coral, including statuesque staghorn and dangerous, red fire coral. The captain made sure Sasha understood the danger of touching the red coral. It proved to be a very rewarding and fulfilling snorkeling adventure. After everyone returned to the boat, the captain was proud to show Sasha and her parents two very beautiful, deserted beaches on distant islands. Each island was shaded by green pines and a few low palm trees and boasted the whitest, finest sand beaches. The beaches were framed by peninsulas, which created cove-like lagoons filled with calm, translucent aqua-colored water. On the first island, Sasha spotted two goats, but it seemed otherwise deserted; the other island was pure and uninhabited.

Perhaps the most exciting part of this first boat trip for Sasha was her search for giant conch shells and sand dollars. The captain knew the most promising place for her to search, and he took the group to a massive sand bar that was mainly exposed when the tide was low. It gleamed so brightly that everyone needed sunglasses to protect their eyes from the sun's strong glare off the pure white sand. Sasha found several large conch shells along the sandy shore, left behind by the critters that once lived in them, and she chose one to take home. Its deep red and pink interior was truly beautiful. She also stumbled across a few sand dollars. They were more difficult to spot since they were partly submerged in the sand and water. Some sand dollars were dark and easier to see, but the captain told Sasha they were still alive and advised her to leave them in the sea. Finally, she found two white ones: they were round, pure white, and marked with symmetrical lines in a star shape. The sand dollars turn stark white when dead, and these were the only ones the captain allowed Sasha to take.

This boat ride was so enjoyable that the family decided to hire Captain Shaw and his yellow-hulled open boat for a second day. This time they invited him to bring along his ten-year-old daughter, Darlene, to meet and play with Sasha. She came, and as Sasha learned later, she was extremely eager to join her father and meet a new friend. The two girls had a wonderful time together jumping off the boat into the pristine waters. On each lagoon, Sasha showed Darlene some of her gymnastic tricks in the water and along the beach. They both tried some acrobatic dives from the boat—some successful, some not, but all fun.

Darleen and Sasha at a cave on Eleuthera Island in the Bahamas

On this second outing, Captain Shaw took Sasha and her family to two of his favorite beaches, each with pristine white sand, incredibly calm aqua blue waters protected by small peninsulas on either side, and featuring a small reef in front to protect the beach from the waves and large fish flowing in from the nearby ocean. He also took them to some of his favorite fishing spots. First, he instructed Sasha how to fish for bonefish. The captain trolled slowly between two small islands. There Sasha saw several fish, but they weren't interested in her lures and swam away. While casting lures to the bonefish, she saw several medium-sized green turtles that followed her lures up to the wake of the boat. When the captain left the bonefish flats, the water depth was six feet or less. He trolled for jacks next, and Sasha's mom caught a small blue runner jack. He then drove to another coral reef where everyone enjoyed some snorkeling. This reef was home to one thousand small gold grunts that brilliantly lit up the dark coral. Darleen showed Sasha a multitude of fish and many colorful large sea fans moving silently with the tide as they snorkeled over the very busy reef.

The highlight of this boat trip wasn't the magnificent fish teaming on deserted reefs, but rather a visit to Preachers Cave—a large coral formation that lay about one hundred meters in from the surf, shaped in a half arc like an amphitheater. It provided shelter to the first settlers of Eleuthera, whose boat sank on a reef beyond the island in 1648. Captain Shaw told Sasha the story about these pilgrims who were seeking a place where they could freely practice their religion when their ship wrecked on the reef. They decided to call the island that they landed on and eventually settled Eleuthera, which in Greek means "freedom."

Their second boat ride ended, and Sasha's one-week vacation in the Bahamas was drawing to a close. On their last day in Eleuthera, Sasha and her parents settled by the infinity pool, swam in the north cove, and prepared to leave the quite pristine beach location. On her trip home, Sasha thought back to the story of these brave European pilgrims and savored a small taste of the freedom and relief they must have felt in the sweet sea air and waters of Eleuthera.

21

Thanksgiving in Havana

INSTEAD OF PREPARING A TURKEY with all the fixings for Thanksgiving, Sasha and her family boarded a flight to Havana, Cuba. Cuba became the twenty-second country that Sasha had visited in her first twelve years of life.

Cuba had just begun to open its doors to the rest of the world after spending the past seventy years cut off from global influences, and signs of decay were present everywhere. Buildings in the center of Havana were crumbling from neglect. Wi-Fi was available in pitifully few locations, and even then the signal was weak. Stores, hotels, and all services did not accept US dollars. All foreign currency had to be converted into Cuban pesos, and ATMs did not accept US credit cards. This made the trip extremely complicated and very frustrating for Sasha's family.

Upon their arrival, Sasha and her parents were greeted by an English-speaking taxi driver in a Russian Lada vehicle. The influence of Russia on Cuba is omnipresent, especially in the capital, Havana. Sasha witnessed how the average Cuban lived in old Soviet style: concrete block buildings, laundry hanging from windows, and only a few electric appliances visible, although old electric wires were hanging from poles everywhere. Moreover, there was little evidence of modern electronics.

Cuba has to be the country with the fewest cell phones on earth, Sasha later thought.

Their taxi also drove past the ubiquitous fleet of antique US automobiles gaily painted in bright Caribbean colors. A fleet of convertibles graced the front of their hotel, the Iberostar Parque Central. It was located across the street from a small park. The far side of the park was lined by large hotels; a magnificent, baroque opera house and museum; and a colossal parliament building, a gigantic replica of the US Capitol building. The opera house was built more than one hundred years before the revolution and fortunately had been conserved in prime condition.

Likewise, the hotel was old but well preserved. It offered Wi-Fi, but only in the lobby. Like all other businesses on the island, the hotel wouldn't accept American credit cards. The family immediately made dinner reservations with the concierge and then took his suggestion to have a tapas lunch at the rooftop pool of the adjacent Parque Central building. The hotel roof had a spectacular view of Old Havana, the Caribbean Sea, and the inlet that led ships into the inner harbor toward the commercial docks.

After finishing their tapas, Sasha and her parents went down to the street and conveniently accepted a ride in a horse-drawn carriage, which took them through some of the old city. They passed by the harbor and Revolution Square with its many military artifacts celebrating the arrival of Fidel and his troops and memorializing the Bay of Pigs invasion and the short-lived introduction of Russian missiles. The entertaining carriage driver next took them to a small bar that celebrated the Beatles in pictures throughout the shop. There Sasha's parents had the opportunity to make their own mojitos with fresh lime and mint. The barman even offered Sasha the chance to make a virgin mojito, which she immediately proceeded to undertake with great enthusiasm.

Dinner that night was in a small, privately owned restaurant called Ivan Chef Justo, which was recommended by the concierge. The food was very good. The presentations were attractive and mainly consisted of fish, lobster, and chicken. Sasha liked her choice: chicken fricassee. Her parents used most of the cash they had on hand to pay for dinner, and Sasha wondered how they would cope the next day: Thanksgiving Day.

Since they had walked to dinner, Sasha and her parents had to walk back to their hotel along the dark and dusty streets. Surprisingly, walking through the streets of old Havana at night and passing locals waiting for transportation or just milling around did not inspire fear, as one might expect in most American cities. Many other visitors and the hotel staff had offered the advice that streets in old Havana were safe. And they were. When Sasha and her parents arrived back at the hotel, they sat for a bit and listened to a noisy salsa band before retiring for the day.

Sasha woke early on Thanksgiving morning and proceeded down to the hotel dining room to enjoy a sumptuous breakfast of juice, fruit, eggs, and assorted pastries. The plan for the day was to hire an antique American convertible and tour the old city more extensively than they were able to on the horse-drawn carriage the day before. The car, a pink 1953 Chevrolet convertible, came with a driver and an English-speaking tour guide. They first visited Havana University, home to fourteen thousand students, and then drove to Fifth Avenue, the most luxurious street in old Havana. In the past, it was where the wealthy Cuban families lived. After the revolution, the government took over the real estate there and leased the buildings out to foreign embassies, which now occupied most of the old mansions. Farther along, on their way to see Revolution Square, they passed by a real forest of undeveloped parkland filled with huge trees that were thickly covered with vines. Finally, they visited San Francisco Square, the place where slaves were traded before 1888, when slavery was officially banned in Cuba. When they'd completed their hour-long ride, Sasha believed that they had seen most of the major sites in the old city.

After a delicious lunch at the Kempinski Hotel, which was constructed in 1894 and gloriously renovated in 2017 to preserve the historic building and to sustain its commanding view of the harbor, Sasha and her parents ventured down Obispo Street, one of old Havana's most famous walks, to mingle with the locals and window-shop at the few stores that offered merchandise in a city without much retail business. Sasha stopped at one of the very few souvenir shops, actually a roofless set of stalls, and asked her parents to purchase a bracelet for her. Finally, after walking down the length of the street, Sasha came upon two chocolate shops. They sat down at one of them to sample a chocolate drink, which Sasha enjoyed, but her parents preferred to have a Cuban coffee at a nearby street café.

Friday morning came and greeted Sasha with another warm, sunny day. The family's plan for this day was to select a colorful antique convertible and drive to El Morro Castle to visit the fort that defended Havana Harbor against roving bands of pirates in the days of Spanish expeditions. Havana Harbor had only one narrow inlet that led into a wide bay where the Spanish galleons stocked up on the provisions they needed to make the long sea journey back to Spain with their cargoes of gold and silver taken from South America. The pirates lay in wait, ready to plunder the Spanish ships when they left the safe confines of the harbor.

Sasha and her parents chose a blue Chevy convertible and arrived at the fort before it opened. To kill time, they took a detour to see the ten-meter statue of Jesus Christ that overlooks the harbor from a promontory, reminiscent of the Christ statue in Rio de Janeiro. Back at the castle a little later, they walked through the silent corridors to check out the cannons, which faced the inlet, and spent a moment in a tiny chapel to experience the devotion that must have been there centuries ago when the troops were defending the harbor. The castle also housed a small museum dedicated to Che Guevara; items on display included his desk, some pictures, and a box containing his remains.

They left the castle in another old convertible and drove to the Hotel Nacional de Cuba. All of the hotels, the land, and the businesses are owned by the Cuban government. As was evident from a casual view of Havana, government ownership has stifled the Cuban economy. The Cuban people pay 70 percent of their meager earnings in taxes to the government and receive free health care and education. However, the streets are littered with potholes, the buildings are crumbling, and there is no infrastructure. People don't need much money since there is so little to buy in any of the stores. The facades on the colonial buildings are painted in bright colors; however, the insides of the buildings are falling apart even though people are still living there. The strikingly colored real estate, like the brightly colored old automobiles, are handed down from generation to generation. The people are friendly, educated, and polite, but the communist system forbids entrepreneurship, stifling innovation and choking ambition and initiative. There is no place in this system for risk-taking or change. Yet the people seem relatively cheerful and happy—many seem to enjoy smoking cigars, drinking rum, and listening to live bands play salsa music on most street corners in old Havana. It gave Sasha a new perspective into the different ways people find their happiness.

The Hotel Nacional is situated on a promontory overlooking the harbor. It had plenty of chairs and service stations selling coffee and mojitos on the grassy slopes for tourists to enjoy the views. Sasha ran up and down the grassy slopes while her parents sat on one of the slopes drinking rum drinks and gazing at the castle across the inlet. After a lunch of traditional Cuban food consisting of rice, beans, and pork at one of the hotel restaurants, they wandered through the grounds and eventually made their way inside to see the pictures hung throughout the lobby celebrating the many famous guests who had stayed there in its long history.

In the afternoon, while Sasha was resting at the hotel and taking advantage of the Wi-Fi in the lobby, her parents went in search of another side of Cuba's history. Havana is known to be the home of many famous bars with storied histories. Their objective on this afternoon was to find the Roc El Viejo y el Mar hotel and go to the bar at the top of it. Long ago Earnest Hemingway had a room in this hotel and wrote *The Old Man and the Sea* while staying there. Sasha's parents never found the hotel, but one night they did pay a visit to El Floridita, another of Hemmingway's old haunts. The tavern was also famous for its daiquiris. They had two while they watched the female salsa band playing and dancing to lively Afro-Cuban music.

Great drinks are a signature of Cuba, and Sasha joined her parents for a tour of the distillery at the old Havana rum factory. The tour ended with a sample of their seven-year dark rum, and even Sasha took a very tiny sip.

On another warm and sunny day, the family started out in a red Ford convertible with an old-fashioned external spare tire on the back to tour some of the city's famous cathedrals. Sasha's first stop was at the Cathedral of the Virgin Mary of the Immaculate Conception. It was a dark, Gothic-style building in the center of Havana. The moment she walked into the cathedral, Sasha was reminded of northern European churches,

Sasha in a 1950s Ford convertible in Havana, Cuba

particularly in the United Kingdom. The fact that this cathedral lasted through the communist period, when it could not have been used, was a testimony to its sturdy construction.

From there Sasha went to the Plaza de la Catedral to visit another cathedral, this one done in Southern European tradition. It was a lovely baroque-style church dressed in gold from its Spanish benefactors. The square contained a flower market where local women were selling brightly colored cut flowers while dressed in equally bright attire. On the other side of the square was a famous hotel and restaurant, La Bodeguita del Medio, where many famous artists have gathered for coffee, mojitos, food, and conversation.

Along the way, Sasha and her parents drove to one of the famous Cuban cigar factories, just a few blocks from the giant cathedral. Unfortunately, they needed tickets to enter this government-owned enterprise, which they didn't have enough Cuban currency to buy, so they left without getting to see how Cuban cigars are made.

On two of the remaining nights in Cuba, Sasha and her parents planned to see a couple of different shows. The first was a performance of *Carmen* at the National Theatre. The theater was beautiful: it was old, elaborate, almost rococo in design, and had a very tall ceiling, multiple levels of seats, and a large stage. The performance was lively, well executed, and sung beautifully. Sasha enjoyed dressing up and experiencing the beautiful atmosphere of the theater, but after a long day of exploring, she fell asleep in the second act, and her dad had to take her home at the intermission.

The next night, Sasha and her parents had tickets to attend the famous cabaret show at the Hotel de Nacional. The cabaret doors opened at 9:00 p.m., and they were escorted to a great table with an unobstructed view in front of the large stage, thanks to a generous tip Sasha's mom paid one of the ushers. The show was fabulous! Sasha especially liked it, much more than she had enjoyed the opera the prior evening. There were at least twenty-five professional dancers who went through countless costume changes, much to Sasha's delight, and five or six singers. The music was Cuban, and the songs were sung in Spanish, but the beat was so infectious that everyone in the audience was swept along.

Sasha's final day in Cuba started the same as all of the others: perfect, sunny, and warm. She finished her breakfast, and the family decided to take one last walk down Obispo Street until they turned left onto Cuba Street on their way to the Cathedral of Havana. The church door was open that day, unlike the last time they were there. They walked in to take pictures, and Sasha noticed that the altar was being set up for Sunday Mass. Sasha and her parents decided to sit in a pew and watch as the priests formed a procession and went up to the altar and begin serving Mass. They stayed for a while and listened to the singing of Spanish hymns. The baroque church was warm and inviting and had a huge chandelier hanging from a high dome at the top of it. There were no stained-glass windows in the old church, unlike the Gothic cathedral they had visited on Friday. In fact, there were only a few narrow windows located high on the walls of the church.

After Mass, Sasha wandered through the plaza and discovered a salsa band playing in front of five highly decorated dancers on very tall stilts proceeding down the street. The sight was totally unexpected, and Sasha couldn't believe her eyes. She immediately joined the small crowd, mainly of tourists, snapping pictures. After the troupe passed, Sasha and her parents continued on to the famous old hotel the Plaza de Armas, now a tourist site. They walked perhaps two blocks more before coming to a tiny park on a side street off the plaza. It was filled with cats and kittens, including one that could not have been more than one or two months old and could barely walk. Sasha tried to pet the cats but they were wary of people, especially ones they didn't know, or who had no food for them.

Sasha finished the last walk on O'Reilly Street and went back to the hotel to finish packing and check out. Her parents decided to have lunch at a nearby rooftop restaurant before flying back home. Sasha took her last views of old Havana from this rooftop and said goodbye to Cuba.

Sasha learned a great deal from this short vacation. She learned that different races can live together in harmony and people can accept living on the edge of poverty without public protest. She also saw how they contend with very slow service and live with neglected infrastructure and unsanitary conditions. Since nearly all of the people of Cuba are in roughly the same economic condition, there is very little crime and almost no envy, because there are so few material items available to acquire.

Sasha also realized she had just experienced quite a revealing contrast between her life in Singapore and her visit to Cuba. Both are small island nations that commenced their current nationhood status sixty years ago. Yet no two places could be more different. Two charismatic men started their governments sixty years ago and led their countries in dramatically different directions. Singapore is a modern, open, prosperous, first-world nation that has become the crossroads of Asia—a beacon of the future for the rest of Asia and other third-world countries. In contrast, Cuba is old, dilapidated, impoverished, and is a closed society with little exposure to modern technology. It is behind most of the rest of the world in economic and physical development. Both countries had only one leader for most of their history: one leader was a visionary who created a first-world nation with enviable infrastructure and institutions; the other started as an idealist following the wrong ideal and left his country buried in the past.

22

Skiing in Aspen

HER 2019 WINTER SKI TRIP to Aspen was Sasha's first visit to Colorado, the ski mecca of the United States. The family booked a week of skiing at the Viceroy Hotel, a small luxury hotel with only eighty rooms. Sasha really enjoyed the quieter atmosphere, the suite-style rooms, and the wonderful ski-in-ski-out convenience. She began to make insightful comparisons between small, boutique hotels and the much larger ones like the Montage in Deer Valley, Utah.

Sasha started the ski trip with a half-day private lesson at Snowmass, the mountain closest to the hotel, one of four skiable mountains that make up the Aspen skiing experience. Her instructor's name was Leah, and she took Sasha on a very challenging first day of skiing down several advanced mogul runs. During the next day's lessons, Leah and Sasha skied off into the mountains, but their day was interrupted because Sasha was cold in her ski outfit and had outgrown the pants. After dinner that night, Sasha's parents took her to the village mall to purchase new ski clothes. Her Valentine's Day present was a new red ski jacket with a fur-trimmed hood and white ski pants.

Sasha went to ski school the following day and joined a group of children around her age. Unfortunately, she was a more experienced skier than most of her peers and therefore did not enjoy the lessons. Coincidentally, she did see several of her Pine Crest schoolmates who were also taking lessons at Snowmass that week.

Wednesday was Sasha's first day of skiing with her parents. Despite the fact that Sasha was much more advanced than the other students, the ski lessons of the past two days had improved her skiing skills significantly. She skied swiftly, fluidly, and with improved style. Toward the end of the day, Sasha decided she wanted to go snowboarding on the next day. She set aside her skis and spent the last hour trying to remember her snowboarding skills on the bunny run outside of the hotel in preparation for the next day's snowboarding lesson. Sasha also practiced getting on and off the ski lift with her snowboard late that afternoon. This was her first big accomplishment on a snowboard. She succeeded with only one fall and eagerly joined a group of beginners to learn more the next day.

Her experience at snowboarding school was much more successful than her first day in ski school. She immediately bonded with a girl from Chicago, Caroline, and they had a good time learning together. Sasha was a real beginner in snowboarding and therefore did not think that the group lesson was beneath her abilities. When the lesson finished, her coach rated her well; her friend Caroline was slightly older and rated slightly higher.

Sasha decided not to go back to snowboarding school on Friday, but she had difficulty deciding whether to try out her new snowboarding skills or return to skiing. Eventually she decided to ski with her parents on an absolutely beautiful, crystal-clear, sunny, warm day. They skied run after run that day under windless, perfect conditions.

Some ski days are indeed perfect, but Aspen offered a variety of conditions that Sasha had to learn to navigate. Some mornings she awoke to dark clouds in the sky, and skiing was difficult because there was so little light that visibility was very limited. Other days, the sky threatened snow, but it never came. Then there were mornings that absolutely delighted Sasha: She would arrive on the slopes to find that several inches of fresh, perfect snow had fallen overnight. New snow changed the required skiing technique significantly, making each day different from the last. When there were several inches of new snow, Sasha had to avoid making sharp turns with deep carves and instead simply glide over the snow, making tiny, steplike turns. Because of the ever-changing conditions, Sasha had to learn to adjust her technique each day, which made her visit to Aspen a fabulous and instructive week of skiing.

When Sasha and her parents returned their skis at the end of the week, they were all hungry to ski more. So, after a relaxing soak in the hotel's hot tub accompanied by much reminiscing about the skiing they had just finished, the family left to go skating on an ice rink in the center of the mall. This was Sasha's second day of trying to ice skate. She had progressed rapidly and fell only a few times while making several very graceful pirouettes.

Several nights during the ski week, Sasha and her parents ate dinner in the hotel's restaurant, Toro. They were served typical Western mountain cuisine, mostly steak and lamb chops. Sasha tried several entrees there that week; the New York strip was tasty, and the black cod was a pleasant surprise. In between, they had Japanese one night and paid a visit to Il Poggio on another occasion. The latter was a noisy, crowded restaurant, but as soon as Sasha sat down and tasted the food, she immediately understood why it was the most popular restaurant in Snowmass. She and her parents thoroughly enjoyed the pasta, venison, and sea bass, and they all agreed it was the best meal of the trip.

As they boarded their flight home, Sasha reminisced about the ski trip and concluded that Snowmass had the best and most varied set of blue runs of any mountain she had ever skied. There were very few green runs, some surprisingly difficult blue runs, and a few very challenging double black runs. The vast majority of the mountain was blue. Her favorite runs were Sandy Park, Granite, Gunners View, Two Creeks, Cascade, Camp Grounds, and Mick's Gulley. The varied and rewarding ski terrain, along with the Viceroy Hotel's rustic ambiance, convenience, and fine dining options with breathtaking mountain views meant Sasha never wanted to leave Aspen. As their flight inevitably departed, she hoped to soon return.

23

Summer in the United States

New York

Once the school year was over in June 2019, Sasha began an extended tour of the United States. The first leg of her US discovery journey started with a plane ride to New York City. Sasha was in New York to attend Columbia University's Alumni Family STEM Day. It was hosted by the school's alumni to celebrate science, technology, engineering, art, and math with a day of speakers' panels, interactive booths, and even a scavenger hunt. But beforehand, she had a couple free days in the city to explore the sights. The best part of this trip was that she was joined by one of her friends and classmates from Pine Crest, Sienna.

It was much colder in New York City than in Fort Lauderdale, and very cold for June, even in the Northeast. Sasha was staying in the Sofitel Hotel in Midtown, close to everything in Manhattan. On the first day, Sasha walked up Fifth Avenue and window-shopped before heading into Saks Fifth Avenue, the famous department store. The

Sasha in Rockefeller Center, New York City

pinnacle of her free time was lunch in Rockefeller Center, where she watched people of all types—businessmen, tourists, and locals—bustling through the large plaza. After lunch she and her parents walked down to visit the Museum of Modern Art, and then to Bryant Park by the New York Public Library, where they wandered around and browsed among all the temporary stalls set up in the park to sell mostly homemade craft items.

That evening, Sasha's parents had arranged to visit the ABC News TV studios. They had special permission to watch the filming of the daily six o'clock news program live from the studio, and it was Sasha's first time seeing all the equipment needed to make the show possible. Sienna joined Sasha for this visit, and both girls were eager and excited to go in. One of the producers from the studio was waiting for the group when they arrived. She brought them in, introduced Sasha and Sienna to the presenters, and escorted them to seats at the side of the desk where the producers were sitting. They were very friendly and attentively answered the girls' questions. When it was time for the evening show to start, Sasha watched as the anchors made their presentations. After the program finished, the producer brought the group back to the control room where all the computers and equipment needed to put together the show were stored. She introduced Sasha and Sienna to the director, who was controlling the pace of the show and making all of the video selections by switching between the multiple cameras to follow the flow of the presentations. The girls left the studio quite happy and excited about what they had experienced and talked endlessly about the different parts of the show that they remembered as they walked down Broadway to return Sienna to her waiting parents.

On Saturday, Sasha joined Sienna, her family, and some of Sienna's friends for a picnic on one of Central Park's grassy knolls to celebrate Sienna's mom's birthday. During that very pleasant picnic in the park, Sasha ran into some people she knew from Fort Lauderdale—from the Coral Ridge Country Club and from her school. After Sasha left the festive birthday party, she and her parents walked through the park to Central Park West and went to the American Museum of Natural History. She looked at the dioramas, focusing mainly on the fascinating displays of animals and human existence in this hemisphere. Most impressive, however, was the giant model of a blue whale suspended from the ceiling in the museum's Hall of Ocean Life. As Sasha gazed up at this life-sized replica of the largest animal on Earth, she felt both small and in awe of all the wonders in this vast world and in this dynamic city.

Saturday night was Sasha's cousin Alexandrovna's birthday, and the family celebrated together in a Persian restaurant in downtown Manhattan. Alexandrovna brought her son, Nico, who was extremely active and kept everybody busy. It wasn't often that Sasha had time to spend with relatives from the Russian side of her family, making this visit extra special and another opportunity for Sasha to recharge her Russian language skills.

On Sunday morning, Sasha had to make her way uptown to Columbia University for the STEM event that had brought her to New York City. Once Sienna arrived at their hotel, Sasha and her parents quickly flagged a taxi. As they made their way into the street, they had to bob and weave to avoid the participants of the Puerto Rican Day parade, celebrating one of the many cultures that make up New York's melting pot.

Despite the delays, the family soon reached Columbia's campus on 116th Street. It was Sasha's first glimpse at a university campus, but she would visit two more later that summer. Alumni of Columbia's STEM program had set up approximately twelve tables with computers and video presentations about different STEM topics for the visiting students. Sasha's favorite station was a fitness evaluation, which was part of a booth about the neuroscience of how athletes and everyday people use their brains to perform complex movements. Her second favorite was a creative construction of metal foil and iron. Sasha and Sienna enjoyed the various demonstrations, but at the end of the day, they both claimed that they did not like STEM and would probably not pursue it in college. At the end of a brief but highly educational tour of New York City, Sasha repacked her bags, rode to Penn Station, and boarded a train for her next stop on this summer's tour of the United States: Washington, DC.

Washington, DC

As the train was pulling into Union Station in Washington, DC, Sasha saw the cupola of the US Congress building. It was Sasha's first sight of the nation's capital, which she had studied about in school. The plan for this leg of Sasha's trip was to stay in a hotel in Tysons Corner, Virginia, a suburb of DC, and commute in to see the famous sites. She had a full agenda for her visit, starting with exploring the city's many museums.

The first stop on Sasha's Washington agenda was a visit to the Smithsonian Institute to see the full-scale skeletons of dinosaurs and early homosapiens, early undersea life, and several space exhibits. Sasha found it all fascinating, but the museum was too big and overwhelming for her to see and appreciate everything. Her next stop was the Media Museum, which had an impressive collection of news reports of all the major events of the twentieth century. There were exhibitions of front-page newspaper stories and pictures of famous TV personalities who had reported the news over the past seventy-five years. A few of the old news pictures caught her attention, but Sasha was most excited about her next destination: the Spy Museum. In keeping with the theme, she and her parents entered the Spy Museum quietly. She started her investigation by watching movies about spies like Mata Hari who were involved in the two world wars of the twentieth century. A special section of the museum was dedicated to 9/11 and discussed the new brand of terrorism that was originating from the Middle East. Sasha's favorite activity in the museum was a game she played with her father where each player pretended to be a spy and had to decide whether to tell the truth to the other person, who was also a spy and had to answer the same question. The follow-up question posed to both participants was to decide whether the other person was telling the truth. The outcome was a tie; Sasha and her father both believed the other had lied. Sasha's day at the museum ended with an FBI spokesman warning everyone about the dangers of cyber espionage.

The theme of the next day was visiting famous government buildings. Sasha began her day by traveling to the White House, which she unfortunately couldn't enter without an invitation from her local congressman. However, the visitor center had a very sophisticated set of visuals that provided her with sufficient insight into the rooms, furniture, and layout inside the White House.

From there, she and her father traveled up Pennsylvania Avenue to the Capitol Building to see where Congress meets. They joined a one-hour tour, which was quite instructive for Sasha and her father. After the tour, they ate lunch in the Capitol Building's canteen, located in its basement. Sasha learned there were several floors below the basement where members of Congress could seek shelter in the event of an attack on the building. She could never have imagined then, in 2019, how useful this basement would become just eighteen months later. After lunch, Sasha and her father wandered around the city, rented electric scooters, and took a boat ride along the Potomac River. The boat ride took them past the Watergate Hotel, Arlington Cemetery, and some of the sights and monuments Sasha would visit the next day.

The plan for Wednesday was to visit Georgetown University to see its campus and wander around the quaint surrounding village. Sasha entered several of the school's buildings, looked in on classes—some of which were in session—and was amazed at the size of the school's large gym. After she and her father left the university, Sasha walked around the streets of the historic town, observing the tiny houses and commenting on how crammed on top of one another they were. Sasha was very enthused by the school's proximity to the Georgetown area and all its shops. Among them was a kitten café, where patrons could sip their drinks in the company of the store's cats, which were permitted to wander around the premises. Sasha and her father entered the café, and Sasha observed that the kittens seemed exceptionally drowsy. She thought it may have been that they were used to customers coming into the café, so there was no cause for alarm or frantic running around. These kittens were taken from shelters, where they were in danger of being euthanized, and offered for adoption at the cafe. Sasha thought that the café's business was quite humane.

After Sasha and her father left Georgetown, they went to see the great monuments on the mall. The Washington Monument was fenced off for refurbishment, so they walked along the shallow pool separating all of the monuments toward the Lincoln Memorial. Sasha climbed its stairs and looked back toward the Washington Monument, envisioning what the approximate first one hundred years of her country must have been like.

Once they left the mall, Sasha rented a scooter and rode beside her father as he walked past the Federal Reserve Building, one of the places where he worked years before, and then past some of the other Federal Agency buildings alongside the great park.

Sasha's final day in Washington consisted mainly of observing a high-tech display at the Museum of Art Tech. It was a provocative exhibit of science, photography, and art combined into a massive projection. It was made of materials donated by NASA, including pictures from space, which were fed into an AI algorithm that shaped them into magical, slow-moving art forms. The exhibition was creative, inspiring, and easily the best event Sasha saw in Washington, DC. She was fascinated watching the arrays of light slip past. She'd previously thought of science, space, and AI as having to do with a bunch of boring numbers, but seeing them come together in a beautiful display like this made her reconsider her earlier decision and think about possibly pursuing these subjects in school.

Sasha left Washington, DC, with a deeper appreciation for the great figures and events that shaped her country's history and with new curiosity about the emerging technology fields and digital creativity that would chart its course in the future.

San Francisco

The next leg of Sasha's very active summer involved a trip to California. It would be the seventh state that Sasha visited. The weather in Northern California was very cool, more so than in New York or Washington, DC, though the sky was exceedingly bright and sunny. The main purpose for visiting San Jose was for Sasha to tour Stanford University in Palo Alto and visit the well-known high-tech firms located in this part of Silicon Valley.

The first of these famous companies that Sasha visited was Google. It has a huge sprawling campus and permits visitors to walk through the grounds, visit their buildings, and take pictures with their famous icons. There was even a visitor shop where one could buy Google souvenirs. Sasha was also interested in visiting Instagram's and Facebook's offices, but unlike Google, those buildings were closed to visitors, which left Sasha extremely disappointed. These companies did not have a sprawling campus, but instead Facebook's location consisted of two regular-looking office buildings attached together, though they were painted different pastel colors for easy identification. Viewing them from the outside as her father drove through the parking lots behind the buildings, Sasha thought they looked like any other office space despite the innovation happening within.

Sasha left the high-tech giants and drove to Stanford University where she would meet her mother, who would take her on an extensive tour of the school's campus. It was by far the most impressive university campus that Sasha had visited. It was large and very attractive, so much so that Sasha found it very difficult to choose which of Stanford's buildings impressed her the most. The old mission-style church in the center of the campus was enchanting with its Spanish architecture, elaborate interior, wood-beamed ceilings, and colorful stained-glass windows. It was very different from the churches she had visited in Europe.

Sasha was able to visit some of the classrooms at Stanford, since school was not in session. She enjoyed having a drink while walking through the science center, and she stopped by the school's bookstore. Everything about the campus was well planned and laid out. Despite its enormous size, it was very walkable; Sasha also noticed a myriad of bicycles scattered about, indicating that this was how most students navigated the large campus. Sasha left the Stanford campus thoroughly impressed and hesitantly hopeful that one day she would be able to attend this school.

The next day, Sasha left Silicon Valley and drove up to San Francisco to begin her tour of this famous and beautiful city. Her family stayed in the Palace Hotel, a beautiful 145-year-old masterpiece of architecture that featured a massive, glass-domed ceiling above its main dining room, where breakfast and lunch were served. Approximately twelve large chandeliers hung from the ceiling around the dome and many intricately carved sculptures were set along the walls of the immense room. The magnificent building hinted at the wealth and grandeur of life in San Francisco at the end of the eighteenth century.

Sasha's first stop in San Francisco was Fisherman's Wharf, where she had a late lunch of cioppino, a local version of French bouillabaisse. After lunch, she enjoyed seeing the stunning views of San Francisco Harbor from the upper deck of the wharf. She gleefully watched a large sea lion look for food among the fishing boats lining the piers along the wharf and competing against many noisy seagulls. The wharf was bustling with weekend tourists, and Sasha joined them, dipping in and out of the shops lining the piers, soaking up the vibe and the warm California sun.

Sunday dawned much colder in San Francisco; it was a two-sweater day. Sasha and her parents started the day with a visit to the Golden Gate Bridge. The beautiful red bridge was covered in San Francisco's signature early morning fog that blows in from the cold Pacific Ocean. While Sasha and her parents waited for the sun to burn off the morning mist, they walked into the bridge shop to buy some souvenirs. The fog eventually cleared, and Sasha was lucky to get a magnificent view of the bridge's red expanse. They then crossed the Golden Gate and drove into Sausalito, a picturesque town on the lee side of the bridge. This side of the Pacific Palisades offered marvelous views looking back toward San Francisco and its surrounding harbor. After browsing in several shops on the main street, Sasha and her parents decided to take a break and have lunch in this harbor side of town and enjoy another warm bowl of cioppino.

Back across the bridge in San Francisco, Sasha and her parents stopped along the famously sloped Lombard Street and watched as automobiles wound their way down the steep hill and around the rose boxes in the middle. From there Sasha was thrilled to hop on a cable car,

Sasha on a cable car in San Francisco, California

and she rode it down California Street through the center of San Francisco. At the bottom of the street, she and her parents exited the cable car and eventually walked back to their hotel. By this time, Sasha was exhausted and happy after her exploration of this fabulous city.

The plan for Monday, another bright, chilly day, was to take a bicycle tour and explore San Francisco, beginning in Fisherman's Wharf. Sasha and her parents each rode on electric bikes up through Little Italy and then Chinatown, which slowly flowed into the financial center. From there, they rode along the piers and up to Oracle Park, the San Francisco Giants' baseball stadium, and then past the last of the boathouses that were being phased out. They continued up Mission Street to the Castro neighborhood and Haight Ashbury, where they stopped for a quick Vietnamese lunch. After lunch, they rode down to see the majestic domed city hall and then back to Fisherman's Wharf. It was truly memorable for Sasha to see so many districts of the city up close.

The family decided to cap off the trip to San Francisco by stopping at the famous Top of the Mark cocktail bar in Nob Hill to take in the views from the city's highest spot. By now, Sasha and her family had seen San Francisco from every angle imaginable. As Sasha looked out over the rows of houses and hilly streets spread before her, she could feel her California dreams just beginning.

Los Angeles

Sasha couldn't have been more excited to arrive for the first time in her dream city of sunny Los Angeles. She and her parents stayed in the Viceroy Hotel in Santa Monica, located one block from the famous beach and featured in so many famous movies.

Each day in Los Angeles, she and her parents started with a bike ride along the beach in the very cool morning air. The ocean was usually gray at this time, reflecting the dull gray sky above. Sasha rode her bike past the surfers who were preparing their wet suits for the cold Pacific water and, next to them, the homeless individuals who were strewn over most of Venice Beach. Having worked up a healthy appetite, Sasha and her parents often ended their bike ride with breakfast at the Shutters hotel along the beach at the border of Marina del Rey.

After breakfast, Sasha would walk up Ocean Avenue to the famous Santa Monica Pier. The end of the long pier was lined with fishermen, their fishing poles leaned against the railing in the hopes of catching something big. Although the waves along the surf were moderate, there were very few bathers brave enough to test the cold Pacific waters. Sasha wandered through a few souvenir shops that lined both sides of the broad pier looking for a new LA T-shirt. Then she discovered there were rides in the permanent amusement park at the middle of the pier. Sasha quickly decided to go on the roller coaster, a swivel ride, and a rotary ride, and enjoyed them all. Farther up from the beach and perpendicular to it, there were a few streets that were closed to traffic. These streets became a pedestrian mall with trendy shops lining each side of the walkway. Sasha went from one store to the next, enjoying her freedom to shop for clothes among so many teen-friendly stores. Even during the middle of the week, the street was crowded with tourists from near and far.

Sasha's weekend started out with a drive along the coast. Overnight, their family friend Tatiana Ohm, who was in San Francisco on a business trip, joined them to explore the West Coast beaches. Sasha, her parents, and Tatiana began Saturday with breakfast at a landmark California highway restaurant, Patrick's Roadhouse, right on Route 1. It was a quaint, diner-style restaurant with pictures of famous movie stars who had dined there in the past and plenty of World War II memorabilia. Curiously, the diner was staffed by Russian-speaking waitresses, which permitted Sasha the opportunity to try out her Russian vocabulary.

Farther north along the Pacific Coast Highway, the group encountered one of the trip's highlights, the Getty mansion and museum. It was more museum than mansion as it featured many Greco-Roman art works, coins from ancient Rome, and statues comparable to those found in any major big-city museum. The building stood on the cliffs overlooking the Pacific Ocean and was designed with no expense spared to be a replica of a Roman villa that had been destroyed by the eruption of Mount Vesuvius more than two thousand years ago. The details of the construction were executed meticulously, from the layout of the gardens and courtyards to the design of the rooftops and arches. The building's architecture was awesome. It was a true revelation that only a man with wealth, inspiration, imagination, and desire could create.

After taking many pictures, Sasha, her parents, and Tatiana left the museum and continued north up the coast to the Malibu Café, located within a beautiful resort and ranch high up on the cliffs of the Pacific Palisades, but too high to afford a view of the sea. The café was populated by enthusiastic tourists and locals indulging in good food and drink, listening to live music, and relaxing in a very comfortable, rustic setting.

Once the group finished their drinks and lunch, they set out to find the Pepperdine University campus. It was an immense campus situated high on the Pacific cliffs with a spectacular view of the Pacific Ocean from all of its many levels. The campus looked new, with multiple modern buildings for instruction and living quarters and an abundance of well-manicured sports fields. The campus fulfilled its reputation as a world-class school for the well-heeled.

A thousand exclamations later, the travelers drove out of the Pepperdine campus and headed back onto the Pacific Coast Highway to find Zuma Beach, which was highly recommended to them as having the cleanest ocean water on California's southern coast. Apparently, its virtues were well known, because the beach was packed with bathers. The ocean water was cold, the waves were quite high, and the undertow was very strong. Consequently, the beach had to be patrolled by many lifeguards. Sasha tested the water and immediately decided it was too cold to venture into. She later had an unfortunate incident with a large seagull that relieved itself all over her. Nevertheless, the time Sasha spent on the beach was a welcome and much-needed rest after all the driving and exploring they had done earlier in the day.

On the way back to Santa Monica, Sasha stopped at another famous spot: the Malibu Pier. It is probably as long as the pier at Santa Monica, but not as wide. It is, however, equally famous, as it has also been featured in many productions of the nearby film industry. Sasha enjoyed an ice-cream cone and looked in all of the pleasant shops, some quite whimsical, that lined the pier, which was perched high above the roaring surf. Similar to the Santa Monica Pier, it had a full complement of fishermen standing along the length of its boardwalk. The sun was setting as they left the pier and headed down the Pacific Coast Highway to Santa Monica.

No trip to Los Angeles would be complete without visiting some of the famous Hollywood film locations. The next day, Sasha and her parents first drove to Bel Air to admire the magnificent homes. Sasha gasped at the size of some of them. She was hoping to see some celebrities, but eventually had to settle for guessing who was having a heavily catered party at one of the imposing homes. They left the breathtaking houses of Bel Air and drove past some of the private golf courses in Hollywood on the way to Rodeo Drive, perhaps the most famous luxury shopping street in America. Sasha stopped to do some window-shopping there before going to view the stars set in the pavement on Sunset Strip. The actual pavement was filled with tourists and hawkers trying to sell souvenirs and tours of the area. Unfortunately, the sidewalks were simply too crowded to observe all the Hollywood stars' handprints famously imprinted in the cement. Over lunch, Sasha commented on how much less crowded Rodeo Drive was than Sunset Strip, and how much better dressed the shoppers were.

None of Hollywood's glam compared to getting a glimpse of where the magic was made. A friend of Sasha's mother, Sonja Joo, worked at 20th Century Fox and arranged for Sasha and her parents to visit the movie and TV studios one afternoon. The visit started with a formal lunch with Sonja in the Shirley Temple room. Lunch ended with the signature plate of warm cookies, straight from Shirley Temple's past, which everyone consumed with pleasure. They then walked around the grounds of the very large movie-making facility. Sonya was a well-informed host: she pointed out all the sights as they walked past. She gave some history along the way, including telling Sasha that the production costs of the movie *Cleopatra* almost bankrupted the company and later *Die Hard* and *The Sound of Music*, two very successful movies, restored it back to financial health.

Sasha had another studio visit planned for the next day, this time to the Warner Brothers (WB) Studio in Burbank. The WB studio lot was immense; it contained even more studio facilities than 20th Century Fox. Sasha booked an official tour with a guide, who constantly reminded the group of the size and history of the company. There were truly many famous movies created at these studios and filmed along the interior street sets. The street scenes brought back many pleasant memories of

Sasha on the set from Friends TV show in Los Angeles, California

movies Sasha had seen in the past. She sat and took pictures on the sets for *The Ellen DeGeneres Show* and *Friends*, saw ongoing construction for new programs, and was thrilled when she caught a glimpse of some of the famous unique vehicles used in the *Batman* movies.

The final studios Sasha visited were the Netflix studios, which are also located in Burbank. Sasha had been invited by her mother's YPO members to attend a screening of a new film. She was part of a group of fifteen-to-seventeen-year-old high school students who were invited to volunteer their opinions about it. Sasha liked the movie, a romance with a happy ending, but she was embarrassed and therefore declined the organizers' prompts to offer her opinions about it.

It was finally time to leave Los Angeles, but unfortunately, it was also rush hour, and traffic was at its daily peak. Sasha and her parents meandered through the back streets of central LA to avoid most of the traffic, which was mainly concentrated on the major freeways. Eventually they passed the congestion, reached Highway 101, and proceeded to travel south toward their next destination, Long Beach. On the way, they passed through the Long Beach port facility, the largest port in the United States. Sasha and her parents were astonished by its immense size and sprawl, which truly must be seen to be believed. The amazing port had huge gantries reaching almost to the sky everywhere. Containers were stacked high throughout the gigantic facility and challenged everyone who tried to unravel the colossal mystery of where each container would have to be shipped to.

It was dinnertime, so Sasha and her parents decided to stop at Shoreline Village for a quick bite. They ate at the Pelican House, which was situated in full view of the *Queen Mary*, the largest cruise ship ever built at more than one thousand feet long. It is now permanently moored in the Port of Long Beach. The restaurant's staff informed the group that there were plans to convert the cruise ship into a luxury hotel. Following dinner, they wandered through a few souvenir shops along the harbor front and eventually climbed back into the rental car to drive the remainder of the way to Laguna Niguel.

The Surf and Sand Resort beckoned as Sasha approached this ultra-trendy, attractive, and casual beachfront community. Sasha's room had a fabulous view of the Pacific Ocean, and it came with the constant sound of waves crashing along the coastline. Sasha opened the windows to beckon in the salty aroma from the sea. She didn't realize how perfect the room was until the next morning, when she looked out on a typical California beachfront.

Breakfast at the hotel was one of the best Sasha enjoyed on the trip. It was served in a room with a stunning view of the ocean. Later in the day, she and her parents had a late lunch in the bar room, which was located several feet above the breaking waves as they rushed to within three feet of the hotel wall at high tide. The family was only scheduled to stay one night at the Surf and Sand, but it was so perfect that Sasha wanted to stay longer. Unfortunately, this was high season and the hotel was already overbooked for Saturday night. Therefore, she spent the entire day enjoying the hotel's facilities and rushing into the waves before she and her parents had to pile back into the car and drive down Highway 101 to Dana Point to visit the famous Ritz-Carlton Hotel.

The Ritz is perched high up on a cliff above the beach. From this vantage point, Sasha enjoyed watching surfers trying to catch a wave and wished she could have joined them, although she admitted that her surfing skills weren't practiced enough to contend with such huge waves. Consequently, she turned back and wandered down the hill to a park along the beach where an open-air rock concert was going on. It was a perfect California setting!

A little while later, Sasha and her parents were back in the car driving down Pacific Coast Highway past Dana Point and onto the 5 freeway. They continued to see glimpses of the sea and occasionally surfers waiting beyond the breakers for the big one to ride. They exited the 5 at Encinitas and continued driving south along Pacific Coast Highway toward Del Mar and Torrey Pines. Del Mar proved to be a lively town filled with noisy bars, restaurants, and fashionable shops. Torrey Pines is a large golf and recreation facility, famous for being host to many PGA golf tournaments. Finally, Sasha and her parents arrived in La Jolla and searched for their hotel, the Grande Colonial—an old hotel in the center of town that had been recently refurbished. After dinner, she and her parents walked around a few of the streets in La Jolla close to their hotel, window-shopping in the multitude of tourist-oriented shops, before retiring for the day.

The next morning, the air felt much warmer in La Jolla than it had in Laguna, and the sea was much calmer—especially in the giant cove that the town of La Jolla partially surrounds. The cove is a federally protected nature preserve and is used as a laboratory for marine research by scientists from the University of California at San Diego. Since the cove was a protected area, the animal and bird life were varied and extensive.

Sasha wanted to see the highly recommended La Valencia Hotel, which had been totally booked for the nights of her stay in La Jolla. Consequently, her family chose to have breakfast there. Breakfast was served on a terrace overlooking the pink-walled gardens of the property, and though the food was nothing special, Sasha was glad to have seen this famous old hotel even without having stayed there. Once they finished breakfast, Sasha and her parents slowly walked around the uncluttered streets of La Jolla, stopping occasionally in some of the stores. It was a much more subdued atmosphere than the crowded, noisy streets of Los Angeles and Laguna.

Later that afternoon, the family drove to San Diego's Gaslamp district and strolled along the fair-filled streets, stopping for a late afternoon lunch at a touristy Italian restaurant. After lunch, they drove across the causeway to Coronado to visit the Hotel del Coronado, a huge, grand hotel with over a century of history. It is still a very popular resort and continues to command very high prices. In spite of its fame, it reminded Sasha and her parents of a giant factory. They walked along the streets of Coronado and listened to various bands playing different styles of music in several corners of the town. The atmosphere was exciting, but Sasha decided that La Jolla was a much nicer, quainter place to stay. Dinner on Sunday night was at George's, a restaurant that emphasizes its sunset views from its tables perched high above the cove instead of its haute cuisine. Unfortunately, Sasha arrived too late to catch the sunset, so the family settled for salads and a glass of California wine. Not to be left out, Sasha had a large, iced virgin Mojito.

Sasha's mom had to go to work at her San Diego office the next day, and therefore Sasha's day started early. Since it was also her final day of this very long and highly varied California vacation, Sasha and her father walked along the Pacific Coast Highway to Duke's restaurant, named for the famous Hawaiian Olympic-gold-medal swimmer and surfer from the 1940s and 1950s. The restaurant was decorated in Hawaiian style and so was its menu, which consisted of macadamia nut-and-coconut-crusted pancakes, real Kona coffee, lilikoi-scented butter, and PPOG juice, a tantalizing mix of pineapple, passion fruit, orange, and guava juices. Everything tasted delicious! Sasha also enjoyed looking at old pictures of the Duke in some of his various endeavors.

After consuming such a decadent breakfast, Sasha and her father needed some exercise, so they walked along a path on the edge of the cliff overlooking the Pacific Ocean and the calm waters in the cove. The beach below was littered with black seals and brown sea lions belching loudly at one another, swimming in the surf, sleeping on bird rocks and other gigantic boulders, and begging for food from the many accommodating tourists. Birds filled the air with their sounds as they walked on the sandy beach below. There were large gray pelicans, white and gray seagulls, and black long-necked sea birds searching for fish in the sea or drying their shiny black feathers as they rested on the boulders. Sasha watched as the black birds and pelicans perched on the bird rock, sporadically dove into the sea searching for fish, splashed around in the water, and flew back onto the bird rock to finish their sunbath as the warm sun dried their feathers. Sasha continued walking and discovered a path that led down to several caves that had been dug out by Californians more than one hundred years ago. Sasha's curiosity compelled her to climb down to the bottom of one cave to inspect it and see that it funneled down to the sea.

The waters close to shore were filled with multicolored kayaks bunched together, grouped according to their colors. Each group of colored kayaks was led by a different private tour group instructor. The calm, clear waters offered kayakers and snorkelers crystal-clear views of the fish life and coral formations at the bottom of the cove.

A little more window-shopping plus an ice cream cone tided Sasha over until her mother returned from work. Next Sasha wanted to visit Sea World, so the family decided to drive south to San Diego's famous amusement park. Once inside the park, Sasha watched dolphins being trained and fed, stingrays swimming in a circular pond, and a large aquarium filled with sea turtles and Pacific Ocean fish. But the main attraction for Sasha was the ultra-tall roller coaster, which had a severe drop and several twisting up-and-down turns. She rode the roller coaster twice and finished the ride each time with a wide grin on her face. Sasha chose a few more rides, but none as challenging as the roller coaster, before it was time to go back to the hotel.

At the end of this very long day, Sasha said goodbye to her mother, who still had many business appointments in San Diego, and she and her dad drove north along the coast to the Los Angeles airport, where they would fly back to Fort Lauderdale the next day.

24

Europe's Urban Capitals: Paris and London

Paris

In the second half of summer 2020, Sasha returned to Paris for the first time since she was quite young. While she and her father waited in the Miami airport, they began to discuss Sasha's first trip to Paris back in early 2011, when she was just four years old. Sasha remembered little of this trip, but her father described to her how he, intent on showing her the city's great museums, would bundle her up in a wool hat, scarf, and her warmest clothes, put her into a stroller, and push her around the streets of central Paris. Aside from Sasha's age, the biggest difference between the two trips was the weather. Paris in early February, when Sasha visited nine years ago, was very cold and blustery, and the streets were scattered with snow and broken ice. Everyone was dressed in their warmest clothing. This time it was midsummer, and Paris was suffering through its hottest heat wave in seventy-two years. The temperature rose to forty-two degrees Celsius on Sasha's second day there.

On this trip, Sasha stayed at the Maison Albar Hotel, a small hotel just a few steps from the Arc de Triomphe and located at the pinnacle of the most famous boulevard in Paris, the Champs-Élysées. The hotel had a small dining room, but Sasha preferred to try the cafés, bistros, and brasseries of Paris. Maybe the city's reputation for exquisite cuisine made Sasha more adventurous, because she tried foods that she never sampled before. She ate crepes, croissants, and brioche for breakfast, salmon avocado sandwiches and gazpacho soup for lunch, and all manner of French dishes including oysters, snails, langoustines, and pastas for dinner, and she enjoyed every bite.

The first morning in Paris, Sasha and her dad walked past the exquisite Paris Opera House on their way to the Louvre, hoping to enter and explore this most famous museum. Once there, they discovered that they needed to buy tickets online and tickets were sold out days in advance, so they were forced to regroup. Because of the intense heat, they decided against walking up through the Tuileries to the center of Paris and chose instead to walk across the street toward the palace of King Henry IV's brother, which had been destroyed in 1871 and was later rebuilt.

The tree-filled secret park behind it was lined on both sides with tiny, trendy boutiques, and over lunch in a great French restaurant toward the opposite end of the park, Sasha and her father decided to visit the Louis Vuitton museum (Fondation Louis Vuitton) since they had been denied the Louvre that day. This museum was built next to a large park on the outer edge of central Paris and was designed by the world-famous architect Frank Gehry. The museum's profile is distinctly modern, designed with the intent to be a serious contrast to the Louvre and all of the other wonderful eighteenth- and nineteenth-century buildings nearby. From a distance, Sasha remarked that its profile looked like an ancient sailing ship. The art collection inside the museum was far less impressive than the building's structural features, making Sasha even more anxious to visit the Louvre another day.

Because tickets for the Louvre were difficult to come by, Sasha was glad that her father purchased tickets to a guided tour through the Greco-Roman-period part of the museum, which gave her access to the whole museum. The guided tour included artworks from the Renaissance, including the *Mona Lisa*, the *Venus de Milo*, and *Aphrodite*. Sasha listened attentively as the guide talked about the beginning of Greek mythology and gave an excellent explanation of the symbolism behind the early Greek statues. One startling fact Sasha learned from the presentation was that all the famous Greek statues in the Louvre and in Notre Dame were originally painted in the most vivid colors, but those colors had faded over time to their present dull tan.

On Sasha's next day in Paris, she and her parents signed up for a bike tour that lasted four hours and took them past the Palace Gardens, the Louvre, St. Mary's Church, Notre Dame—where Sasha observed the terrible damage done by the massive fire six months earlier—down to the St. Germain district for ice cream, up the Seine past the Museum d'Orsay, and to the Eiffel Tower, across the Seine, down toward the Petit Palais and the Place de la Concorde, and finally back to the bike shop. It was an incredible journey through central Paris, and while the bike ride was tiring, it gave Sasha a true sense of the beauty of Parisian culture.

Sasha returned to the St. Germain area often throughout her trip in Paris to sample the cuisine at some of the restaurants and window-shop throughout the arrondissement. She and her parents enjoyed both the atmosphere and the food in this neighborhood, and Sasha spent hours there shopping or riding around the streets on a rented scooter.

Midway through Sasha's stay in Paris, the weather suddenly became much cooler. An evening breeze sprang up and brought in some light rain, causing the temperature to drop precipitously as night fell. It rained all that night, and the temperature had fallen to seventeen degrees Celsius by morning, fifteen degrees lower than the day before. Sasha was very happy she had packed a few sweaters for this trip as she bundled herself up for her walk through the Luxembourg Gardens, one of the most beautiful parks in Paris.

Sasha and her parents made a special trip to Montmartre to visit the Sacré-Cœur Basilica and marvel at the breathtaking view. From its vista at the top of the highest hill in Paris, Sasha could see the entire city lying at the feet of this glamorous church. The Sacré-Cœur is one of the most beautiful churches in Paris. Its handsome arches, gorgeous central dome, and exquisite stained-glass windows are all elegant, but the painted arched ceiling above the altar was the most memorable and heavenly sight that Sasha saw. She lit several candles, said a prayer, and as she left, she said she would keep it in her mind forever.

Next, Sasha walked around the exterior of the magnificent church and into the main square of Montmartre, which is now a vast dining area (a decade ago it was just an open field). Several artists nestled along the periphery of the square offering sketches, portraits, and other art for visitors to purchase. Sasha's family circled the square twice to discover the right artist to have Sasha's picture painted. Eventually they chose one and showed him a photo of Sasha's portrait that had been painted eight years before in the same French square. The artist worked for the next half hour creating an updated portrait of Sasha. The painting turned out well, and Sasha was overjoyed by it. Like the first, it made her look older than her years.

After dinner, Sasha and her parents walked down the hill to the Latin Quarter. Her objective was to see the Moulin Rouge, the famous cabaret theater with the iconic red windmill on its roof. The Latin Quarter is known to be a rough neighborhood, and Sasha was startled by some of the risqué window displays along the boulevard. Nonetheless, she was thrilled to see the marquee of the notorious Moulin Rouge theater. The ten-foot signs in front of the theater advertising the current performances were brilliantly red and vividly risqué.

On Sunday, Sasha watched from her hotel window as police poured into the Champs-Élysées area in preparation for controlling the crowds that would gather at the finish line of this year's Tour de France. The famous bike race would end in front of the Place de la Concorde, where viewing stands had been erected. The police were everywhere, and they had blocked all of the streets leading to the Rue de Rivoli where the Tour de France bikers were directed to pass on their journey through the center of Paris. By late afternoon, the Rue de Rivoli was totally packed as the bikers from the Tour de France, floats, and a closing parade were coursing along the street. Consequently, Sasha and her parents had to take several detours that day.

They crossed the Tuileries and then headed across a bridge over the Seine to the river's left bank. While they were walking across the bridge toward the Musée d'Orsay, Sasha's parents purchased a lock, printed their names on it, and attached it to the bridge, where it sat alongside thousands of others symbolizing endless relationships. From the peak of the bridge, Sasha could see the bikers sprinting down the Quai de Tuileries. It was an exciting day to be in Paris, and it was very special for Sasha to get to witness the close of this famous bike race, the most famous and popular sporting event in France.

That evening, after a filling dinner of pasta carbonara, Sasha found another scooter and rode past the Invalides and the National Assembly toward another bridge that crossed the Seine. From this bridge, she could see the lights from the Eiffel Tower sparkling spectacularly in the clear, dark night. Eventually, she and her parents made their way to the Champs-Élysées and walked under the Arc de Triomphe, marveling at the beauty and grandeur of these famous monuments that were all lit up at night.

Sasha would return to the Eiffel Tower the next day; her family had booked brunch on the first level of the iconic structure at the famous Jules Verne restaurant. Brunch was delicious, and the views of Paris from all sides of the tower were awesome. Afterward, they walked around the entire first-level platform, taking many pictures and soaking up the glorious views. Wanting an even better view, Sasha decided to climb up the

Sasha and her dad on the Seine River bridge in Paris, France

stairs to the second level. The view from this level, 350 feet above street level, was breathtaking. From this vantage point, Sasha could see all of the most famous buildings in Paris.

Next, Sasha's family decided to visit her dad's favorite place in the city: the Place Vendôme. Sasha circled the octagonal square with the obelisk statue in the center, looking in the windows of the very expensive shops, and eventually walked into the famous Hotel Ritz. The family entered a courtyard to the side of the lobby, chose a table, ordered some drinks, and tried to soak up as much as they could of the patrician ambiance of one of the most exclusive hotels in the world. As the sun was setting,

Sasha and her parents had one last dinner in Paris at the Brasserie La Lorraine, indulging in the succulent crustaceans and snails they were served and enjoying a final glass of Louis Roederer champagne to toast their wonderful trip to Paris.

London

It is foolish to visit Paris and think that you have seen Europe. It is necessary to also see London, the second major city of Europe, and observe the striking similarities and profound differences between these two distinct cultural capitals. Upon leaving Paris in the afternoon, Sasha and her parents took the high-speed Eurostar train from Paris to London by way of the famous English Channel. The weather in London in midsummer was sunny and hot. They taxied to their hotel, the May Fair, in the center of London and very convenient to all the city's major attractions, and then had dinner at a lively Italian restaurant next to the hotel.

The next day Sasha and her parents jumped aboard a hop-on-hop-off bus to enjoy an extended tour of central London, which included historic castles, old churches, extensive parks, and crowded shopping centers. The Union Jacks, hung from nearly every building, were fluttering in the gentle breeze as the bus drove past Piccadilly Square and on to High Street where retail shops proliferate.

Sasha's first stop was at St. Paul's Cathedral, London's response to St. Peter's Cathedral in Rome. As Sasha walked through this massive and magnificent gothic building, she kept remembering her visit to St. Peter's and began comparing the artworks, the stained-glass windows, and the size of the altar and side altars. She had lunch at a tiny café underneath the tall tower of the monastery and said she thought it wasn't as bright as St. Peter's, although still very impressive.

After climbing back aboard the bus, Sasha traveled to the London Eye, a huge Ferris wheel on the banks of the Thames River. The crowds trying to board the wheel were immense, and Sasha could hardly wait her turn. Once on and circling around the wheel's giant pivot, Sasha was rewarded with a glorious panoramic view of London. That night the family had dinner at the Sexy Fish, another restaurant close to their hotel that was packed with young people having a loud, joyous time.

The next day, Sasha's principal goal was to visit the London Zoo. But before getting there, she and her family made a couple stops along the way. The first stop was at the Sherlock Holmes Museum, which was set in a 200-year-old multistory wood-framed house on Baker Street. The museum had dioramas based on scenes from the famous exploits of Mr. Holmes, with statues and realistic props lying everywhere. They then passed through the Regent's Park and paused to take many pictures of the incredible number of multicolored rosebushes in the gardens along the path. Finally, Sasha made it to the zoo. There she saw animals from all over the world and many examples of birds of prey, including eagles and owls, but her favorite was a show where the trainer was coaxing a couple of meerkats to perform tricks.

After leaving the zoo, Sasha and her parents stopped for lunch on Marylebone Lane at a small charcuterie. Once they finished their treats, they left to go to the main London aquarium, which is housed in a large building along the Thames River and close to the London Eye. The open space between the two very popular sites was jammed with visiting tourists. This aquarium was much larger and more interesting than the area for marine life in the London Zoo. It contained large tanks filled with sharks and stingrays, a crocodile in another area, plus several smaller tanks displaying many colorful types of coral, and a fascinating tank filled with a large group of piranhas.

That night, Sasha and her parents had dinner in a Russian-owned Italian and Asian restaurant, Novikov. An unusual combination of cuisine, but innovative dining ideas are prevalent in London's busy dining market. The restaurant was filled with Arabs, Indians, and many other non-English patrons.

Sasha at the Museum in Tower Bridge, London

On the third day, Sasha visited the Tower of London and viewed all the precious jewels, royal crowns, and massive armaments, and she learned a substantial amount of history about the British royal family. As she left the Tower and walked along the Thames River, the murders and scheming among the family members titillated her imagination.

On the route back to the hotel after lunch, Sasha walked through the Leadenhall Market. This centuries-old covered market was filled with restaurants and pubs, and most were host to businessmen drinking large steins of beer. In the past, it was a true food market filled with farmers selling their produce. Today, it has been designated a landmark. Good thing, because the old market is surrounded by new construction as the city is actively trying to modernize the old neighborhoods.

Sasha's last day in London began with a trip on the underground to the British Museum, which houses a fabulous collection of historically important relics from the past. The United Kingdom had an extensive overseas empire over the centuries, and British officials brought back to London wonderful examples of art and artifacts from these civilizations. The museum was featuring two special exhibits at the time, and Sasha chose to explore both. The first one concerned the origins of Sicily and revealed how this Italian island was subject to many different invasions by diverse armies coming from everywhere in the Mediterranean region, and even from as far away as the Baltics.

The second exhibit was about the ancient, buried cities of Egypt. Both were superb and highly educational. Sasha learned that some ancient cities in the Nile River Delta sank into the sea more than one thousand years ago. Their remains were discovered twenty years ago, and an excavation is still ongoing. These cities were Egypt's most important ones in that era. They were conquered by Alexander the Great in 370 BC and ruled by Ptolemy and his heirs until the Roman invasion in 30 BC.

Sasha enjoyed learning about the Egyptians the most. She was intrigued to learn some of the Egyptian mythology, and slightly confused by the merging of Greek mythology and their gods with the Egyptian gods that occurred after the Greek invasion. After absorbing all of this fascinating history, Sasha wanted to walk through the museum's permanent Egyptian collection to learn more about this ancient culture. She became especially interested in the Egyptian hieroglyphics that were found on the old statues.

Sasha was hungry when she left the cavernous museum, so she and her dad took the tube to London's most famous department store: Harrods. There Sasha rode the escalators decorated in Egyptian style several times, soaking up the ambience and marveling at the surrounding architecture. Then she had lunch in the massive food court at the center of the store. Sasha enjoyed lamb chops from the rotisserie and left the landmark building after indulging in a quick cappuccino.

Another trip on the underground brought Sasha to Regent Street, another British shoppers' paradise with Union Jacks flapping prominently in the breeze. While there, Sasha wanted to visit Hamleys, a world-renowned children's toy store, to buy a gift for her young nephew.

Dinner that night was at a small French restaurant, Le Boudin Blanc, in Shepherd Market. The market is a small collection of local streets, each with a number of quaint but diverse restaurants offering cuisine from every ethnic group imaginable. Sasha and her father had dinner with Benoir and his wife, Lisa, who were former classmates of Sasha's mother and now were becoming business partners with her old firm. The conversation was lively; however, after a long day visiting historic British buildings and learning about the ancient Egyptian culture, Sasha fell sound asleep in the restaurant. A taxi took Sasha back to her hotel and her bed.

Friday came too quickly. Sasha and her parents had to pack quickly, travel to Heathrow Airport, and board their flight back to the United States. Sasha couldn't make up her mind about which European capital she liked most. Paris and London both had very prominent advantages; however, she continued to ruminate about the Egyptian artifacts that she saw in the British Museum.

25

New Year's in Punta Cana

NEW YEAR'S FOUND SASHA and her parents making their first trip to a Club Med resort. The one in Punta Cana in the Dominican Republic was highly recommended to Sasha's mom by the new head of Club Med in North America, a fellow YPO member in the Miami chapter. Sasha's family made the decision to go with just a few weeks' notice, wanting to take full advantage of Sasha's winter break from school.

Sasha, her parents, and her grandmother arrived on Saturday, December 28, and were met at the local airport by Club Med representatives. The drive to the resort took Sasha through typical parts of the Caribbean island where she noticed roadside debris, vegetation, and low-income living quarters. Getting a glimpse of the humble daily life on the island made Sasha wonder if (and how) the Club Med resort helped the local economy, or if it was truly a world apart. She would learn a partial answer to her question when she left the resort.

When Sasha arrived at Punta Cana, she was greeted by the welcoming staff, who provided her and her family with iced tea and an introduction to the area. The Club Med director then showed them to their rooms. Sasha would be staying with her grandmother in the family section of the resort, while her parents had a room in the Zen quarter, a separate section of the resort designated for adults and meant to be a quiet, meditative space. Naturally the room in the Zen quarter was larger than Sasha's, and it included a peaceful, private garden area. The two zones were well planned and provided an active, noisy, energetic, swimming environment in the family area and, in contrast, a tranquil peaceful area for quiet relaxation in the Zen section.

The resort was gigantic—it took Sasha and her family a few days of wandering around its premises to appreciate its scope. It had two main pools, one for each section. They were both humongous, at least the size of back-to-back Olympic pools, and that still does not adequately describe their immense size. Sasha was anxious to jump into the family pool, which she did immediately after lunch, and she refused to get out until it was time for dinner.

Dinner on Saturday night was in a buffet restaurant next to the sea called Hispaniola. The family sat in the cave area adjacent to the general seating area, where all through dinner they enjoyed a persistent, fresh, cool breeze blowing from the sea, which was just below their table. Sasha and her family ended their first day at the resort with a long walk back to their respective rooms. The night air was cool, which made the long walk tolerable, and it inspired Sasha to begin looking for stars in the clear night sky. She would inform everyone with enthusiasm when she spotted a recognizable constellation, and she wanted to have a contest with anyone who would join her to see who could spot and name the most constellations.

Dawn broke early on Sunday, but everyone was tired. Sasha awoke much later than usual, dressed quickly, and set out for another day of exploring. Along the way to breakfast, she noticed a trampoline and a huge trapeze set up in an area by the sea. The trapeze was high above the ground with safety nets strung below it. Sasha was anxious to try both. After a quick meal and a few hours by the pool, Sasha convinced her

Sasha swinging on the trapeze in Punta Cana, the Dominican Republic

family to venture down to this area, which was called "the circus." It was a large circular space that featured a rock-climbing wall, a trampoline, and a trapeze.

Upon seeing these giant fixtures up close, Sasha grew hesitant about trying these activities, but then she learned that a training session for her age group would begin at three o'clock. Her excitement quickly returned, and she resolved to try the giant trapeze. Although she had never performed on a trapeze before, after she did three swings on it, she was able to improve her technique with each attempt. She thoroughly enjoyed this new activity. Next on her agenda was the trampoline, and there she demonstrated her backflip and other techniques she had learned from years of gymnastics. After a few attempts, her backflip improved to near perfection. Success came once she managed to gain more height on each jump before executing the flip. She hoped that if she could demonstrate to the staff her proficiency in aerial flips and turns, they would instruct her to do more dangerous tricks on the trapeze. But that decision would have to wait for another day.

Everyone left the circus area to prepare for dinner after making a heartfelt promise to return on Monday so Sasha could improve her trapeze technique. Dinner that night was again at Hispaniola, and once more the buffet tables were filled with a bonanza of delicious choices from all types of salads, meat and fish preparations, pasta, risotto, cheese, soups, and cold meats. It was a prodigious display of very tasty food, and Sasha enjoyed it all. As dinner was winding down, Sasha and her family remained sitting in the open-air space and were treated to a cabaret show that had been set up in the center of the resort.

There was quite a large stage, booming sound equipment, and multicolored dancing lights. The music that night was old-fashioned American rock and roll from the 1950s and 1960s. The dance acts were performed by members from the Club Med staff, and many of them were terrific dancers. Sasha learned during the intermission that the cast of the show came from thirty different countries, each bringing a slight amount of ethnic spice to their participation. All performed energetically and quite well. The French general manager of the resort was the MC for the night, a role he earnestly enjoyed, and it sparked everyone's enthusiasm. It was a great performance by the hotel staff, and Sasha wished she could have danced along to all the exciting, energetic dance numbers!

Monday started out very breezy and overcast, a real contrast to the weather Sasha had enjoyed over the past few days in Punta Cana. The swirling created some large waves that complicated the family's plans for a boat trip that day. After an early morning swim, followed by breakfast and much splashing in the family pool with some young girls Sasha had met in the pool the previous day, the weather finally cleared enough that it looked like the boat ride would materialize after all. After lunch, Sasha and her family hastened back to their rooms to prepare for the much-anticipated boat voyage. They took a path along the beach and walked to the Club Med nautical center.

The seas were still rough, so the family had to jump aboard a flat-bottomed open boat that would ferry them out to a larger, double-hulled, two-level vessel. Once everyone was aboard, the larger vessel slowly made its way downstream, meandering past tiny sailboats, windsurfers, and multiple reefs that were visible to Sasha as they motored over them. Seeing young people on windsurfing boards caused Sasha to think about pursuing this water sport—something to try, perhaps, after the boat ride.

The boat cruise took them down the eastern coast of the island of Hispaniola, where Sasha could see several other vacation resorts that faced the sea, a golf course next to the beach, and some very large mansions. They continued on for a while, past a tiny river with a large breakwater that was sheltering a small private marina, and that became the furthest point of the cruise. As the boat's captain turned the boat to head back to the Club Med, Sasha spotted a large fish that dove down toward the sandy bottom, but no one could identify what type of fish it was in spite of Sasha's curiosity. While they were cruising back toward the Club Med resort, the boat's captain obligingly stopped over a sandbar—a shallow patch of brilliant white sand situated between two small coral reefs—to allow everyone to swim in the clean, clear water. Sasha and her family posed for pictures in this pristine setting, and Sasha frolicked in the water like a happy fish. Once back aboard the boat, they slowly proceeded back toward the sandy dock. As the boat approached it, Sasha saw several stingrays in the water. Eventually the boat had to pass through the array of tiny sailboats and windsurfers to reach the dock. The cruise ended when everyone jumped from the boat into the surf, and Sasha and her family clamored out of the water and walked happily back to their respective pools to chill out until dinner.

The sun was bright and warm the following day, the wind had died down, and the elements set a tone of high excitement for fun activities on New Year's Eve. The day started off as usual with an early morning swim and then breakfast, followed by some time at the beach. After a hearty lunch, Sasha took pictures in front of the surf and watched in fascination as the pelicans dove into the ocean searching for fish to eat. As the afternoon progressed, Sasha was eager to go back to the circus and perform on the trapeze. Her first two attempts were perfectly executed backflips, a real improvement from her first try on Monday. Her triumph left Sasha on a high note as the day was winding down, and soon it would be time to kick off the evening's festivities.

Sasha and her family dressed colorfully for New Year's Eve. The resort center was filled with partygoers, all equally festively dressed, drinking New Year's Eve cocktails—mainly Aperol spritzes. Sasha joined the crowd at the center of the trapeze arena to celebrate the end of the year and the decade. With cocktails in hand and a juice for Sasha, the family split off from the crowd to claim their reserved table. The tables were tightly bunched together; everyone wanted to be near the center because it provided great views of all the initial celebrations.

Dinner was superb! It began with large scoops of black caviar and blini, patés of all compositions, and piles of Alaskan king crab legs. Farther inside the restaurant were tables filled with delectable salads, fish (cold and hot), a special scallop dish with an appetizing French sauce, a rack of lamb, and too many assorted trays and overflowing saucepans to individually name. Deserts were even more enticing and elaborate, especially the ice-cream-filled profiteroles. Sasha celebrated the end of the year with her loved ones and enjoyed the excellent food, along with two bottles of French champagne for the adults.

When dinner was complete and everyone was happily stuffed, Sasha and her family walked back toward the circus just as a trapeze demonstration was unfolding. Sasha watched intently, hoping to pick up some new tricks and techniques to try out the next day. From there they walked to the beach, where a giant screen and stage had been set up for the year-end show. The beach was already crowded with partygoers, and it was only going to become even more crowded as the last day of 2019 drew to a close. Sasha had a hat and noisemakers, and her parents had more French champagne for the midnight toast as the family listened to the DJ playing music. Finally, the MC began the countdown. At the stroke of midnight, a brilliant fireworks display shot skyward. "Happy New Year!" Sasha shouted, grinning from ear to ear. It was a momentous evening to celebrate the end of a decade and welcome in a new one.

Shortly after welcoming the New Year, Sasha's family repacked their things and left Club Med with a completely different idea of the resort from the one they held when they arrived. Everyone found something to love in the wonderfully well-planned facility, its enormous spaces filled with exciting and calming activities that appealed to all age groups. The staff was courteous, friendly, and very helpful, especially Sasha's parents' social manager Audrey, who was from Vietnam. Sasha had fun speaking with Audrey about the places she had visited in Vietnam a few years ago. Audrey was perfect for her role at the resort because she could speak French, having learned it in school in Vietnam. Most of the clientele at the Club Med were French, with a scattering of other European and Latin guests and very few Americans. The guests were of all ages, but most were families like Sasha's.

Sasha asked Audrey why she had learned to speak French in Vietnam and was told that some parts of the country clung to their old colonial customs. That brought up more questions for Sasha because she had learned when she was there about the Americans in Vietnam, but not the French. Regardless, Sasha left Club Med with a suitcase full of wonderful memories and a souvenir T-shirt emblazoned with a large number "45." This is the number of the Punta Cana resort among Club Med's resort collection, and it denotes that this resort was built forty-five years after the first Club Med resort was constructed. Sasha also learned that the resort provided thousands of jobs and much income for the local residents of the Dominican Republic.

Ski Weeks in Vail

SKI WEEK AT PINE CREST SCHOOL is a tradition that many Pine Crest families partake in, and one that Sasha would enjoy with her classmates over multiple winters. The first time Sasha joined her classmates and their families in Vail, Colorado, in February 2019, Sasha's mom booked a week's accommodation in the Arrabelle Hotel, located right in the heart of Lionshead Village, the newer section of the Vail resort. Lionshead Village is anchored by several five-star hotels and located a five-minute bus ride from the original Vail Village. It includes a large skating rink, a gondola that takes skiers three-quarters of the way up the massive mountain, several ski shops bulging with rental equipment, and many restaurants offering a variety of Alpine fare.

The Arrabelle has a comfortable design for a ski-in-ski-out hotel. There was a wonderful hot tub located on the roof of the main building, a couple of restaurants serving food typical for mountain resorts, and a very tiny lobby. The bar/bistro next to the concierge offered a cozy spot for an après ski drink and conversation, which often led to an informal dinner. Breakfast was served in the same small dining room. The hotel's valet service was unique: They took care of ski boots—keeping them on warmers overnight—skis, and helmets, and they made getting skis on and off very convenient.

Sasha arrived in Vail on Saturday afternoon with a special agenda. She was excited about this ski trip because many of her friends from school would be there too. Soon after Sasha and her parents arrived at the Arrabelle, she met up with one of her school friends, Chloe, with whom she would be skiing and snowboarding throughout most of the week. There were many other classmates in Vail this week as it was the favorite ski location for many Pine Crest families.

Sasha's first responsibility on this and all ski trips was to visit the ski store to select and rent skis, poles, a helmet, and boots and arrange for ski lessons and lift tickets. When Sasha went to meet her ski instructor, she made sure to arrange to be in the same group with her friend Chloe. Each morning, their group skied off with their instructor to enjoy the slopes for a full day and didn't return until around 3:30 p.m. They were joined by another of Sasha's classmates, Sienna, who arrived a day later than Sasha. This trip was extremely special for Sienna because she had never seen snow before.

Skiing the first day got off to a rocky start for Sasha, and she didn't appreciate that her instructor was totally insensitive to her concerns, especially after she fell skiing and developed a headache. Her parents were concerned about Sasha's headache and believed it could be due to the high altitude in the mountains. The Colorado Rocky Mountains are the highest in North America, and Sasha would be skiing at eleven to twelve thousand feet.

The second day went better, as Sasha had a new instructor whom she ended up liking much better. She skied in a group with Chloe, and at the end of the day, she decided to venture into skiing in more challenging locations: the massive bowls at the back of Vail Mountain's ski area. Sasha convinced Chloe to go with her on this adventure, though Chloe was a better snowboarder than skier and had trouble with the severity of the slope and the wide-open snowscape with no trails.

Tuesday was snowboarding day for Sasha and her friends; she was joined by three girls and six boys from her seventh-grade class at Pine Crest. Sasha and her friends weren't happy with the snowboarding instruction, so they decided they would rather ski the next day. That morning, the girls gathered early at ski school and worked hard to find a more accommodating ski instructor. Once they found an instructor they liked, they immediately took off, leaving the boys behind to struggle with snowboarding. Skiing proved much more satisfying for Sasha and her girlfriends, possibly because they were free of the boys that way.

As the week drew to a close, ski school ended for Sasha and Chloe, and some of their friends left to return home to Florida. Sasha's skiing style had evolved further over this week of instruction. When Sasha skied with her parents on her last day in Vail, she fast outpaced both of them. She still did not use her poles or shift her weight early onto the downhill ski; she just skied down the fall line. Sasha also wanted to ski more difficult terrain than her parents did, and many times she veered off the traditional run to ski in between the trees, or on a more difficult black diamond alternative.

It wouldn't be long before Sasha would "graduate" from ski school entirely. On her next trip to Vail the following year, 2020, she really didn't need any more ski instruction as she was competent enough to be fearless, whether searching out new terrain, skiing flat out downhill, going up and down moguls, or diving between the trees.

Sasha was becoming more independent off the slopes, too. Most evenings after skiing, she would go with friends to Vail Village to wander past the enticing store windows, stopping now and then to explore a shop, and ultimately having dinner together without parents. Only one night did Sasha join her parents for dinner at the Four Seasons Hotel in Vail. Dinner there proved to be exceptional, with delectable food served in a beautiful dining room—far fancier than the places Sasha usually went with her friends.

Another night, an amusing dinner situation occurred. Sasha and her friends were together at a large table at the back of the Blue Moose pizza restaurant. They were having lots of very boisterous fun, while Sasha's parents had a casual dinner with Sienna's mom and younger sister at a much smaller table in the front of the restaurant. Neither group minded being in the same restaurant, as each was just where they wanted to be.

Skiing with her classmates made the mountain experience so much more special for Sasha. A highlight of the trip came one evening after skiing all day when approximately thirty Pine Crest families showed up precisely at five o'clock at the bottom of the main gondola to have a group picture taken. It was truly awesome to realize how many families came to this resort from one school in South Florida to ski with one another. In true form, once the pictures were taken, Sasha and her friends rushed off to take the gondola up to the top of the mountain to go snow tubing down the resort's massive, steep tube tracks before having dinner together afterward. The temperature at the top of the mountain by the tube tracks dropped significantly as the sun set and the wind picked up. By the time Sasha returned to the hotel room to change clothes, she was freezing and needed to take a very hot shower to regain her equilibrium.

Valentine's Day usually fell during ski week. Sasha and her mom slept late on Valentine's Day morning. They managed to find great snow that day and had some good skiing, first in Game Creek Bowl and later in Sasha's favorite run, the Sun Up Bowl—a very steep, open bowl with mixed fall lines. When Sasha and her mother finished skiing, they took the Orient Express lift up to Two Elk Lodge to have lunch at the top of Vail Mountain with its incredible views of the adjacent snowcapped peaks. The building, made of local pine, was reconstructed in 2000 after arsonists burned down the original structure in 1998. It was always packed; reservations were required, even for lunch.

Sasha and her parents then skied the front side of the mountain down to Vail Village before taking the lifts back up to the Lionshead area so they could ski down to their hotel. Sasha's family celebrated Valentine's Day with dinner at the Hyatt hotel, where they enjoyed duck ravioli and cannelloni along with some extravagantly sweet deserts.

Sasha could not have asked for better ski conditions for her vacation. It snowed the entire week she was in Vail. Most mornings, she woke to fresh snow that had fallen overnight, and most days started off overcast with a few snowflakes falling. The gray clouds promised more snow coming soon. Every once in a while, the clouds would part, permitting a few glimmers of partial sunlight to filter down on the ski slopes. A few rare mornings, Sasha was lucky enough to have skied out under a brilliant, crystal-clear sky. Those days were perfect for picture-taking in the clear, high-mountain air with evergreen trees blanketed with piles of heavy white snow. The resort's grooming technique on the Lionshead side of Vail Mountain was to groom the center of the trails and leave the sides to chunk up, or stay as moguls. By the end of a busy day of skiing, all the snow on the slopes would be chunked up, and the moguls would have grown bigger.

Snowball fight in Vail, Colorado

This was the case on the last day of Sasha's school's ski week, when the slopes were also filled with skiers beginning their first day of skiing during the week following President's Day, when all the public schools across the country began their winter vacations. Conditions on the mountain deteriorated greatly from what they had been in the previous few days. Lift lines and waiting times were long, and the runs were crowded with all levels of skiers and snowboarders. Consequently, Sasha decided to ski in Game Creek Bowl, which usually had fewer skiers than other areas, before retiring her rented skis for another year. It snowed all that night and into the next morning, adding to the excitement and enjoyment for all the holiday week's visitors. It was a fitting end to a glorious, snow-filled ski vacation in Vail for Sasha and her family.

Sasha would return to Vail for ski week the following year, 2021, with her Pine Crest classmates. It was the week before President's Day again, but this year's trip was entirely different, as it occurred during the COVID-19 pandemic. Only a few of the families that would normally take advantage of the school's winter recess to go skiing risked flying on airplanes to travel to Vail. As a result, Sasha and her family had the pleasure of skiing on slopes that were much emptier than they had been in past years.

They started their journey with everyone in the airport and on the plane covered in masks and plastic gloves to reduce the risk of contagion. Sasha's parents booked a private car service to and from the airports for the same reason. When they arrived at the Arrabelle, they learned that reservations for food service had to be made in advance because of the restrictions the community made to ensure social distancing during the pandemic. The Vail community proved to be very strict about occupancy in restaurants and enforced the wearing of masks everywhere. Early in the 2020–2021 ski season, the resort staff had to live through an extended period of quarantine and closure, so management at the entire resort was careful to take and enforce precautions. Sasha's parents were glad they'd gone ahead and made dinner reservations for every night before they arrived.

There was also a reservation system in place for access to the hotel hot tub on the top of the main building. The hot tub was relatively small, but being on the roof provided tired skiers with expansive views of the surrounding mountainsides while taking a relaxing soak. This year, reservations were required so only one family could enjoy the hot tub at a time. This restriction actually made this facility more enjoyable than in the past, because Sasha and her family could now enjoy the tub in privacy.

Sasha was very lucky that she was able to enjoy the company of her friend Chloe again on this ski trip. Most nights, she decided to eat dinner with Chloe and some of the other students who had come from Pine Crest School. She did join her parents for dinner one night, the last night, after her friends had already flown back to Florida.

All too soon it was time for Sasha to pack her bags and head to Vail's Eagle County Regional Airport, which was uncharacteristically empty. The ski vacation was over, and Sasha was very sad to leave because she realized that skiing was her favorite and best sport. She and her parents headed home with many good memories from this unusual year and were very glad they managed to make the trip despite the COVID-19 epidemic.

SASHA'S FOURTH SKI WEEK in Vail was no ordinary trip, either. Her family had moved from Florida to Brussels, Belgium, during the prior summer. Even though there are many wonderful and famous ski resorts in Europe, Sasha preferred to return to Vail to spend time with her Pine Crest schoolmates. She worked extra hard to achieve excellent grades in her new school in Brussels to please her parents, who had made it clear that she could make the trip to Vail as a reward.

The journey began with the truly humongous effort to travel from Brussels, Belgium, to Vail, Colorado. The trip required three different airplanes. The first was from Brussels to Frankfurt, Germany, and this is where the trouble started. The first flight arrived late in Frankfurt because of technical problems, causing Sasha's family to miss their connection from Frankfurt to Denver. The minute they arrived in Frankfurt, Sasha and her parents ran through the long Frankfurt terminal to their United gate only to find they were fifteen minutes too late. Fearing she would not arrive in Vail in time to meet and have dinner with her friends, Sasha burst into tears. She then spent several hours at the Frankfurt airport cursing her bad luck while her parents created a revised itinerary that would reroute them from Frankfurt to Chicago and then from Chicago to Denver. Once in Denver, they had to organize car service to Vail since the new flight arrived too late to connect with the originally scheduled last flight from Denver to Vail. Twenty-eight hours after leaving their home in Brussels, Sasha and her parents finally arrived at the hotel, thoroughly tired, frustrated, and annoyed. On the long road to Vail, Sasha began to accept the fact that unforeseen incidents occur, and that when they do, she needs to be flexible and persistent to ultimately achieve her goals.

Arriving a day late wasn't Sasha's only problem: Her family arrived at the Arrabelle Hotel late Sunday night, but without any of their luggage. All of it had been lost or delayed in transit. Thus, they had no clean clothes, no toiletries, and nary a bit of ski equipment. Sasha and her parents repeatedly checked in with United Airlines' lost luggage service to try to track down their bags, but unfortunately, the phone calls only added to their frustration, since they were told so many conflicting stories. Sasha began to believe they would never see any of their six pieces of luggage again.

On Tuesday night, three days after their arrival, Sasha's parents learned from the airline that five pieces of luggage were delivered to Eagle County Airport. To retrieve them, they had to hire a limousine to drive to the airport. The sixth piece of missing luggage was brought to the hotel in Vail on Wednesday, four days late. Nevertheless, they were relieved to have their luggage back and finally have clean clothes to change into.

Sasha was inconsolable that first night after missing a day and night with her friends and having no ski attire—or any other clothes, for that matter. The purpose of this ski trip was mainly for her to spend time with her friends, whom she hadn't seen in months, and she wanted to enjoy as much time with them as possible. That first evening, Sasha texted her friends to see if they had any extra ski clothes she could borrow so she could go skiing with them in the morning, and luckily they were able to help out. Sasha's parents supplemented some of the borrowed ski clothes with rental ski gear, and Sasha was at least able to join her friends and ski the next day.

Sasha's mood brightened as she waved goodbye to her parents that day and ran off to meet her friends. They had much to discuss as they waited in the lift lines and in the cable car as they soared up the mountain to the top of the slopes. Sasha was bigger, stronger, and more confident in her ski technique. She was also fearless and immediately began leading her friends down the slopes, through the trees, and over the moguls. She was always the first one down the mountain, waiting for the others to catch up. She was happy to show off on the mountain during the day, and at night she followed the lead of her friends to the Vail restaurants.

Sasha quickly learned that COVID-19 protections were not enforced as strictly as they had been the previous year, though many skiers volunteered to wear a mask or pulled up a gator when they were in lift lines. Restaurant reservations were still mandatory, but the hot tub restrictions were not enforced. There were also more skiers on the slopes and in the hotel than the prior year, but life at the ski resort was not completely back to the way it had been before COVID-19. The village was quieter, with fewer skiers and families, and it was everything

Sasha had wanted. She enjoyed skiing and spending time with her friends, learning what was happening at Pine Crest, and informing her friends about what life was like in Belgium.

The trip back to Brussels was stress-free, with both planes—from Vail to Chicago and then Chicago to Brussels—leaving and arriving on time. There was no long car ride to contend with, and Sasha sat happily the whole time reliving happy memories of her ski vacation with friends. She also began to assimilate the value of resilience as she learned that she could achieve most of her objectives by being flexible and persistent.

27

Life in the Heart of Europe: Brussels, Belgium

DURING A TUMULTUOUS AND DIFFICULT year in Fort Lauderdale, Sasha's mother made an important decision to change jobs. Her new position would require the family to move to Brussels, Belgium, for two years. This meant huge changes for Sasha: she would have to leave her friends at Pine Crest, attend a new school, and adapt to an entirely new and different social scene. It also meant learning to navigate a world where everything was written and spoken in French and Dutch, both new languages for Sasha.

Sasha's mom would have to make her way into a new corporate environment in a different industry and begin developing a relationship with a new CEO. Sasha's dad would have to learn the routes around town, the streets that would bring him to grocery stores and other daily necessities. He would need to acquire a car, set up utilities and insurance in a new country, open a new Euro-denominated bank account, and obtain a Belgian identity card. These identity cards were required for what seemed like every service the family needed in Brussels, even finding a veterinarian who would care for Sasha's dog, Lucky. Sasha accompanied her father on these many errands their first days in Brussels, and it gave her an idea of how troublesome yet worthwhile it was to live abroad.

The family's new residence was a very modern building with many glass walls that opened out on an extensive back yard and the forest beyond. The house was set back from a lonely side road and was hidden from vehicular traffic, making it feel peaceful and secluded. It was in the middle of a much larger property that had been subdivided into four very generous lots completely enclosed by high, thick hedges. The property enjoyed complete privacy and refreshing silence, making it a joy to live and work in. Sasha's mom had her choice of two rooms for her office, and she used both at different times. Sasha's dad had a huge kitchen to cook in and a complete view to the spacious green garden through wall-to-wall glass doors. And Sasha had a lovely new bedroom, plenty of space to enjoy her hobbies, and a whole new country to explore.

But perhaps the family member that benefitted from and liked his new home the most was Lucky. He had a huge yard in which to roam around. It was totally fenced in, so he could run everywhere, chasing birds and squirrels without danger of escape. Most days, Sasha also took him for long walks in the nearby forest where he explored new scents and met many other neighborhood dogs. The forest was also a hiker's and runner's paradise, their only competition being the mountain bikers. Occasionally, Sasha passed by a few horses walking with their riders, which made Lucky bark furiously. There weren't many animals that lived in the forest, at least that Sasha saw. In the fall, she spotted a couple of foxes, and there were road signs warning drivers of deer crossings, but Sasha never saw any.

Sasha and her family would have to get used to the cooler, rainier, and darker weather of Brussels in the fall, so unlike the warmth of Florida and Singapore. It was too cold when they arrived to enjoy the outdoor amenities they had—a patio table and chairs, a huge grill, a Ping-Pong table, badminton net, and even (Sasha's favorite) a trampoline. Until spring brought warmer weather, the family mostly stayed indoors and took advantage of the projector screen and surround sound system in the living room to bring light and warmth into the house on the long, cold winter nights.

But to Sasha's delight, when spring did finally come, buds began to show on the trees, and some grew into beautiful flowers ranging in color from white to pink, red, and deep purple. As spring progressed into summer, the forest became a dense green, interspersed with the giant red oaks that added the contrast of red leaves to the verdant forest. This large forest behind their house showed Sasha's family how wonderful the change in seasons was in a temperate climate zone with a varied and colorful deciduous landscape. Sasha only realized the next fall when she was back in Florida how much she enjoyed seeing the full seasonal changes to the trees and foliage in Brussels. The forest turned from dense, impenetrable green when she first arrived to multiple shades of reds, oranges, and browns as the leaves slowly dried and fell. When winter arrived, the forest became virtually barren, and she could easily see between the lonely tree trunks. At times the ground was covered with white snow, creating yet another impression.

Sasha initially refused to like her new school, the International School of Belgium (ISB), claiming it was not as challenging as her former school was, at least not in math. She didn't want to make new friends, although there were many friendly students in her classes who, like her, were new to ISB. Of course, not all courses seemed to be a repeat of what she had learned at Pine Crest. Sasha had to start taking French, and she also had to take chemistry as her science class; she had never studied either subject before. As time passed, she began to like some of her teachers and even the subjects they taught, and despite her best efforts, she even began to make new friends. Most of her teachers were impressed by Sasha and liked her very much (and they eventually gave her outstanding recommendations when the time came for her to transfer back to Pine Crest).

While at ISB, Sasha stumbled upon an unexpected talent that has since developed into one of her foremost academic skills: creative writing. It all started because she disliked her computer course, so she chose to not attend those classes and instead joined her friend who was taking creative writing during the same class period. Sasha completed the writing assignments and thoroughly impressed the teacher, but none of it counted toward a grade as she wasn't registered for that course. Nevertheless, creative writing is a skill that has stuck with Sasha ever since.

Brussels also hosted an assortment of sports clubs and professionals willing to provide instruction. Sasha's mom and dad joined the nearby tennis club, called the Racing Club, and played there once a week. Sasha started to take tennis lessons there with two French-speaking girls, but she quit after a few sessions because their skill levels were mismatched: the French-speaking girls being much more advanced tennis players.

More successful was her golf training. She took lessons from a highly sought-after French golf coach, Jean-Christian Lassagne, at the Seven Fountains Golf Course. He taught several professional European golfers and often went to Spain to coach other clients. He helped Sasha first by changing her grip and then her swing. Sasha also learned how to shape the flight of a golf ball, and she became a much more adept golfer. This golf training in Brussels became very important because it gave her access to joining the Pine Crest golf team when she returned to Florida in the next school year. In addition, Sasha took Krav Maga lessons every Tuesday after school. Her coach had been trained in Israel, was very fit, and inspired Sasha to enjoy the self-defense training.

In between school and her extracurriculars, Sasha liked to explore Brussels and spent many hours with her new friends in the city's central square. This huge square is surrounded by magnificent and ancient buildings, many of which are internationally designated landmarks. They represent the architectural accomplishments of a very wealthy and prominent European country over several long centuries. As such, they attract millions of tourists annually from around the globe. Branching off from the square are a myriad of tiny passageways and pedestrian streets with a host of small shops and restaurants serving both local cuisine and international fast foods. Sasha spent many fun afternoons visiting these sites and shops. There she tasted Belgium's world-famous chocolate and learned to enjoy Belgian waffles. But wandering through the multitude of small shops with her new French friend, Lucy, was Sasha's favorite. They had fun comparing their small purchases made in the various shops celebrating Belgian themes.

While in Brussels, Sasha couldn't help but soak in some of the city's political significance. It is the political center of the European Union with its many administrative buildings and huge assembly center for member delegates. Naturally, Brussels is filled with embassies from nearly all nations, especially those that want to interact politically or commercially with the twenty-eight countries of the EU. In addition, Brussels is also headquarters to NATO and therefore home to an abundance of advanced military personnel from all member countries and an assortment of defense industry contractors eager to sell their products to NATO members. Consequently, there are a multitude of modern office buildings surrounding the center of Brussels housing all of these prominent expats. On top of all this, of course, Brussels is also the capital of the Belgian government.

The scope of Brussel's international importance was unknown to Sasha when she arrived in Brussels, but gradually as she met children from different countries and learned what brought their parents to Brussels, she began to understand the global role that Brussels plays—and that she was now in the center of it. This new insight into international affairs has stayed with Sasha, such that on recent university visits in the United States, she has made it a priority to examine each school's course offerings on international economics and political science.

The Ukrainian tragedy also began while Sasha was living in Brussels. Being at the center of the European government during this tense time increased Sasha's awareness of the support Europe was mounting for the Ukrainians, and she saw the migration of Ukrainian people filtering into supportive Belgian homes. The issue of the Ukraine tragedy was constantly spoken about in Sasha's circles, and she often saw the large blue-and-yellow Ukrainian flags flying from Belgian government buildings and throughout all the cities in Belgium she visited. Sasha vividly remembered some of these European issues and fears when she began visiting universities in the United States, further reinforcing her interest in international affairs.

Around Thanksgiving time, Sasha began thinking of inviting her friend Philip and the Ohm family for Thanksgiving dinner. The families had spent many Thanksgiving dinners together in Singapore. The Ohms had recently moved back to their Hamburg, Germany, home and were therefore relatively close to Brussels. In addition to sharing Thanksgiving dinner with friends, it also offered Sasha the opportunity to explore Brussels with Philip. None of the Ohm family had seen Brussels before, so it was an exciting visit for them. The families spent most of their short weekend visit walking through the city center and seeing the extraordinary colorful night lights that exhibited the ancient buildings in a most picturesque manner.

After Thanksgiving, the Ohms invited Sasha and her family to visit them in Hamburg, which they did one month later. It was colder, dark, and gray in Hamburg in December. This historic port city on the Elbe River, which empties into the North Sea, has been one of the most important trade routes for Europe. The families spent most of their brief time together watching the enormous cargo ships navigate tricky turns in the narrow confines of the river to achieve their docking births.

While living in Brussels, Sasha took the opportunity to visit other parts of Belgium. Belgium is divided into three provinces: Brussels in the center; Wallonia, the southern and mainly French-speaking province; and Flanders, the northern province populated mainly by Dutch-speaking people.

Christmas in Brussels Square, Belgium

Each province has its own historic treasures. For example, Liège in Wallonia is an educational center filled with universities and populated mainly by young students and a variety of centuries-old churches. Sasha felt almost at home when she visited Liège. Flanders has Antwerp, the diamond-cutting capital of Europe and host to a multitude of expensive jewelry shops, which opened Sasha's eyes as she browsed past all of the lavish pieces and began to realize what it would take to own and wear some of them. Finally, she visited Bruges, a seaport town on the border of the Netherlands and the North Sea. It, too, was the setting for many colorful historic churches and architectural landmarks. Sasha loved walking on the chilly beach, gasping at how close the huge tankers passed as they steamed past on the North Sea. She could picture in her mind how close England was across the cold water, and she realized how central Belgium is to the many countries of Europe.

… 28 …

Skiing at the Top: St. Moritz

ONE ADVANTAGE OF LIVING IN Brussels, located in the center of Western Europe, is the ease of traveling throughout Europe relatively inexpensively either by high-speed train or short, inexpensive flights. Sasha and her dad took advantage of this proximity and went to ski in the European Alps. The last time Sasha had visited St. Moritz was near the end of the great train ride through Switzerland in the summer of 2014. She remembered the brilliant cerulean lake reflecting the deep sapphire sky and the massive brown mountains above it that seemed to be waiting for the first snowfall to paint them glistening white. This time Sasha would be returning in late February, when temperatures drop to minus eighteen degrees Celsius, the lake is frozen, and the mountains are encrusted in snow. The intense sun that seems to always pour light over this magnificent valley was one and the same. Seeing the lake and mountains again but anew, Sasha realized that St. Moritz was a very special and scenic place.

Sasha left Brussels early Sunday morning for this father-daughter ski trip. They took a flight to Bergamo, Italy, and then picked up a rental Volkswagen and drove the 160 kilometers north to St. Moritz, Switzerland. The route took them along Lake Como, through tunnels under mountains, and past little villages and commercial communities in Northern Italy. The scenery changed dramatically as they crossed the border into Switzerland, ushering in the magnificent Alpine terrain. Mountains were everywhere, and it was getting colder. As they drove north, the buildings became fewer, and those they did see had dark wood siding and steeply peaked roofs. There were a few villages with church steeples built midway up the mountains, and Sasha pondered how they could be constructed, how long it took to bring building materials up, and what effort it would take for present-day homeowners to purchase groceries and other necessities.

Suddenly, the roads led to the face of a huge mountain laced with switchbacks going as high as Sasha could see. Her father drove cautiously around many 180-degree turns that led up the mountain while Sasha nervously imagined what would happen if a big truck or bus came driving down the mountain on the other side of the road. They both prayed that it wouldn't snow while they were driving, knowing that icy conditions on this road would be deadly—they later learned that the road closes during snowstorms. Their anxiety subsided when they reached the top of the mountain, where they were overcome by a magnificent view of the Swiss Alps. Huge, steep mountains were seemingly falling straight down to a series of lakes below them. As they drove past, Sasha saw people walking their dogs, skating, and Nordic skiing on the lakes. It was becoming darker, as the day was ending; the air was much colder and pristinely clean. After three hours of driving and climbing to just over six thousand feet, Sasha and her dad finally reached their hotel in the middle of St. Moritz.

St. Moritz is the quintessential Alpine resort, and in the brilliant morning sun the following day, Sasha thought it looked just like a Christmas card. The architecture is Alpine in style, with roofs iced in snow and warm wood paneling, and the streets were filled with high-end designer boutiques. Sasha wasted little time before setting off to explore these famous designer shops, though the biting cold made her outdoor walk short-lived. Sasha rapidly returned to her hotel. This became a theme of the trip—short brisk walks outside in the cold followed quickly by shelter in someplace warm.

After renting boots, skis, and poles from the ski shop on their first morning, Sasha and her father were dismayed to learn they now had to carry their gear to a gondola, which was a twenty-minute walk in their ski boots from the hotel past a traffic circle and up two flights of steps to reach the entrance. Sasha tried to put the discomfort from the long walk past her as she looked out the window of the gondola that brought her up the mountain. She focused instead on the ski days ahead, which seemed full of promise.

It was at mid-mountain that Sasha learned how different skiing was going to be at St. Moritz compared to the conditions in the American West. These mountains hadn't received a major snowstorm since Christmas. In the absence of new snowfall, the ski mountain management employed grooming as a strategy to hold the snow for future skiers. Consequently, the snow becomes extremely hard and requires deep-edged carving ski techniques to navigate. Underneath the groomed surface is ice. By midday, the early-morning skiers and boarders would scrape away the top, leaving a slick, icy surface that defied all but the staunchest carving techniques. The middle and lower slopes frequented by children and less-experienced skiers and boarders were especially slippery. Sasha and her father learned to limit their ski times by quitting early in the afternoon rather than skiing until the lifts closed.

Sasha observed another significant difference about skiing in the Alps versus the Rockies or the mountains in Japan when she and her father ventured higher up the mountain on their second day. There were no trees at mid-mountain and higher. Up toward the top of the mountain, the surface was entirely covered in white; it was brilliant in the direct sunlight, and the reflection was blinding. There were no trails, no moguls to ski on, no trees to ski between—nothing to break up the enormous white space.

Sasha's first day on the mountain was not the happy day she thought it would be. First, her rented skis were too short and did not offer enough weight to carve into the hard snow. After two runs, she decided to go back to the village and replace her skies with another pair while her father remained on the mountain skiing until she returned. It was a good idea, but unfortunately, Sasha did not know how to find the right gondola to return to the village and accidentally took one that returned her to the bottom on the other side of the mountain in another village. Consequently, she had a forty-five-minute walk to return to St. Moritz. It was her second long, unplanned walk of the day, and by the time she returned to St. Moritz, she was tired and frustrated.

Sasha called her father on her cell phone as she was hiking back to town, and he decided to meet her in St. Moritz. But he, too, took the wrong gondola down the mountain and had to walk to a bus stop and wait for a bus that brought him, sweaty and tired, back to their hotel much later.

Dinner that night proved to be another exasperating adventure. The concierge at the hotel booked a quaint, Alpine-style restaurant for Sasha and her dad, which she said was a ten-minute walk from the hotel. It wasn't ten minutes, but rather a twenty-five-minute walk in minus-sixteen-degree temperatures, and the whole experience rekindled all the days' frustrations. Sasha and her father enjoyed their Swiss-Alpine style dinner, but returned to their hotel by taxi, and thereafter decided to limit their walking around town to a block or two from the hotel.

As Sasha was walking to the gondola the following day, she learned what the loud cow bells and crackling sounds she'd been hearing all morning were about. It was the first day of March, and the local Romansh people were observing a traditional seasonal rite to banish winter and welcome spring. Sasha was fascinated as she watched the local school children, dressed in traditional garb, cracking long bull whips in the air and ringing their loud cow bells. Many parents and other tourists were also standing around observing this colorful performance. After asking a few locals who were watching nearby, Sasha quickly learned that they were in the fourth region of Switzerland where the native people speak Romansh and follow the old customs. Their language was slowly giving way to German, which was now the principal language taught in the public schools in this fourth and smallest area of Switzerland; Sasha learned that Romansh was spoken mainly at home.

Sasha and her father spent the following days skiing at the top of the mountain more than 3,050 meters above sea level. One steep, sharply turning trail that took them down the back of the mountain would have easily qualified as a double blue or black trail in the United States. Another steep black run took them down the mountain's front

The top of St. Moritz in Switzerland

side. Sasha wanted to stop for a break to have lunch in a high mountain café—so high that Sasha mused about how the restaurant suppliers brought food and beverages up to this very isolated spot near the top of the mountain. She concluded it must have been by helicopter.

As their ski days counted down, Sasha was sad to leave the beautiful region with its snow-draped mountains and glittering frozen lake. She also was troubled at the thought of having to negotiate going down the mountain pass, only this time she and her father made the trip from the decline side and in the bright sunlight. Sasha was again apprehensive and soon became nauseous watching all the sharp 180-degree turns as they wound their way down the face of the mountain. Other than the switchbacks, the drive reminded Sasha of Switzerland's pristine beauty, which she remembered from her summers in Neuchâtel. She hoped to have more opportunities in the near future to return to this beautiful mountain region.

29

Easter Week in Spain

SPAIN IS A VERY RELIGIOUS Catholic country, as Sasha learned when she visited the south of Spain during Easter week in 2022. All the churches were elaborately decorated, and even houses in the neighborhoods close to big churches had colorful banners hanging from their windows. Processions were everywhere, and most of the city centers were cordoned off from auto traffic to permit the faithful to observe the religious ceremonies. Many people were dressed in old religious garb and joined the parades, and others drove mule-drawn carts into and around the processions.

Sasha and her parents traveled to Spain during ISB's Easter week vacation to visit an apartment they'd purchased as a vacation home above the Calanova Golf Course in the Costa del Sol region of Spain near Marbella. It recently had been furnished, and finally all the appliances and electronics were installed. When Sasha's family arrived on the Saturday before Palm Sunday, the maintenance people were cleaning away the residual brown dirt that had blown in from a massive rainstorm originating in North Africa a week before. Even the main pool of the condominium complex and all the small pools on the individual terraces were covered with this brown dirt. The condo, newly renovated, looked very attractive to Sasha as she wondered around inside, looked at the pictures that were hung on walls, and checked out all the new furniture on the balcony.

The weather in southern Spain was fantastic this time of year: warm days, cool nights, and very sunny. It was a pleasure to sit on the balcony with a warm drink in the early morning as Sasha often did. The view from the balcony overlooked the enormous Calanova Golf Course below, and it constantly reminded Sasha and her parents of a need to play this very challenging golf course. Sasha's dad finally found the time to play a half round of golf on the famous course toward the end of their trip. It was extremely challenging, with massive elevation changes and no level lies from which to hit golf balls. Sasha wasn't quite ready to attempt this course yet, but there was much more for her to see and do while in Spain.

After unpacking their things and going for an early dinner at the Beach House Restaurant near Marbella, the family stopped in El Corte Inglés department store to begin purchasing the many items needed to make the apartment a functioning vacation home. It was something Sasha would return to do throughout the week. They even went back to the store on Palm Sunday for more things they discovered the house was still lacking.

On Monday morning, Sasha's mom's work required her to make a trip to Murcia, about a five-hour drive from their residence. The plan was to have dinner in Granada, which was about half the distance to Murcia. After getting a late start, the family ended up stopping for a light dinner at a roadside restaurant along the highway toward Murcia instead. Granada would have to wait for another time. This brief road trip gave Sasha and her dad a chance to go exploring while her mom was occupied with work.

They decided to explore the port city of Cartagena. It proved to be a small, nondescript harbor town on the southern coast of Spain. Sasha learned that this small town had given its name hundreds of years ago to a much larger city in Venezuela when settlers from Spain landed and founded a vibrant South American city. When they arrived back in Murcia, Sasha wanted to visit the city's massive basilica, where one of the most grandiose religious ceremonies she ever witnessed was taking place. On the cathedral's main altar was the archbishop of the local diocese, wearing a very tall miter hat and flanked by two bishops. The three were consecrating a solemn-high ceremonial Easter Mass. There must have been more than one hundred priests in attendance—more than Sasha had ever seen gathered together at a Catholic ceremony before—positioned around the altar and in the front pews of the church. There were also two separate choirs, a large organ, and hundreds of parishioners. The service was beautiful and inspiring, the church was very grand and elaborate, and it left a strong imprint on Sasha's young mind. The extensive scope of the service and the immense number of parishioners in attendance also reinforced Sasha's view of how religious Spanish people are.

On the drive back home from Murcia, Sasha and her parents did finally stop at Granada, which is a ski town in Spain during the winter snow season. Sasha called out that she could still see snow on the tops of the nearby Sierra Nevada Mountains. They drove up some narrow winding roads to a famous hotel, which had been converted from a beautiful monastery where nuns used to be confirmed. It offered the family a magnificent view of the city below while they consumed some delicious Spanish pastries.

Another day, Sasha and her dad drove up the mountain to a village, whose buildings were completely painted in white, high above the sea in search of a communal store that featured Spanish ceramic designer products. The drive up the mountain on a single-lane road with hairpin turns and no protective fencing was probably more dangerous than the road they took with all the switchbacks driving up to St. Moritz. Similarly, this drive was treacherous and time-consuming, especially considering it served as a two-way passage. At the top of the winding road stood the village of Mijas all in white. The small town was completely engaged in a Holy Week ceremony of its own, and all of its tiny churches were participating in hosting processions with marching bands. The narrow cobblestone streets were lined with townspeople dressed in traditional religious clothing. There were also donkey carts decorated for the processions on the single-lane roads of the village. Driving through all the people and carts was quite tricky, but eventually Sasha and her father arrived at the ceramics store. It was everything its website had promised and more. Sasha was in awe of the fine craftsmanship achieved on everything that was sold in the commune and helped choose many of the colorful plates and bowls that her father purchased.

Another night, Sasha and her dad drove to Málaga to find a new restaurant for dinner that was highly recommended. Unfortunately, all the choice restaurants in Málaga were located in the old center of the city. As they drew near the center, traffic became heavier, and they soon realized why: the center of Málaga was completely closed off for the religious processions and ceremonies that would wind their way through the old quarter and to provide viewing space for all the visitors who wanted to observe the ceremonies. After several attempts at circumventing the roadblocks to reach the restaurant district, Sasha and her dad decided to head home.

Sasha later learned that Málaga is famous for hosting one of the largest Holy Thursday ceremonies during Easter Week in Spain, and it attracts hundreds of visitors from across the country. Sasha also learned from this dinner disappointment and from other trips made in Southern Spain during Easter Week that Spanish cities and monasteries compete for the biggest and best religious observances during Holy Week. The procession in Málaga was inspiring to see, in spite of having to head home disappointed and hungry. From this and her other brief trips around Spain during Easter Week, Sasha learned that it is a country full of history and strong religious faith, making her curious to return during a non-holiday time to explore these same streets and cities.

30

Mother's Day on Santorini

FOR THE PAST FEW YEARS, Greece had been high on the travel list for Sasha to visit. Finally she had her opportunity. Sasha and her family arrived on the Greek island of Santorini in May to celebrate Mother's Day. It was another of the many trips that Sasha took from Brussels to nearby European destinations. The weather was perfect: warm days with a cooling breeze and cooler nights that required a sweater or light jacket. It was also a perfect time to be there before the hot summer weather arrived and the tumultuous crowds descended on the Greek islands during July and August. Santorini is the most popular Greek island for visitors, attracting an estimated one hundred thousand tourists a year, mainly during the summer months.

The best part of this brief trip was the resort and villa that Sasha's mom chose for the family's visit. The Mystique Hotel in Santorini is regarded as one of the best on the island. It is located in the small village of Oia on the extreme north coast of this very rugged, mountainous island. The extensive villa they stayed in looked out over an azure bay from high up on the cliffs. Sasha was constantly looking down from her mini balcony to see several catamaran sailboats that were tied to buoys in the placid waters below, inviting visitors to rent them for short excursions to the many surrounding islands.

The villa was painted completely white inside and out, as is the tradition in Santorini. More than a tradition, actually, it's an island regulation for all structures facing the sea. The white buildings make a vivid contrast to the black lava lying across the island's cliffs, a welcome sight for visiting sailors arriving to Santorini. The white buildings can be seen from miles away, and they set Santorini apart from the multitude of Greek islands strung across the Aegean Sea.

Sasha spent most of her time on Santorini alternating between sunbathing on the deck of her villa and cooling off in its private pool. Most meals were taken in the resort's main dining rooms, which were located at the edge of the cliff and faced down to the sea and across to the nearby islands. The resort featured a Michelin-starred chef, and therefore the food was quite good and deliberately innovative. Dressing for dinner was simple: Since everything on the island was blue and white, people tended to wear blue and white as well. Sasha and her family naturally fell in with the local custom and dressed accordingly. It was no surprise that Sasha soon proclaimed that this resort with all its amenities and polite service qualified as one of the best she and her family had ever stayed in.

In addition to enjoying the local produce, the creative menus, and the famous Santorini wine that was served at the resort, Sasha and her family also visited the famous Ammoudi Fish Tavern, located at the bottom of the cliff in the tiny Oia harbor on the northernmost point of the island. The seafood at this restaurant was fresh and good, but the most memorable part of their Saturday night dinner was the adventure it took to get to the restaurant. They had to walk through the entire village of Oia, which is confined to one road starting at the top of the cliff and lined with hundreds of clothing and jewelry shops and many small restaurants as the path winds its way down the island. As Sasha and her parents traveled down this road, they stopped from time to time to browse through some of the merchandise. At one tiny jewelry store,

Sasha's dad bought her a tiny ring to remind her of her trip to Santorini, which she put on immediately.

The real adventure began just before they reached the end of the village and came upon a long, winding stairway. They began to climb down this narrow stairway comprising three hundred cobblestone steps in the dark and encountered many unexpected batches of donkey manure along the way. It took Sasha and her parents one exhausting hour to reach the restaurant from their hotel. They did finally arrive, but much later than planned.

Sasha taking pictures of Athens from the Acropolis in Greece

Sasha and her father had started their journey to Greece on the Thursday before Mother's Day on a flight from Brussels to Athens to meet Sasha's mother, who was already there on a business trip. While in Athens, Sasha and her father took the opportunity to go sightseeing. Their first stop was Plaka, the ancient neighborhood in the center of Athens just below the Parthenon. It was now a bustling tourist destination filled with many small restaurants and shops selling mostly tourist collectibles.

After walking through Plaka, Sasha chose a small restaurant in a quiet square that was surrounded by other small restaurants. Everything that was served was traditional Greek food and was very good—a wonderful first introduction to Greek cuisine for Sasha, who liked the pita bread and the fresh fish and vegetables the best. Following this delicious authentic Greek meal, Sasha and her dad hired a taxi and took a three-hour ride through the bustling city to visit all of the many well-known ancient attractions. Sasha marveled that most were erected hundreds of years before Christ and the modern era. She could have spent more time in Athens to visit more ancient sights, but Sasha was anxious to get to Santorini. When they passed through Athens again on the return trip to Brussels, Sasha was even more convinced that she needed to spend more time in Greece to sightsee in Athens and travel back to Santorini to enjoy all the island's merits.

31

Mom's Birthday on the Côte d'Azur

THERE WERE NOT MANY DAYS between Mothers' Day and Sasha's mother's birthday. This year Sasha and her family would celebrate her mother's birthday on the Côte d'Azur in France. It would prove to be the family's last short trip in Europe from their home in Brussels, as Sasha would soon move back to Florida to finish high school at Pine Crest. The short journey from Brussels to France started in Nice on the Mediterranean coast with a quick lunch at a very famous seaside brasserie that featured photographs of many international stars who had dined there. After a short walk along the beach's boardwalk, Sasha and her parents left Nice and made the short drive up through the mountains to Monte-Carlo. Crossing into Monaco let Sasha add one more country to the long and growing list of countries she had visited.

Sasha's father parked near the famous Hôtel Hermitage, and the family got out to do some shopping in the famous stores that decorate this incredibly affluent place. While Sasha and her mother browsed through the many high-end stores, Sasha's father sat in a mini park in front of the hotel observing the visitors drinking Veuve Clicquot champagne in a park-side stand. The pop from the opening of another new bottle interrupted the sound of roaring engines and squealing tires of Formula One race cars as they competed in a Grand Prix auto race, which was occurring just minutes from the hotel. The automobiles parked around the hotel and mini park were as extravagant as the hotel and stores themselves.

Finally, once everyone had spent enough time perusing the expensive shops, it was time to leave this storied wonderland and journey on to the final destination of this trip: Saint-Tropez. The road out of Monaco climbed immediately up the steep cliffs away from the harbor of Monte-Carlo and led to a speedy toll road: the A8. Sasha's family drove along it for a while, but soon decided to leave the modern highway and drive instead on a local road closer to the sea for a better view of the French Riviera. This road was considerably slower and full of turns as it traveled up and down the Alps that flowed parallel to the coast along the entire distance from Monaco. When Sasha finally arrived in Saint-Tropez, three hours after leaving Monaco, the family still had to wind their way through the narrow streets of Saint-Tropez to arrive at the Hôtel Byblos.

The hotel was constructed more than half a century ago and had grown incrementally from its inception. It was a perfect representation of Provence. The walls of the buildings that made up this wonderful hotel were painted in colorful pastels, and they surrounded several interior courtyards. The first courtyard hosted the restaurant Arcadia, where Sasha and her parents ate their first dinner. It also contained a large, deep circular pool. The courtyards were fringed by an abundance of varied vegetation: palm trees, cacti, pines with large cones, elegant tall rubber trees, and many green hedges and shrubs.

Sasha and her parents were hungry after a long day of traveling, so they quickly changed clothes, went down to the courtyard, and had dinner under the stars in a picture-perfect setting with very pleasant weather. The food was delectable, and the service was most friendly. After some encouragement from her parents, Sasha tried out her school

French with the waiter, who was more than happy to indulge her with simple conversation.

The waiters also recommended that Sasha's family go to the hotel's disco club just below the courtyard and told them that if they were to go, they needed to be there early. Apparently, it was the most popular club in Saint-Tropez. Sasha's parents intended to investigate the famous club after dinner; however, after they returned to their room, fatigue set in from the long eventful day, and they missed their opportunity to join the midnight revelers.

Saturday was Sasha's mom's birthday. The day began with birthday wishes and birthday cards, which were exchanged at breakfast under the sun beside the deep blue pool. The weather couldn't have been more hospitable: warm sunshine and a cooling breeze. Since it was Sasha's mom's birthday, she had the pleasure of structuring her day. It turned out shopping was the desired activity. They all set out from the hotel and walked along the narrow streets that led from the hotel to the harbor. Every street was filled with small shops selling a great assortment of designer clothes and jewelry, interspersed with eclectic collections of upscale resort garments.

The day quickly turned into a shopping frenzy with a late afternoon lunch break at one of the restaurants that lined the waterfront. While Sasha and her parents ate, they were able to observe the huge yachts docked along the edge of town and speculate about their length and cost. The most spectacular was a pair of enormous, glistening black-hulled boats, one engine-powered and the other a sailboat. Sasha later learned that the engine-powered yacht was 165 feet long and cost 25 million euro at its initial sale. The sailboat was a single-masted vessel and equally long. Every inch of both boats was polished and gleaming in the sun and all of their lines were jet black and very impressive. It made Sasha whisper that these yachts were bigger and more impressive than the ones she had seen at Puerto Banús in Spain, another port for super wealthy boat owners.

Although lunch was delicious, the real birthday celebration came at dinner that night at the hotel's main restaurant, Cucina. The Italian restaurant was located below the main hotel and adjacent to the storied nightclub. Sasha and her parents were shown to a very nice table under the stars. It was just mild enough to enjoy eating outdoors. After the food was eaten and the table was cleared, the restaurant's lights flickered, the sound system played "Happy Birthday," and the staff brought a strawberry and ice cream dessert with sparklers to the table, which stimulated the other dinners to applaud. It was incredibly festive, very unexpected, and even a little embarrassing for Sasha's mom.

That night, Sasha's parents endeavored to go to the celebrated disco. It opened at midnight, would fill up around two in the morning, and didn't close until five. Since it was a warm, pleasant Saturday night, they expected that the club would be packed—and it was! Though her parents urged her to come along, Sasha was too embarrassed to go to a club she thought would be filled with old people dancing and drinking. So while she went up to bed, Sasha's parents arrived at the rope entrance to the club. There was a long line of people waiting to be admitted, most of them apparently in their late teens and early twenties. All were well dressed in fashionable evening clothes and very anxious to gain admission.

Because the hotel management had added Sasha's parents to the guest list, they jumped the line and entered with a warm greeting from the gatekeeper. The place was semi-dark, with music blaring from several sets of large speakers, making it near impossible to hear anyone speaking even if they were standing only one foot away. The club had two professional DJs who were selecting the music program. The dance floor became crowded early, and some of the young girls climbed onto mini stages around the floor and immediately began gyrating in time with the music. Sasha's parents may not have been the oldest people in the club, as there appeared to be one or two others who wandered in to refresh their memories of times past dancing in clubs. Sasha's parents walked around, watched the revelers, had one drink, and then decided to give their ears a break and return to some semblance of sanity outside of the cacophonous club. As they left, they noticed that the line to gain entrance to the club was now much longer and packed thicker with young people than it had been earlier. They were glad to have experienced the fun and were happy to end the very long day of shopping, walking, eating, and finally clubbing in Saint-Tropez.

Morning came too soon for everyone, even Sasha. She began her last few hours in Saint-Tropez by walking the narrow streets and wandering through the trendy shops. Finally, it was time to return to Byblos, check out, and depart from this picture-perfect French provincial hotel on the Côte d'Azur. For her last experience, Sasha opted to stop in Nice for a quick lunch on the beach and watch the bathers and late afternoon sun worshippers sipping their aperitifs. It was a fitting end to a relaxing and enjoyable visit. While waiting to board their flight back to Brussels, Sasha's mom admitted that it was one of her best birthdays. However, the best one was yet to come.

32

Back to Pine Crest

SASHA'S MOM'S BIRTHDAY AT the Côte d'Azur was the family's last trip together in Europe from their home in Brussels. In June, while Sasha's mother attended to her work assignments in Brussels, Sasha and her dad would return to the family home in Florida so Sasha could finish high school at Pine Crest. She missed her friends and her life there immensely, and she couldn't wait for the school year to begin. Her first class that summer was a creative writing class, where she amazed her teacher with her skillful and imaginative writing ability. Sasha enjoyed creative writing, and the stories she'd written while attending ISB gave her a boost of confidence to continue this pursuit at Pine Crest.

Sasha fit back into school as if she had never left. Her friends embraced her and wanted to know about her year in Europe and how her classes were in comparison to those at Pine Crest. Sasha dove headfirst into her classes and earned a spot on the school's honor roll in her sophomore year. She also earned a spot on the girls' varsity golf team, a nice reward for the hours spent on golf lessons during the cold, rainy days of Brussels.

School at Pine Crest wouldn't be complete if Sasha and her parents didn't observe the school's ski week. Thus, Sasha went back to Vail again in February of 2023. It was her fourth year of skiing in Vail with her Pine Crest friends. Her mother flew over from Brussels without incident, and the family met at the Arrabelle hotel. This year, the village was full of skiers and tourists. As soon as Sasha and her friends went to the lift lines, she noticed that everything was back to the way it was before COVID-19. No masks or pulled-up gators, and no restrictions around the hotel. Being another year older and much more confident in her abilities on snow, Sasha began to quickly outpace her girlfriends, and therefore, after completing a run or two, fell in with the boys from her school who wanted to ski more demanding trails. She also had no interest in snowboarding and wanted to concentrate all of her time on skiing more difficult terrain.

Dinners were the same as other years at Vail—shared mostly with her friends from Pine Crest, and each meal became the start of a new adventure. There were always new restaurants to try and old favorites to savor. Because Lionshead and Vail Village were relatively small, Sasha would sometimes run into her parents as she and her friends were roaming around, and she made a point to share some skiing time with them, too, harkening back to her earliest days of skiing on her family's trips.

Soon another Vail ski trip ended happily; this one did not have travel disruptions or COVID-19 restrictions and was simply satisfying for Sasha. Her skiing improved significantly, she deepened her friendships with her schoolmates, and her love of traveling and exploring the world's snowy terrains only grew stronger.

WHEN SASHA FINISHED HER sophomore year, her father and mother scheduled visits to colleges and universities throughout the United States. Her parents broke up the trips into different regions of the country. The East Coast and West Coast school visits were with her mom, and schools in the middle of the country were visited with her dad. Sasha enjoyed her visits and was anxious to learn about each school: the campus and campus life, the class offerings, and the setting, whether urban, rural, or in between. Most importantly, she learned that she needed to prioritize these many school attributes and create a list ranking their importance to her. Not surprisingly, Sasha's top school changed with each new campus she visited; however, her rejections remained steadfast.

It wasn't long before summer ended and junior year began for Sasha. Traditionally, this is the most important year of high school because in this year, aspiring college applicants must prove their scholastic and extracurricular value to the intended college. Thus, Sasha prioritized studying over traveling, though she did make time to go to Vail with her classmates for Pine Crest's annual ski week in February 2024.

Thus ends Sasha's childhood journeys around the world with her parents. Soon she will be traveling to college and beginning her next journeys through life. Sasha is now mature enough to establish priorities for spending her time and effort this year to maximize her chances of achieving her near-term goals. Her worldly experiences of observing poverty, limited motivation and mobility, and extravagant luxury directly enabled her to realize that focusing on appropriate near-term goals would help her successfully reach lifelong ambitions. Thus, from August through May, Sasha focused predominantly on elevating her academic profile, especially employing her linguistic skills, and again she earned a place on the school's honor roll for her junior year. Her ambitions, while not yet fully formed, would always be internationally oriented because of her years of global travel and her experiences of befriending children from all over the world.

33

Sasha's Words

AS I SIT HERE REFLECTING ON the past seventeen years of my life, I am amazed by the richness of my experiences. My memories are full of countless countries, cultures, and encounters. Each journey, each adventure, has played an important role in shaping the person I am today. Each destination offered its own unique lessons and left an indelible mark on me.

One of the most important lessons I have learned from my travels is the value of diversity. Growing up in the melting pot of Singapore, I was introduced early on to a diverse culture. The city's mix of Chinese, Malay, Indian, and Western influences taught me to appreciate and respect different ways of life. This lesson was only deepened as I explored other countries. In China, I saw how ancient traditions and modernization existed together. I learned that embracing diversity means recognizing the strengths of different cultures and understanding that there is no single way to live one's life.

Learning different languages has been one of the most rewarding aspects of my travels. Each language allowed me to experience new cultures and connect more deeply with the people I met. In China, my attempts to speak Chinese in public were met with encouragement and taught me the value of effort and respect. Each language was a new way of thinking, a different lens through which to view the world. This taught me that communication is not just about words but about understanding and connecting on a deeper level.

Food has been another universal language throughout my travels. Each cuisine held a story of a country's background and way of life. In Italy, I learned to savor the simple yet delicious flavors of fresh pasta and pizza. The Japanese art of sushi-making taught me the importance of precision and experimentation. Indian spices were extraordinary, and each dish was a celebration of complexity and harmony. Belgian chocolates and Swiss cheeses introduced me to the art of indulgence and craftsmanship. Cooking traditional dishes from the countries we visited became a way for me to keep those cultures alive in my own home. Through food, I learned that the act of sharing a meal is one of the most genuine forms of human connection.

Immersing myself in different cultures has been a transformative experience. In China, the mix of ancient traditions and modern innovation opened my eyes to the constantly changing nature of cultural evolution. Italy's Renaissance art and architecture started my passion for history and creativity. Russia's history and ballet introduced me to new forms of artistic expression. These cultural immersions taught me to look beyond the surface and appreciate the depth and complexity of human experiences.

Through my travels, I have grown in ways I never imagined possible. I have learned to be adaptable and explore unfamiliar environments with curiosity and confidence. I have developed a sense of understanding that everyone has a unique story shaped by their cultural and personal experiences. My interactions with people from different backgrounds have taught me to approach life with a spirit of compassion. These experiences have shown me that despite our differences, we are all connected by our shared humanity. The kindness of people and the wisdom of diverse perspectives have all contributed to my personal growth.

I am about to become an adult, and I plan to carry all the lessons and memories of my travels with me as I build my future. I have seen the world through many lenses, each offering a different perspective on life. This global outlook has taught me to be open-minded and seek out new experiences with passion. I have learned that the world is so large and full of wonder that there is always something new to discover. This sense of adventure and curiosity will guide me as I step into the future and prepare me to face new challenges and new opportunities.

As I reflect on my journey, I am filled with gratitude for the experiences that have shaped me. I am grateful for my family's opportunity to travel to so many wonderful places. I am thankful for the people I have met along the way, each contributing to my understanding of the world. I am appreciative of the lessons I have learned and the memories I have made. These travels have not only expanded my horizons but also given me the understanding that we are all part of a larger, interconnected world.

In conclusion, my travels have been more than just visits to different countries; they have been a journey of self-discovery and personal growth. Each destination has added a new perspective to my understanding of the world and my place within it. I have learned to appreciate diversity, the power of language, and various foods and cultures. As I look back on my seventeen years, I am proud of the person I have become and excited for the adventures that lie ahead.

My experiences have taught me to embrace uncertainty and see it as an opportunity for growth. Traveling to new places, often where I didn't speak the language fluently or understand the traditions completely, pushed me out of my comfort zone and forced me to adapt quickly. This adaptability is a skill I will carry with me, ready to face any challenge that comes my way.

The most important takeaway from these travels is that they have instilled in me a lifelong love for learning. Each country I visited sparked my curiosity and inspired me to learn about its history, culture, and traditions. This passion for learning extends beyond academics; it's a curiosity about people, their stories, and the world around me. It has shaped my dreams and driven me to seek out knowledge and experiences that broaden my perspective. My travels have also highlighted the importance of global citizenship. In a world that is increasingly interconnected, understanding and respecting different cultures is more important than ever. I feel a sense of responsibility to contribute positively to this global community and to advocate for understanding and cooperation. The friendships I have made around the world remind me that, despite our differences, we share common hopes and dreams.

—Sasha Fabbri

About the Authors

"**BRIAN FABBRI** is a very good economist, if only we knew what continent he was on," wrote the head of trading at one of Brian's former firms on his annual review. It was an apt description that characterized most of his professional life as an economist for several large global banks. He had the privilege of being sent around the world to speak with governments, central banks, and investors about global economic developments and financial markets. As a result, he visited more than one hundred countries and discussed global economic affairs with professional people of all backgrounds. Brian was fortunate to be a professional economist during the great globalization era of the last decades of the twentieth century and early twenty-first century. His profession whetted his appetite for travel, which he eagerly indulged in both professionally and privately. Travel led him to see different regions of the world, meet diverse peoples, and learn their cultures; it was these experiences that inspired him to share the world with his daughter.

SASHA FABBRI, a senior in high school, discovered her passion for international relations early on, as she grew up all over the world. Attending Pine Crest School, she excelled in world history and language classes, which shaped her aspirations for a future career in global business and her goal of making a meaningful impact on the world. Sasha is now ready to venture off on her own and start a new journey in college, but she wants to continue traveling the world with her family by her side.

Made in United States
Cleveland, OH
25 April 2025